Advanced Host Intrusion Prevention with CSA

Chad Sullivan, CCIE No. 6394
Paul Mauvais
Jeff Asher

Cisco Press
800 East 96th Street
Indianapolis, IN 46290 USA

Advanced Host Intrusion Prevention with CSA

Chad Sullivan

Paul Mauvais

Jeff Asher

Published by:
Cisco Press
800 East 96th Street
Indianapolis, IN 46240 USA

Printed in the United States of America 1 2 3 4 5 6 7 8 9 0

First Printing May 2006

Library of Congress Cataloging-in-Publication Number: 2005931071

ISBN: 1-58705-252-0

Warning and Disclaimer

This book is designed to provide information about the Cisco Security Agent product from Cisco Systems, Inc. Every effort has been made to make this book as complete and as accurate as possible, but no warranty or fitness is implied.

The information is provided on an "as is" basis. The authors, Cisco Press, and Cisco Systems, Inc. shall have neither liability nor responsibility to any person or entity with respect to any loss or damages arising from the information contained in this book or from the use of the discs or programs that may accompany it.

The opinions expressed in this book belong to the author and are not necessarily those of Cisco Systems, Inc.

Trademark Acknowledgments

All terms mentioned in this book that are known to be trademarks or service marks have been appropriately capitalized. Cisco Press or Cisco Systems, Inc. cannot attest to the accuracy of this information. Use of a term in this book should not be regarded as affecting the validity of any trademark or service mark.

Corporate and Government Sales

Cisco Press offers excellent discounts on this book when ordered in quantity for bulk purchases or special sales. For more information, please contact: **U.S. Corporate and Government Sales** 1-800-382-3419
corpsales@pearsontechgroup.com
For sales outside the U.S., please contact: **International Sales** international@pearsoned.com

Feedback Information

At Cisco Press, our goal is to create in-depth technical books of the highest quality and value. Each book is crafted with care and precision, undergoing rigorous development that involves the unique expertise of members from the professional technical community.

Readers' feedback is a natural continuation of this process. If you have any comments regarding how we could improve the quality of this book, or otherwise alter it to better suit your needs, you can contact us through email at feedback@ciscopress.com. Please make sure to include the book title and ISBN in your message.

We greatly appreciate your assistance.

Publisher	John Wait
Editor-in-Chief	John Kane
Executive Editor	Brett Bartow
Cisco Representative	Anthony Wolfenden
Cisco Press Program Manager	Jeff Brady
Production Manager	Patrick Kanouse
Development Editor	Betsey Henkels
Project Editor and Copy Editor	Deadline Driven Publishing
Technical Editors	Larry Boggis and Joe Stinson
Editorial Assistant	Raina Han
Book and Cover Designer	Louisa Adair
Compositor	Tolman Creek Design
Indexer	Julie Bess

Corporate Headquarters
Cisco Systems, Inc.
170 West Tasman Drive
San Jose, CA 95134-1706
USA
www.cisco.com
Tel: 408 526-4000
800 553-NETS (6387)
Fax: 408 526-4100

European Headquarters
Cisco Systems International BV
Haarlerbergpark
Haarlerbergweg 13-19
1101 CH Amsterdam
The Netherlands
www-europe.cisco.com
Tel: 31 0 20 357 1000
Fax: 31 0 20 357 1100

Americas Headquarters
Cisco Systems, Inc.
170 West Tasman Drive
San Jose, CA 95134-1706
USA
www.cisco.com
Tel: 408 526-7660
Fax: 408 527-0883

Asia Pacific Headquarters
Cisco Systems, Inc.
Capital Tower
168 Robinson Road
#22-01 to #29-01
Singapore 068912
www.cisco.com
Tel: +65 6317 7777
Fax: +65 6317 7799

Cisco Systems has more than 200 offices in the following countries and regions. Addresses, phone numbers, and fax numbers are listed on the **Cisco.com Web site at www.cisco.com/go/offices.**

Argentina • Australia • Austria • Belgium • Brazil • Bulgaria • Canada • Chile • China PRC • Colombia • Costa Rica • Croatia • Czech Republic Denmark • Dubai, UAE • Finland • France • Germany • Greece • Hong Kong SAR • Hungary • India • Indonesia • Ireland • Israel • Italy Japan • Korea • Luxembourg • Malaysia • Mexico • The Netherlands • New Zealand • Norway • Peru • Philippines • Poland • Portugal Puerto Rico • Romania • Russia • Saudi Arabia • Scotland • Singapore • Slovakia • Slovenia • South Africa • Spain • Sweden Switzerland • Taiwan • Thailand • Turkey • Ukraine • United Kingdom • United States • Venezuela • Vietnam • Zimbabwe

Printed in the USA

About the Author

Chad Sullivan is a founder and senior security consultant with Priveon, Inc., which provides leading security solutions to customer facilities around the world. He is recognized as one of the premier CSA architects and implementers. Prior to joining Priveon, Chad was a security CSE with Cisco Systems, Inc. During that time, Chad wrote the first Cisco Security Agent book and assisted customers with numerous Cisco security product implementations. Chad holds numerous certifications including three CCIEs (Security, Routing and Switching, and SNA/IP), a CISSP, and CHSP. He resides in Atlanta, GA with his wife and children.

Paul S. Mauvais has been securing and administering varying operating systems ranging from most UNIX flavors available to VMS to VM/CMS and to Microsoft Windows for 18 years. He currently holds the position of senior security architect working in the Cisco Corporate Security Programs Organization, where he has worked for the past six years to secure Cisco and improve Cisco security products. Paul was responsible for leading the deployment of Cisco Security Agent inside Cisco and speaks on many occasions to customers on endpoint security. He has worked for a wide range of organizations including Portland State University, Apple Computer, and University of California LLNL.

Jeff Asher is a network systems engineer at Internetwork Engineering in Charlotte, NC. Jeff has focused on security and storage technologies for the last eight years and has a degree in geography from Virginia Tech.

About the Technical Reviewers

Larry Boggis, CCIE No. 4047 (R&S) is a senior security consultant with Priveon, Inc., based in RTP, NC. He has a strong background in host and network security design and implementation. At Priveon, a premier security consulting organization in the U.S., Larry's focus is on security design, consulting, and research. Larry previously supported large enterprise security projects throughout the U.S. as a security consulting systems engineer for Cisco Systems, Inc. for over eight years. Beyond his CCIE certification, Larry holds many network and security certifications including CISSP. He is an avid cyclist and he also enjoys camping, hiking, and fly-fishing in his down time. Larry's greatest joy comes from his wife Michelle and their two children Logan and Alex.

Joe Stinson, CCIE No. 4766 (R&S) is a consulting systems engineer with Cisco Systems, based in Atlanta, GA. He is currently the lead engineer responsible for architecting and building the internetworking solutions demonstrations for the Cisco Atlanta Commercial Customer Briefing Center. His responsibilities heavily utilize the networking, security, and IP telephony skills he has acquired, as a security-focused systems engineer for Cisco. Joe is a CISSP and is currently working toward his CCIE Security certification. He is a graduate of the Georgia Institute of Technology with a B.S. in information and computer science. His greatest joy comes from his wife of 15 years, Brenda, and their three beautiful children Jabria, Janai, and Joseph III.

Dedications

Chad Sullivan: This book is dedicated to my wife Jennifer, my daughters Avery, Brielle, Celine, and Danae, and my son Elliot. Thank you for providing me all of the energy and smiles you do on a daily basis.

Paul Mauvais: This book is dedicated to my wife Jessica and my son Ryan. This would not have been possible without their constant support, love, patience, and encouragement. (Yes, now Daddy can play, Ryan!)

Jeff Asher: My work on this book is dedicated to Jennifer, Sarah, and the rest of my family. Your support means more to me than I can express.

Acknowledgments

Chad Sullivan: I would like thank God for giving me the wonderful family and friend support team he has provided. Thanks to my wife and children for understanding when Daddy needs to write and cannot play. Thanks to my parents and sister for driving me to continue to exceed my own expectations. Thanks to my mother- and father-in-law who help our family more than they may ever know. Thanks to Larry Boggis for joining me on my ride into entrepreneurship. A special thanks to the technical editors and Cisco Press staff who kept our book on target with countless suggestions and advice. As always, thank you to Seth Judd and Lamar Tulley for the companionship while racking up endless sky miles. To Tyler Durden for always keeping it real. Finally, I would like to thank TiVo.

Paul Mauvais: Special thanks for their patience and support of my time and writing skills (or lack thereof at times) are due to Chad Sullivan and Jeff Asher, coauthors on this adventure, and to Brett Bartow and the editors and staff at Cisco Press for their patience with my concept of timelines and time management (or lack thereof).

Thanks to the management team at Cisco (John Stewart, Michelle Koblas, and Nasrin Rezai)for their patience in my repeated bleary-eyed attendance at morning meetings. Thanks also to Steve Acheson and Doug Dexter, team members who convinced me a long time ago that if I didn't like the way a Cisco product worked, do something about it and fix it! A special thanks to all of my contacts (now coworkers) in the Cisco Security Agent business unit, especially Alan Kirby, Ted Doty, Paul Perkins, Marcus Gavel, and Joe Mitchell who supported me with numerous answers along the way during this process.

Finally, thanks to the wonderful folks at Blizzard Entertainment for providing me the outstanding *World of Warcraft* environment to allow me to work out my frustrations after editing my chapters late at night.

Jeff Asher: I'd like to first thank Chad Sullivan for involving me in this project. I really appreciate the opportunity you've extended and the confidence in my abilities. Thanks also to Paul Mauvais for his work and help along the way. Thanks to the staff of Internetwork Engineering, particularly the engineers and management. Your work with CSA has continually made me explore the subject and given me ideas for material to include that others will hopefully find useful. Your help and assistance made my participation in this book possible.

I'd also like to thank my brother David Asher for calling me and asking me questions about CSA and challenging me with "strange" scenarios.

Finally, I'd like to thank the production team at Cisco Press for making everything that I've done on this book presentable. I am amazed at the way Betsey and the technical editors have been able to make the stuff I originally submitted look so professional and smart.

This Book Is Safari Enabled

The Safari® Enabled icon on the cover of your favorite technology book means the book is available through Safari Bookshelf. When you buy this book, you get free access to the online edition for 45 days.

Safari Bookshelf is an electronic reference library that lets you easily search thousands of technical books, find code samples, download chapters, and access technical information whenever and wherever you need it.

To gain 45-day Safari Enabled access to this book:

- Go to http://www.ciscopress.com/safarienabled
- Complete the brief registration form
- Enter the coupon code 53G3-1EYI-8IB5-12I3-GIC7

If you have difficulty registering on Safari Bookshelf or accessing the online edition, please e-mail customer-service@safaribooksonline.com.

Contents at a Glance

Table of Contents

Command Syntax Conventions

The conventions used to present command syntax in this book are the same conventions used in the IOS Command Reference. The Command Reference describes these conventions as follows:

- **Boldface** indicates commands and keywords that are entered literally as shown. In actual configuration examples and output (not general command syntax), boldface indicates commands that are manually input by the user (such as a show command).
- *Italics* indicate arguments for which you supply actual values.
- Vertical bars (|) separate alternative, mutually exclusive elements.
- Square brackets [ ] indicate optional elements.
- Braces { } indicate a required choice.

Braces within brackets [{ }] indicate a required choice within an optional element.

Introduction

The Cisco Security Agent product is extremely successful in protecting endpoints around the world. The power it provides must be understood to use it effectively and efficiently. This book attempts to provide guidance and examples to help CSA users worldwide do just that.

Who Should Read This Book?

This book is intended for anyone currently using the CSA product as well as anyone targeting its implementation. Although this book is a useful resource for the implementation and tuning teams, it also provides a great deal of information pertinent to project managers and IS/IT managers who are tasked with overseeing a CSA project or implementation.

How This Book Is Organized

This book is intended to be read cover-to-cover or used as a reference when necessary. The book is broken into five sections and two appendixes that cover a CSA overview, CSA project planning and implementation, CSA installation, CSA policy, monitoring, and troubleshooting.

- **Chapter 1, "The Problems: Malicious Code, Hackers, and Legal Requirements"**—CSA is capable of preventing day-zero attacks and enforcing acceptable use polcies. This chapter covers the threats posed by targeted hacking techniques and corporate espionage, as well as the rapidly evolving legal requirements many industries face.
- **Chapter 2, "Cisco Security Agent—The Solution"**—This chapter covers how CSA can provide the controls necessary to address the concerns mentioned throughout Chapter 1, ranging from various online threats to legislative requirements.
- **Chapter 3, "Information Gathering"**—This chapter provides some guidance on what information is important when collecting predeployment information.
- **Chapter 4, "Project Implementation Plan"**—This chapter provides direction for the various implementations in your environment from the pilot up through the production installation and configuration.
- **Chapter 5, "Integration into Corporate Documentation"**—This chapter illustrates the necessity of project documentation and also provides information on how CSA should be incorporated into an organization's documents.
- **Chapter 6, "CSA MC Server Installation"**—This chapter provides step-by-step processes covering the various management heirarchy installation options ranging from single-server to multi-server and also from built-in database usage through MS SQL server installation and configuration.
- **Chapter 7, "CSA Deployment"**—This chapter provides detailed information on the CSA agents and information regarding various installation options, such as manual and scripted installation.
- **Chapter 8, "Basic Policy"**—This chapter covers policy components and usage as well as a discussion of what out-of-the box policies are available.

- **Chapter 9, "Advanced Custom Policy"**—This chapter covers custom policy creation and usage along with samples where pertinent.
- **Chapter 10, "Local Event Database and Event Correlation"**—This chapter covers using the information provided in the CSA event logs and also how to appropriately filter the data provided.
- **Chapter 11, "Troubleshooting Methodology"**—This chapter covers CSA troubleshooting by using agent and management server logs as well as built-in troubleshooting tools that are available to the administrative team and CSA users.
- **Appendix A, "Best Practices Deployment Scenario"**—This appendix attempts to cover many of the topics mentioned throughout the book to tie the many components and objectives discussed into a fluid summary.
- **Appendix B, "Cisco Security Agent 5.0"**— This appendix covers many of the new features of version 5.0 and provides screen shots to help you better understand the latest features and functionality that have been added.

PART I

CSA Overview

CHAPTER 1

The Problems: Malicious Code, Hackers, and Legal Requirements

Today's corporate security landscape changes too rapidly for most organizations to effectively react. These changes are not limited to random outages caused by malicious code. The new landscape of threats includes targeted hacking techniques, corporate espionage, and the rapidly evolving legal requirements many industries face. Each of these issues has had a real and lasting impact on many organizations, and therefore, it is likely that you have also faced one or more of these issues in your daily activities. Throughout this chapter, we discuss the high-level problems that you face, and we strive to provide a solution for these problems through the application of the Cisco Security Agent (CSA).

Part I, "CSA Overview," of this book, we look at some of the problems security personnel are required to solve and how the CSA can solve them. This chapter covers issues facing the security industry that demand solutions. We cover security threats and compliance as follows:

- Malicious code
- Hackers
- Compliance legislation

Malicious Code

Malicious code is the security issue most commonly faced by an organization's technical support employees. These employees include desktop and server support and helpdesk personnel. In addition, malicious code is the most common security disruption computer and system users in organizations and homes around the world face. For this reason, it is typically one of the most visible security issues and the one most reported on in the press. Along with the widespread visibility of malicious code comes the possibility of rapid and widespread negative impact. Because of today's high-speed networks, which connect computer systems worldwide, and because of the ubiquitous methods by which every user communicates (such as e-mail and Internet web access), it is highly likely that new exploits will cause outages that might shut down businesses and even critical national infrastructures. There are numerous types of malicious code. This chapter introduces you to the most common: the virus, worm, trojan, bot, adware, and spyware.

Viruses

The term virus has come to mean many things to various people and is often used when referring to specific malicious code types. A virus is typically defined as a piece of software that when installed or executed on a system causes undesirable behavior. Among a host of other symptoms, the behavior exhibited might be system instability, random or targeted file deletion or corruption, and system slow down. After a virus makes its way onto a system, it often attaches itself to other files on the infected system to increase the likelihood of spreading to other systems when the newly infected files are accessed. The malicious code is called a virus because it spreads through a computer system in a manner similar to the way a medical virus spreads through the body.

Viruses have traditionally been prevented and removed through the use of antivirus programs that are installed on workstations and servers. Antivirus programs commonly use a technology known as signatures to identify viral code. Signatures are pattern-matching strings that filter software on the protected system. Typically, the filtering is performed as regularly scheduled system scans and on demand upon software transfer to the computer or when the viral code is executed on the system.

Previously, antivirus technology was successful in identifying and eliminating viruses, but over the last several years, the implementation of this technology has been difficult to successfully maintain. Why is this the case? Because viruses are transmitted via high speed networks with a global reach, it is imperative that any antivirus implementation be as up-to-date as possible at all times. If a new virus is written and released on the Internet, your systems might not be protected until they receive a signature update that includes a pattern-matching string for this specific new piece of malicious code. Unfortunately, in some cases, all or some of your systems might not receive their antivirus update before the actual virus infects the system. If the system is already infected, the antivirus program meant to protect the system is no longer a preventative measure but an after-the-fact, clean-up tool. For this reason, it is important to look for newer technology based on behavior rather than pure, simple pattern matching that can defeat these previously unknown viruses and prevent unnecessary system downtime. The CSA can provide the protection required against previously unknown or day-zero infections.

Worms

Worms are often referred to as viruses; however, there is a single differentiator between these two types of malicious code. This differentiator is based on how the malicious code propagates from system to system. Viruses rely on the user for propagation. For example, you might unknowingly transmit the infection via email with a file that you do not know is infected. In contrast, worms automatically attempt to propagate without this user reliance. Worms typically have the capability to spread to other systems automatically because they attach and send themselves via email to every address in the user's address book. Alternatively, worms can spread by scanning the network to which the infected system is located to identify an unsuspecting system that might be vulnerable to compromise. The capability to move from a system and to automatically spread to unattended systems along their paths gives worms their name. The actual payload of a worm is typically viral in nature, and after infection, a system needs to be cleaned in the same way viruses are removed. The CSA has the capability to prevent the viral infection and to prevent the worm's capability to connect to a protected system.

Trojans

You have probably heard the story of the Trojan War and the Trojan horse that was used against the Trojans. In this story, the Greek army built a large wooden horse and left it at the gates of Troy. The Trojans thought it was a gift to their city and brought it inside the city walls. The horse contained many well-trained Greek soldiers waiting for the right moment to exit the wooden horse and attack within the protective walls of Troy. The legend indicates that the Greeks won the war through this surprise attack.

The computer term trojans refers to malicious programs installed on systems. These programs seem innocuous and act like other trusted pieces of software. However, interacting with this software ensures that the untrusted malicious code has access to whatever is passed through it, such as usernames and passwords, social security numbers, and credit card information. After the trojan gathers information, the information can be transmitted to a location where the author of the malicious software can collect it. The benevolent appearance of the software likens it to the legendary Trojan horse.

Bots

Bots are another type of malicious code. Bots are often left behind by viruses and worms, as are adware and spyware. Bots are software programs that run on systems waiting for instructions to act. Often, these programs communicate with a centralized location on the Internet where the bot controller can monitor the health of the systems infected, the number of bots available, and their location.

When the individual who controls the bots decides to act, she can easily and quickly send attack commands to thousands of the infected systems and instruct the systems to attack a determined destination. At this point, the infected system typically begins to generate mass traffic toward a destination in an attempt to perform a Distributed Denial of Service (DDoS) attack. This impacts the destination network and often severely impacts the network in which the bot-infected computer resides. In addition, the fact that the system is under limited control by a remote entity typically means that the system is "untrustable" and the integrity of the system is questionable. As a result, the system most likely requires a complete reinstallation.

Adware

Adware, or Ad Supported Software, is a relatively new form of malicious code and is unfortunately often mistaken as benign. In reality, this type of malicious code is quite dangerous to the systems used within an organization and even on home computers.

Adware is typically free to the user who installs it in exchange for the slight nuisance of seeing advertisements displayed while using the program. The hidden danger is that the software usually installs additional software that tracks system and Internet usage and reports back to Internet collection points that gather marketing data. The amount and type of software installed is commonly disclosed in the End User Licensing Agreement (EULA). Unfortunately, most users quickly skip past the EULA to get to the software they wish to install.

Occasionally, the software allows the user to choose a pay-for option that is supposed to disable the advertising and data collection capabilities in exchange for financial reimbursement. However, sometimes software packages still install a few of the tracking and monitoring applications even if this option is selected. The invasive monitoring characteristics of adware are what make it such a potential menace to corporate intellectual property and an annoyance to the general public.

Spyware

Spyware is another well known type of malicious code that has become extremely common on most systems throughout the world. Recent studies have shown that about 80 percent of the workstations connected to the Internet run some form of spyware. Spyware is software that runs on a system with the sole purpose of gathering information about the computer, its software, and its usage.

The spyware information collected is often more sophisticated than the identification of software and Internet usage. Spyware also contains keystroke captures that gather damaging information, such as usernames, passwords, social security numbers, addresses, credit card information, and other personal data or intellectual property. Spyware is often installed as part of the adware that was discussed in the previous section. Occasionally, spyware is installed using the same exploits taken advantage of by viruses and worms, but after installation, they have different goals. Virus and worm code typically attempt to destroy data, whereas spyware attempts to remain undetected and collect data from the system. Although spyware "attempts" to remain undetected, it is often poorly written and is noticeable because of the performance issues it can cause. To the surprise of system users, it is not uncommon to locate several types of spyware on systems during CSA evaluations and pilot installations.

The previous security threats discussed are automated and do not rely on a malicious user. The following section discusses hackers who attempt to perform similar actions but in a manual fashion.

Hackers

The term hacker means different things to different people. In a benevolent context, the term hacker commonly refers to someone who attempts to find innovative solutions to problems or an unintended way to accomplish a goal. In the media, hackers are commonly referred to as the subculture of individuals who attempt to break into systems and covertly obtain data for financial gain. In this section, we use the latter definition. This type of individual often uses multiple methods and malicious code to breach security measures of an organization. This can make a hacker as dangerous as several virus, worm, and spyware outbreaks combined into a single threat. The larger issue with hackers is that they typically have specific targets, and unlike malicious code, they have the ability to think and adapt to situations.

Script Kiddies

Script kiddies are individuals who use prewritten, downloadable software in an attempt to gain access and rights to unauthorized systems. These scripts are readily available on the Internet and come in various types and serve several purposes, such as monitoring and obtaining access to wired and wireless networks, gaining access to remote systems, and remotely corrupting and rebooting remote systems. The individuals who must rely on prefabricated software are often not mature programmers capable of writing their own new exploits and are branded as kiddies. Although these individuals rely on common attack software, they do not represent a minor threat. Because script kiddies drastically outnumber the capable exploit writers, they are a real threat. Therefore, it is important that systems are appropriately secured to ensure that they are not exploitable by the common and unending thwart of attacks used by script kiddies. CSA can provide protection against script kiddies and the methods they use when attempting to access privileged data.

Targeted Espionage

Individuals engaged in targeted espionage can be more damaging than script kiddies. Targeted espionage covers numerous threats: corporate espionage targeting a specific corporation; individuals seeking access to specific projects that are jointly owned by both educational and military institutions; military and financial targeted espionage; and cyber terrorism. Many people believe that targeted espionage attacks are uncommon and it is more a story line in today's cyber thriller novels than a reality. On the contrary, this threat is quite real.

Many large corporations have been specifically targeted, so that a remote individual can gain access to intellectual property that can be either sold to other individuals or to corporate competitors. In addition, the information might be held as blackmail in exchange for large sums of money.

As you might expect, target espionage attackers are not common script kiddies. Instead, they are the elite code writers and true hackers whose out-of-the-box thought process is often many years ahead of the security mechanisms that are meant to keep them out. Regardless of the advanced thought processes and mechanisms used by this type of individual, one thing remains constant. Certain operating system and application functions should behave only in well defined ways and any deviation can trigger the CSA to defend the system and prevent access.

Insiders

The last type of individual threat we discuss is the insider. The insider threat is often overlooked because it is typically from trusted individuals who are permitted access to data and are therefore not commonly questioned when a log shows that they have accessed proprietary information. These individuals commonly cross the line and become threats after an event occurs that makes them angry with the organizations, such as a missed promotion or firing. Additionally, individuals can become untrusted insiders when approached by individuals outside the organization looking for unauthorized access to information. This type of event is not uncommon and might even seem benign to the individual being approached. For example, a friend asks an insider for some information that is proprietary or requests simple information about corporate processes. Although the request can seem innocent, the information sought might easily be used by a person skilled at social engineering to then gain further pieces of information from other individuals.

NOTE Social engineering is the practice of gaining access to information through social interaction rather than digital hacking. Social engineering is almost impossible to prevent because it typically takes only a single individual's error to provide just enough information for the social engineer to then access the next piece and so on. It is important that your organization treat this as a real threat and address the possibility through regular security awareness programs.

Legislation

Previous sections covered security threats that require a solution, such as malicious code and hackers. This section covers a different type of issue facing security professionals: government- and organization-mandated compliance in the form of legislation. The cyber threats many organizations have faced in the past several years have forced governments around the world to rewrite laws so they can enforce this new type of nonphysical crime. In addition, many of these crimes have impacted not only organizations but more importantly, the customers and the customers' private data, such as social security numbers and credit information. This can cause a single incident to impact hundreds, thousands, or even millions of individuals. The following sections discuss a few pieces of this legislation and more specifically, the CSA's role in assisting with corporate compliance with this legislation.

HIPAA

The Health Insurance Portability and Accountability Act (HIPAA) was originally designed to cut health care costs that result from a lack of standards that surrounded payment processing. In addition, part of this legislature mandated the protection of patient data in two states: as it moves through electronic networks and when data is at rest, such as in electronic storage. The data that is protected is known as electronic personal health information (ePHI). A group of rules define the patient data set and specify what types of data, when combined, must be protected. For example, patient data can include the patient name, address, and medical exam record.

HIPAA affects many organizations primarily in the healthcare field, such as healthcare providers, health plans, and healthcare clearinghouses. Unfortunately, understanding these guidelines and implementing the required controls is not easy. To assist organizations in compliance, it is commonly recommended that the organizations start by following the Center for Medicare and Medicaid Services Acceptable Risks Safeguards document (CMS ARS). This document provides guidance that makes compliance easier.

NOTE To review the CMS ARS document, browse to http://www.cms.hhs.gov/it/security/docs/ars.pdf.

The CSA can assist organizations to comply with several HIPAA requirements, as laid out in the CMS ARS document. The following list outlines how CSA assists organizations by document section:

- Section 7: System Maintenance—Enforce immediate installation of vendor-supplied patches and virus definitions within 72 hours or provide a sufficient workaround security procedures.

  The CSA provides exploit protection without the need for an update to the software. Typically, when a new exploit is released and a sufficient patch is not yet available, the exploit is referred to as a Day Zero threat. Because Section 7 requires the organizations to patch or load necessary virus definitions within 72 hours, each time a new Day Zero threat is released, the staff needs to implement these updates immediately. Because CSA does not require updates, yet still provides the necessary protection, organizations can comply without assuming any additional immediate workload. This provides companies with a sufficient timeframe needed to effectively test patches and other updates before implementing them in production environments.

- Section 10: IDS Devices and Software—Implement host-based IDS on critical systems.

  The CSA provides Day Zero intrusion protection as a core function of the product.

- Section 10: Inspection of Critical Files and Directories—Review directories and files for unexpected and unauthorized changes no less than twice per 24-hour period.

  The CSA product provides real-time access control security and reporting for specified directories and files on protected systems.

Sarbanes-Oxley

Sarbanes-Oxley, which is often referred to as SOX, was introduced by the U.S. Congress because of the corporate financial scandals that occurred over the past several years. This legislation requires that corporate executives place strict controls over financial reporting and auditing mechanisms. If found not to be in compliance with the legislation, the corporate executives could face fines and prison terms. There are additional sections to the SOX legislation that specifically refer to the types of audits that could impact the financial records and stability of a company. Because of this, the CSA is a beneficial piece of the corporate security controls. The CSA provides monitoring, reporting, and control capabilities to many financial systems and to the many workstations that have direct user interaction.

SB-1386

Senate Bill 1386 of the California Senate (SB-1386) was designed to protect California residents' personal information from being left unprotected by companies and organizations that have collected and stored it over the years. This legislation is enforceable on any organization that has employees or customers who reside in California. Protecting private personal information is not an easy task and requires that security controls be in place to protect the data. The CSA provides the end-point protection for the systems that protect and access this data and for the auditing capabilities required to control and report on access attempts.

NOTE Although SB-1386 requires only notification of California residents when a breach of privacy has occurred, it is highly unlikely that a company would inform only those individuals whose security was breached, because other nonCalifornia residents would protest. As a result, many companies follow SB-1386 regardless of the customer location.

VISA PCI

Visa PCI, Protected Cardholder Information, is a standard driven by the Visa credit card organization. This standard provides a strict set of rules that must be followed by any company that accepts Visa credit card transactions and transmits or stores the information electronically. Visa PCI was specifically put into place by Visa to protect the millions of cardholders that trust that the companies that accept Visa every day will protect their personal identity and private information, such as name, address, social security number, and credit score. If a credit card vendor is found in violation of the policies, it will be fined, subject to restrictions, and possibly permanently suspended from the ability to accept the Visa card as payment. The CSA can provide many protective mechanisms required to limit or nullify exposure of personal information by providing secure systems and applications.

Summary

There are many reasons to secure systems; some are related to human threats, others are related to automated code-based threats, and others are related to legislative requirements. Although protecting transactions and resting data is a daunting task, it can be successfully implemented with the use of several products installed throughout the infrastructure. A critical component of that solution is end-point protection, such as CSA, that provides the actual controls over the resting data and any exploits that might attempt to gain unauthorized access to that data. The CSA is an effective solution that provides the necessary end-point controls required for countering today's threats, concerns, and requirements.

CHAPTER 2

Cisco Security Agent: The Solution

From reading Chapter 1, "The Problems: Malicious Code, Hackers, and Legal Requirements," you know that the Cisco Security Agent (CSA) provides institutions and corporations the necessary security controls required to deal with today's security challenges including spyware, adware, viruses, worms, and hackers. CSA also helps organizations to comply with recent legislation, such as Health Insurance Portability and Accountability (HIPAA) and Sarbanes-Oxley (SOX). To ensure that protected systems function within defined acceptable security parameters, the CSA product provides configurable rule types and predefined policies that are instantly deployable in most environments. This chapter introduces you to many of the architectural software components and to the configuration hierarchy that provides the baseline necessary to apply to later chapters. This chapter provides an overview of:

- CSA capabilities
- CSA deployment architecture
- CSA components overview

NOTE This book does not include a thorough explanation of the basic CSA components that are necessary to grasp the advanced topics discussed in the following chapters. To better understand the building blocks of CSA, refer to the Cisco Press book *Cisco Security Agent* or the product documentation available at http://www.cisco.com/go/csa.

Capabilities

Due to the way the CSA software interacts and monitors local system behavior, it can granularly enforce its security capabilities. CSA can play several roles within your network, such as personal firewall, host intrusion prevention, application control, security policy enforcement, and so on. The implementation of the CSA product does not require you to provide these mechanisms within every environment; however, you can enable and disable the policies relating to each of the previously listed roles throughout each environment as necessary.

CSA Component Architecture

It is important to understand CSA architecture at a high level to better understand how to deploy, enforce, monitor, and maintain your individual installation. The three major components of the product are: the Security Agent software, Cisco Security Agent Management Console (CSA MC), and the network communications.

Security Agent Software

You must install the CSA software on any system that you wish to protect and enforce policy. The current supported operating systems are listed in Table 2-1 and include various Microsoft, RedHat Linux, and Solaris operating systems. Although it might be possible to install and run the agent on other operating systems, such as Linux variants, you should note that only the specific platforms in Table 2-1 are supported and tested by Cisco Systems, Inc.

Table 2-1 *Supported Cisco Security Agent Operating Systems*

Operating System	CSA Requirements
Microsoft	Windows NT (Workstation, Server, Enterprise Server) SP6A Windows 2000 (Professional, Server, Advanced Server) SP0-4 Windows XP (Professional, Home) SP0-2 Windows 2003 (Standard, Enterprise, Web, Small Business)
Sun	Solaris 8 (64 bit12/02 or higher)
Linux	RedHat Enterprise 3.0 (WS, ES, AS)

After the Security Agent software is installed on the system, it begins to enforce the policy included in the installation executable. The agent then attempts to communicate with the CSA MC to register and check for policy and various parameter changes that might have occurred. The next two sections discuss the CSA MC and communications necessary.

NOTE For the CSA to communicate with the CSA MC, the host must be able to resolve the server's name. This can occur via DNS or a local hosts file entry. This name must match the IP address assigned to the server for a successful connection to be made. In addition to resolution, the name is also important because the agent uses the server's certificate based on that name for all the Secure Sockets Layer (SSL) protected communication.

Security Agent Management Console Software

All policy is configured and stored in the CSA MC, and all security event notifications are stored and viewed in it. The CSA MC is a component of the CiscoWorks VMS software. The only necessary components of VMS are the CSA MC and CiscoWorks Common Services.

The CSA MC installs its own application components and a database for configuration and event storage. As of version 4.5 of the CSA software, the MC can be broken out to run on up to three servers. By breaking out various CSA MC functions and running them on multiple servers, you can scale the architecture to 100,000 agents and gain additional resiliency. When installing on multiple servers, you have the option of installing the following services to other servers:

- Agent Communication Components
- Configuration Management and Event Reporting GUI
- Configuration and Event Database

The following section explains the basic functions of these components.

Agent Communication Components

The portion of the CSA MC product that receives and sends information to and from the remote CSA can reside on its own server or be combined with the Management and Reporting GUI and additionally with the database component in a single-server deployment. Information sent from the CSA to the MC would include policy infractions as they occur and information that results from various Application Deployment Investigation (ADI) or Application Behavior Analysis jobs requested by the administrator. Information that would be transmitted from the CSA MC to the remote CSA includes policy changes, various analysis job requests, and other configuration parameter changes.

Although the Agent Communications Component can be combined with other components on a single server, it can also be separated to provide higher agent counts and additional redundancy. Taking all the communication that occurs to and from agents and running this component on its own server achieves higher agent counts. By breaking out the software in this way, the dedicated hardware can focus on this single function. This prevents the sharing of processing and memory with other components, such as the database. Additionally, breaking out this software functionality allows you to keep a cloned spare of this server available to use in the event that the software, local operating system, or hardware fail.

In the event that the CSA MC is not available, the agents continue to enforce policy as it did before the failure. The database stores any policy changes made, and the changes are transmitted when the spare server starts and begins communicating with the other server applications. Also, the remote security agent stores any security events on the remote agents that would usually be transmitted for insertion into the database for reporting and notification until the communications path is re-established.

Configuration Management and Event Reporting GUI

This portion of the CSA MC architecture provides the management interface to the security administrators. As shown in Figure 2-1, policy is created and edited at this interface, and events are listed and investigated here. This component does not maintain any active settings or data because every configurable item and event within the architecture is always stored in the database, as discussed in the next section. In the event that this component fails because of hardware, software, or communication issues, agent security is maintained because of the locally enforced policy. In addition, any security events received from the agents are still inserted into the database component, provided the communications server and database reside on an actively participating server. The functionality lost until this component is restored includes policy and configuration maintenance and event reporting.

Figure 2-1 *CSA MC Graphical User Interface (GUI)*

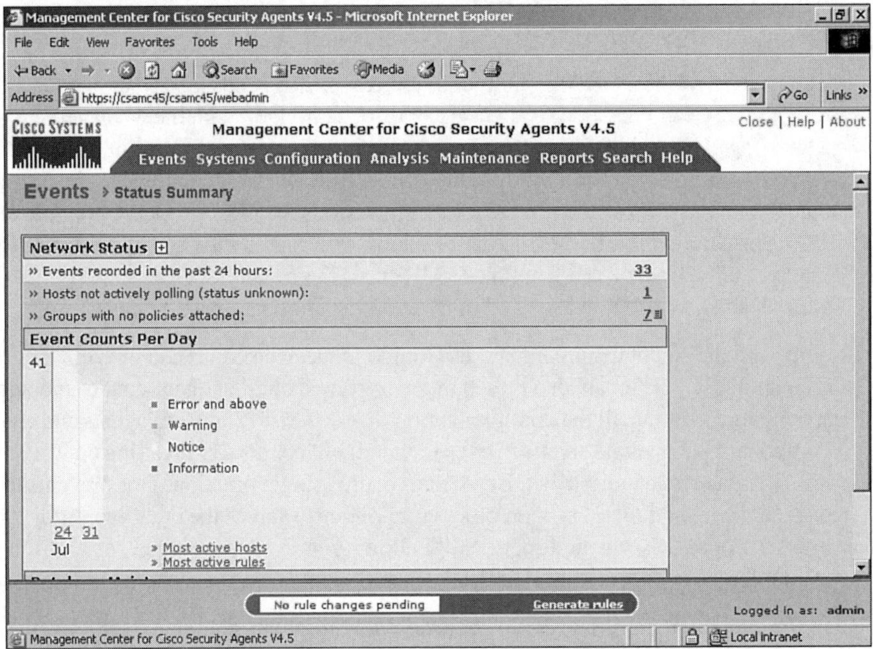

Configuration and Event Database

The CSA MC ships with the capability to install a Microsoft SQL Server Desktop Engine (MSDE) database during a single server installation of the CSA MC application. This type of database is limited to a total 2GB of storage, and therefore, it is supported by Cisco only for deployments consisting of 500 or fewer agents. For deployments greater than 500 security agents, you should install Microsoft SQL server on the single server CSA MC server or on a separate server in a multiple server deployment. This database stores all configurable parameters, policies, and events. For this reason, the MSDE database is the most important component of the CSA MC. Separating this component out from the single-server model is an easy way to take advantage of your organization's current enterprise SQL software and hardware architecture, such as Storage Area Networks (SAN) and other high-availability (HA) mechanisms.

Agent and CSA MC Communication

There are various communication paths that must be available between the agents and the CSA MC architecture to allow seamless updates and security event notification. When sending security events from the remote agent to the CSA MC console, the agent uses an SSL- encrypted connection on TCP port 5401. If a connection cannot be made on that port, the agent uses SSL over the standard TCP port 443. As of CSA 4.5, software updates and policy updates from the CSA MC to the agent are no longer sent through 5401 and/or 443. Today, agents receive this particular information via HTTP on the standard TCP port 80. This change allows these larger file transfers to be cached in various web caches that you might have deployed in your environment to ensure a more efficient mass update of remote agents. Additionally, the agent communicates with the management server at pre-defined intervals and at boot-up.

After your CSA Management Server architecture is deployed and the necessary communication occurs to and from the agents, you need to understand the building blocks within the CSA MC itself that allow you to group the agents in your deployment in such a way that they inherit the policies you desire.

CSA Hosts and Groups

The first two building blocks you should understand in the CSA architecture are hosts and groups. After a remote system installs the CSA software, it immediately attempts to communicate with the CSA MC server to register, verify there is an available license, and check for any changes that might need to be made to current locally enforced security policy. In addition, this initial communication also registers the remote agent with the CSA MC server and assigns it a unique identification, so that multiple systems can have the same name but still be differentiated by the MC. The registration process inserts the remote agent information into the CSA MC database and attaches the system to any necessary groups, as per the agent installation kit. At this point, the CSA MC refers to the remote system as a host.

CSA MC places all hosts into various groups as defined by the security administrator. Groups in the CSA MC allow you to attach certain settings and policy components across your deployment in a consistent fashion. Each host can, and most likely will, reside in multiple groups to inherit multiple policies and appropriate settings. Your groups might relate to various system types, system functionality, user types, applications deployed on the hosts, and every system in your deployment. The next two sections cover Mandatory groups and other ways groups are used outside of policy grouping.

Mandatory Groups

Every system that registers with the CSA MC is automatically placed in one of the three Mandatory groups:

- <All Windows>
- <All Linux>
- <All Solaris>

These groups provide a mechanism by which an administrator can apply high-level operating system-specific policies and settings. In addition, any policies attached to the Mandatory groups are mandatory. This means that you can place any security controls that must be enforced on all operating systems here without worrying that another merged policy attached to another group could override the setting.

NOTE The <All Windows> Mandatory group includes your CSA MC servers. Because of this inclusion, you should verify that the policy you attach to this group does not negatively impact the CSA MC applications, such as necessary communication. A rule applied here that prevents <All Windows> from terminating TCP/80 connections would prevent policy and software downloads to remote systems.

Creative Group Usage

Many CSA groups aggregate various policies that need to be enforced on the remote agents. Other reasons groups can be created include alerting, event filtering, and nonpolicy related group-level settings.

When creating alerts or event filters in the CSA MC, the group that contains the host reporting the event is the component that identifies the hosts. Although you might be able to send an alert notification to an individual in a small deployment based upon a group such as Desktops—Windows in large environments that are geographically dispersed, it might be more advantageous to notify the local support personnel. To accomplish this, you can create a group in the CSA MC named after the specific geographic region, building, or department. You would then add the necessary hosts to this group. This group does not need any policy attached or other settings changed. When the hosts that reside in this and other groups receive their settings, all settings merge appropriately. The administrator then filters events and bases alerts on this functional group.

Other common uses for functional rather than policy-centric groups include TestMode settings, ADI, and software updates. Each of these groups is tied to groups and not to specific hosts. Rather than forcing all hosts in a large group to perform any of the previous tasks, you can simply create groups for these tasks and move agents in and out of the functional group as necessary. For example, it might not be desirable to upgrade all systems to a new version of the CSA software without testing it in a sample of your user base. To accomplish this, create the software update job and tie it to the software update functional group. This group remains empty until you add the test hosts to it, at which time only those systems receive the software update.

After you have laid out an appropriate group hierarchy, you can begin to decide which policies you will deploy to the various hosts. The next section discusses the components you use when building this policy.

Policy Implementation

To secure your environment, the CSA must enforce policy as defined by your CSA administrator. This policy is typically a direct derivative of your written security and acceptable use policies. Security policy within the CSA product is a top-level component that aggregates various rule modules and, therefore, specific rules. For use in starting your deployment, various policies are included during the installation of the CSA MC. These policies are in addition to any policies you need to develop for your own specific needs. To have a clear picture of CSA product policy, the next section begins with the smallest component, a rule, and moves on to rule modules and policy in the hierarchy.

Rules

Rules are the smallest CSA security policy component. Each rule enforces guidelines on specific, attempted actions. Rules vary in what they control on the agent.

The following are Windows rules:

- **Clipboard Access Control**—Controls which applications can access information copied to the Clipboard.
- **COM Component Access Control**—Allows or denies applications access to COM components.
- **File Version Control**—Controls which versions of a file are executed.
- **Kernel Protection**—Prevents certain access to the operating system.

- **NT Event Log**—Allows specific Windows event log events to be reported to the CSA MC.
- **Registry Access Control**—Allows or denies access of the registry by application.
- **Service Restart**—Allows the agent to restart a stopped or non responsive Windows service.
- **Sniffer and Protocol Detection**—Detects and prevents non IP protocols and sniffer drivers detected on a system.

The following are UNIX rules:

- **Network Interface Control**—Allows or denies specific applications from opening a network stream and placing the NIC in promiscuous mode.
- **Resource Access Control**—Protects the UNIX system against symbolic link attacks.
- **Rootkit/Kernel Protection**—Prevents drivers from dynamically loading after system boot.
- **Syslog Control**—Has the remote system send specific Syslog events to the CSA MC when they occur.

The following are Windows and UNIX overlapping rules:

- **Agent Service Control**—Controls the agent service and its stop and start actions.
- **Agent UI Control**—Controls what interaction the remote system user can have locally with the agent user interface (UI).
- **Application Control**—Prevents or allows specific applications executing on remote systems.
- **Connection Rate Limiting**—Controls the number of inbound and outbound connections that applications can begin or terminate.
- **Data Access Control**—Controls certain web servers from specific malformed or malicious web requests within the URI portion of a HTTP request.
- **File Access Control**—Prevents or allows specific file read and write access.
- **Network Access Control**—Controls both inbound and outbound network interaction of applications on the remote agent. These rules provide remote agents with personal firewall functionality.

The previous rules are commonly used as *enforcement rules*. Enforcement rules allow or deny actions from occurring and are also used as *detection rules* that monitor actions or classify processes as actions occur. After being classified by a detection rule, processes are controlled by enforcement rules specifically designed to control the classified processes.

Rule Modules and Policy Hierarchy

Rule modules are collections of various types of rules grouped together to perform a collective task. By grouping rules this way, you can easily deploy the security protection or policy controls they enforce as a single component tied to another layer of grouping called a policy. Figure 2-2 displays a CSA MC view of the Operating System—Base Protection—Windows policy configuration.

Figure 2-2 *Policy Configuration View*

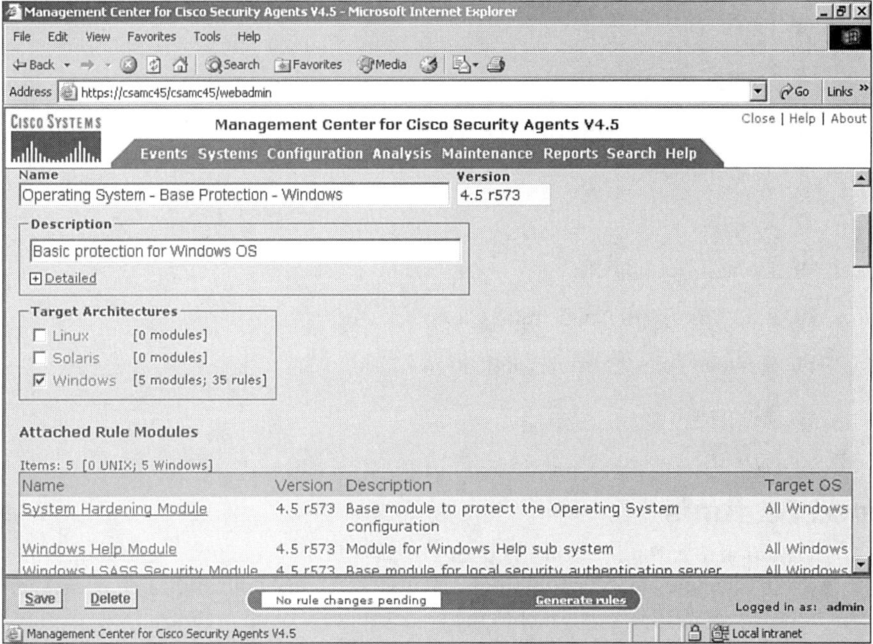

Policies as a grouping mechanism within CSA contain various rule modules that are related to accomplish a certain task or group of security tasks. For example, the desktop policy that is contained within the base CSA MC installation includes several rule modules that in turn contain several rules. Each rule accomplishes the task of protecting desktop systems. When each rule module's rules within the policy are combined, they are ordered according to a specific priority and are enforced just as a typical access control list with higher precedence rules overriding lower precedence rules.

Rule Precedence

As rules are combined into rule modules, and in turn into policies, there is the possibility that there will be conflicting rules in the combined set. The following actions are in order of precedence with the entries at the top taking precedence over lower actions.

1. High Priority Terminate Process
2. High Priority Deny
3. Allow
4. Query User (Terminate)
5. Query User (Deny)
6. Query User (Allow)
7. Terminate Process
8. Deny
9. Default Action Allow
10. Add Process to Application Class
11. Remove Process from Application Class
12. Monitor

Advanced Features

In addition to enforcing security policy and application control to endpoints, the CSA also has other features worth mentioning, such as ADI and Application Behavior Analysis. Both of these features are important to the actual success of an organization's deployment, and it is critical to understand the value they provide.

Application Deployment Investigation

When you attempt to use a behavior-based product, it is easy to protect your endpoints by listing your known environment and tuning the rule set to protect specifically those applications. The problem with this methodology is that the major security issues you face in any organization are not typically relevant to the known, maintained, tested, and patched applications, but rather are relevant to the unknown, untested, and unpatched applications that run on your systems. The ADI that CSA provides gives you a glimpse into what is really installed and used in your deployed user base.

With ADI, you have the ability to run an investigation on a group of hosts over a specified timeframe that collects various pieces of information, such as applications installed and listed in the Add/Remove Windows control panel, processes that are running or that execute while the ADI job is active on the host, and applications that are acting as either clients or servers on the network. Collecting this information and running reports to view the data allows a security administrator to quickly spot applications that should or should not be there and possibly control or prevent application execution, interaction, and usage. A great deal of information is reported from this job when network collection is included. Reported network information lets the administrator see which processes are initiating or terminating network connections and also the source and destination ports and remote IP addresses that are communicating. After you have thoroughly analyzed this data, you can begin to further interrogate suspect processes with the second analysis feature called Application Behavior Investigation.

Application Behavior Investigation

Application Behavior Investigation is another job that you would run on a single CSA protected endpoint that monitors a specific process or group of processes and reports back the related system interaction. The type of information reported includes COM, file, network, and registry interaction of the monitored processes. This detailed information is used to quickly write a rule set to limit or control process and system interaction. Remember, it is not what you know that is most dangerous; it is what you do not know.

Summary

The CSA is an extremely robust, effective, and granular policy enforcement and protective security tool. The rules can control many levels of system interaction in such a way that even if a certain rule is disabled or removed, other rules can still prevent the ultimate exploited compromise of the end system. Only through a behavioral product that is capable of enforcing security controls granularly, such as CSA, can you achieve true defense-in-depth security pervasively throughout the operating system.

Part II

CSA Project Planning and Implementation

CHAPTER 3

Information Gathering

The process of information gathering for a Cisco Security Agent (CSA) deployment is critical.

You must have a good understanding of your computing and network environments before deploying any security package, and you need to take the following into account:

- The types of desktops, laptops, and servers affected.
- The types of standard applications used in your environment.
- How your users typically operate on a day-to-day basis.
- How you best communicate changes to the environment. How your users like to receive notifications of changes to their work environment.
- Nonstandard or applications not supported by your central IT department or central software-support organization.
- Network configuration and deployment.

You must also gather appropriate support and key players who support your rollout of CSA in the environment. Although you do not need an army, you do need to involve the appropriate people to have a successful rollout.

This chapter explores the following topics:

- Reasons to deploy CSA.
- The phases of a successful security software deployment.
- Gathering the appropriate information about your computing and network environment to prepare for a CSA deployment.
- Gathering and involving the appropriate personnel to make your CSA deployment team successful.

Defining Purpose

By examining the first two chapters of this book and exploring the CSA product, you have a basic understanding of the security issues you face and how CSA can help you. Building on that foundation, we can now look into deployment. The next section discusses why and how to deploy CSA.

Why Implement the Product?

There are many reasons why you would want to deploy a product such as CSA; some reasons are obvious, some less so. This section looks at some obvious reasons first:

- For several reasons, you are tired of chasing day-zero exploit issues—by the time you learn of a new critical vulnerability, the folks writing the malicious code that takes advantage of that vulnerability have known about it for weeks, maybe months. Note that in this context, day-zero exploits are defined as vulnerabilities in software exploited or attacked the same day the vulnerability becomes known (zero days from the announcement of the vulnerability to the launch of the attack).
- Your anti-virus vendor is not able to keep up or has missed a few key pieces of malicious code (worms, viruses, and so on). Therefore, you want another layer of security.
- You are interested in the Cisco Network Admission Control (NAC) and having CSA work with the other pieces of software to help your environment adhere to your security and access policies.
- Preventing attacks by using an intrusion prevention product, such as CSA, is more important than just detecting attacks by using an intrusion detection product.
- You need additional visibility into your environment's security posture and want better control of it. BS17799, Sarbanes-Oxley, Health Insurance Portability and Accountability Act (HIPAA) and all the other legal review, certification, and audit issues companies face these days concern you.

CSA can help you in all these areas. Its behaviorally-based policies—which are policies that act based on the behavior of a computer program or system, not the name or signature of a program—can help prevent day-zero attacks or minimize their spread. When you use CSA, you do not have to keep up on signatures or make daily updates. In fact, most enterprise customers do not make more than one or two changes a month after the initial pilot period.

CSA is not a required piece of the NAC security solution, but it can play an integral role in securing endpoints (systems) and helping to secure the end host. It plays this role through its ongoing knowledge of the security of that system and what the network tells it is an acceptable security posture. That acceptable posture includes several factors:

- You run the right version of CSA.
- You point to the correct MC.
- Your CSA is up and running.
- You have not mistakenly disabled the CSA.

The NAC solution then makes decisions based on that information and changes your system's access to the network. These changes are made through the network switches and routers and through CSA via dynamic policy changes called state changes. These changes can raise the security posture of the endpoint system during a period of suspicious activity.

CSA can also give you valuable visibility into the state of your environment, assisting you with inventory, application-usage tracking, and more to aid in your certification or in the ongoing process tracking for Sarbanes-Oxley, BS17799, HIPAA, and other processes many businesses must follow these days.

What else can CSA offer you? The following list outlines just a few of the less obvious areas in which CSA can assist you:

- **Application tracking**—CSA 4.5 and later provides application tracking. Some of this is useful in gauging compliance with software standards such as the following:
  - Is anyone not running Office 2003 Service Pack 1?
  - Is anyone still running a vulnerable version of Firefox?

  Figure 3-1 shows an example of an Application Deployment and Tracking report design screen in which the report searches the database for information on all network applications that listen for connections from the network but have not accepted a connection for a specific number of days. This can be important because, for example, many denial-of-service (DoS) applications might sit dormant on your computers for a long period of time before a connection is made and an instruction given to start attacking.

Figure 3-1 *A Report Design Screen for Application Deployment Reporting in Cisco Security Agent 4.5.*

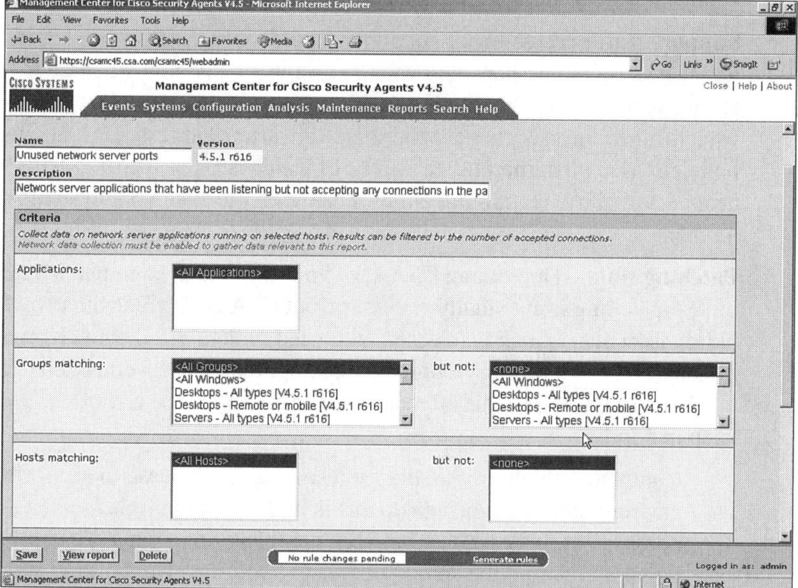

- **Application metering and control**—CSA provides answers to the following types of questions:
  - How many applications do you have that listen as servers and have not received a connection request in the past 30 days?
  - How many applications are not standard server applications. To find the answer to this question, you could request that the CSA show you everything that listens as a server, that is not a Microsoft service, not a known web server application, not a database application, and that did not receive a connection in the past 30 days. Or you might want more information about which applications talk most frequently to which hosts.
- **Forensic analysis**—Perhaps you need some help with the forensic analysis of a worm or piece of vulnerability code. Install CSA on a clean system, establish a set of policies that track every action by any application on the system (such as any file write, read, application execution, buffer overflow, network connection attempt, and so on), but only monitor (logs) the actions. Then attempt to exploit or exercise the vulnerability on your test system to map all the actions taken by a particular piece of code. Note that this is best accomplished within a "safe" virtual PC environment such as VMWare, so that you can control the network access and ensure that you do not attack everyone else. You might suspect that a vendor did something odd in their application but not be sure it is that application. If so, set up a policy for just that application's executable programs and track it!
- **Support staff access**—Your support staff probably needs broad-based access into users' systems, so perhaps you want to design a CSA policy geared to that need to ensure support staff's unrestricted access into every system. However, you do not want to allow the users to have the same unrestricted access. CSA allows you to apply policies based on numerous states, one of which is User or Group. This allows a great deal of flexibility in applying policies based on the state your system is in at that moment.
- **Patching time**—Does using CSA save you from the need to patch again? Well, not quite—patching is eventually necessary, but CSA does give you a window of time. Normally when a patch is released, you need time to test the patch on noncritical systems and run it through a process that might involve several teams' analysis of the patch to ensure no adverse effects on existing applications. Here are some things to keep in mind:
  - Complete full quality-assurance testing before release to a system environment. And you can do this in under an hour, right? Given the almost nonexistent time window between the release of a patch to resolve a vulnerability and the spread of a virus, worm, and so on to exploit that vulnerability, you need more time. The resolution time can be limited to hours these days.

   - Because of the behavioral nature of its policies, CSA allows you to have more confidence that your systems are not infected or data destroyed while you take the time to properly test a patch. As an example, it takes only 30 seconds on the Internet today (on an unfiltered connection) to become infected or compromised, so you need time to both test *and* to get that patch installed.

- **Dynamic application tagging**—CSA behavioral policies take advantage of the ability to dynamically mark an application with various "tags" and then apply policies to that application or the system based on those tags.

  The following is an example of dynamic application tagging. Microsoft Word by itself does not necessarily present problems, but what about opening a Microsoft Word document from your network share? The application is tagged as a **<Network Application>,** and pay a bit more attention to what it does. Now the document you just opened tries to execute some malicious code and open your e-mail address book and e-mail copies of various files on your system to your contacts (along with a copy of the virus). CSA tags that copy of Microsoft Word as a **<Suspected Virus Application>** and puts some more restrictive rules into effect, stopping both the attack attempt and making sure the user does not have to keep answering question after question as the virus keeps repeating its attacks. However, if you open a second copy of Microsoft Word on the same machine, it is treated as a clean copy, so you are back to the first step of this thought process. This means the new copy of Microsoft Word is considered reasonably trusted again until it does something suspicious.

- **Source code or intellectual property protection**—Every company has intellectual property—information that is worth more kept secret than it would be if it were public. For some companies, it is patentable material, for some it is source code, and for others it is product designs. You can use CSA to protect your data and your applications and system.

  The following is an example of protection of intellectual property. You can set up CSA to prevent any data downloaded from an application that talks to the corporate network from being saved to a removable device (such as a writable CD, USB key, and so on). Or maybe you forbid the use of removable media devices altogether. Or you could change the protection "state" of your system depending on where a person is connected, which means that at the office you do not implement as tight a security policy as you do if a person is at the BlackHat security conference in Las Vegas.

In all the areas outlined in the previous list, and in many more, CSA can serve as a flexible tool in your toolbox of security software and can even stretch beyond the area that desktop security software traditionally covers.

Phases

Now that you understand a bit more about what you can do with CSA, this section takes a brief look at the typical phases of a security software rollout and how you should apply them to a deployment of CSA.

To help you understand the deployment phases that apply to your organization and where you might need to apply additional effort, we describe eight broadly defined phases in this section:

- Identification of the Project Team

  In this stage you need to identify and gather early support from the appropriate groups in your organization that help you have a successful deployment. This chapter discusses this in more detail under the heading "Important Individuals."

- Scope Development or "The Problem"

  In this important phase, you should work as a team to identify two or three key areas that define whether your deployment is a success or not. Some possible areas are discussed in Chapter 4, "Project Implementation Plan."

- Prepilot Work (Information Gathering)

  This chapter explains this phase in more detail than the other phases. During prepilot work, you gather all the information you need to properly set and tune your CSA policies and to make key decisions for your pilot and eventual deployment.

- Piloting CSA

  This phase involves mainly the test group and is related to effectively and efficiently (quickly) testing CSA in your environment. You can then begin to take advantage of the security benefits. This is discussed in more detail in Chapter 4, "Project Implementation Plan."

- Postpilot Analysis

  In this phase, your pilot has finished, but what have you learned? Postpilot analysis should feed the metrics you want to gather at deployment time and past that. In this phase, you should also ensure that you gather the data you need to show a return on your investment (ROI).

- Deployment Preparation and Training

  In this phase, you perform the final testing of your production and development CSA environments in preparation for actual deployment. Change Management procedures should be in place and tested, personnel with administrative access to CSA should be aware of their responsibilities, and appropriate support staff should be trained on what to expect during and after the deployment.

- Deployment

  Deployment success depends on everything you do up to this point. Push the big red button! How will it affect your environment? If you carefully performed all the steps outlined in previous phases, you should be able to answer that question.

- Postdeployment Analysis and Ongoing Work

  The deployment successfully completed. Now what? If you are not careful about your planning and preparation throughout your information gathering and pilot phases, you might miss a piece critical to the success of your project. How do you correct those gaps and ensure they do not happen the next time you upgrade CSA? What ongoing training do you need to ensure that support staff, administrators, and users all have the tools they need to do their jobs with CSA in their environment?

It might seem like a huge amount of work, but depending on the size of your environment, many of these phases can be resolved in a few short meetings. However, to carry out an effective pilot and deployment, you must thoroughly understand your environment. The next section looks at what information you need to gather and how to proceed.

Understanding the Environment

CSA might be a host (desktop, laptop, server) security software package, but you need to understand all the aspects of your environment to:

- Maximize your ROI.
- Apply security policies in CSA effectively so they match your expectations for a secure environment.
- Minimize the effects on your environment (network, system, enduser).

You want to accomplish the three tasks listed previously because you do not want to do all the work outlined in the first half of this chapter only to have users select CSA as the first package they try to remove from their workstations after you install it. You would not get much return for your investment (or protection).

Is it possible to use a security package that does not impact users or applications—a package users will not hate? Well, nothing is without impact, especially security packages. However, it is possible to establish a livable balance between security and usability. After all, we all hate reimaging or remediating (for example, cleaning up) machines that have been infected.

Network

First, take a look at your network. You should gather information on several things—none unusual to any large deployment of a software package.

You need to answer some key questions first:

- Are all your users in one location or spread geographically?
- How are the sites interconnected? Fast lines? ISDN? DSL? Dialup connections?
- What is the bandwidth between your sites? If most have pretty good bandwidth available, are there any stragglers (slow sites)?
- How do you distribute software applications to your users/systems?

The following examines these questions and discusses their implications.

Having all your users in one location should typically eliminate all the other main issues. Local bandwidth is easy to come by (100 M Ethernet or Gigabit-Ethernet are fairly common).

If your users are spread geographically, what might the CSA issues be? The CSA issues would be typical of any other software package and could be categorized as follows: regular bandwidth usage (in the case of CSA, sending events to the server and receiving notifications from the server) and other bandwidth usage (full policy updates, deployment of the initial agent software package, and software updates to the agent itself).

There are ways to work within whatever network bandwidth level you have available to your environment, but CSA typically uses the following bandwidth in version 4.5 and later:

- Agent sending the management console an event: 3 KB-10 KB for an average event upload.
- Agent receiving a "hint" message to poll the management console for a new policy: 1 UDP packet per deployed agent, however only if NAT has not occurred for the host on which the agent is running. If NAT has occurred, the management console detects this and does not send hint messages.
- Agent polling: 2 KB–3 KB if there are no changes. 50 KB–100 KB depending on the size of the ruleset picked up by the agent.
- Agent receiving a software update from the management console: currently 8 MB–9 MB (the size of an agent kit).

As you can see, the largest network bandwidth load is the software update (or "Scheduled Software Update" in the management console software). If you have 100 people downloading that update at the same time across a T1 link, it keeps that link fairly loaded until those updates complete.

So take a look at how your users are distributed, and start thinking about how you would like to distribute both the initial copy of the CSA and updates. Ask yourself some questions about your environment:

- Do you have any prepositioning spots available? For example, do you have the Cisco Application and Content Network System (ACNS) or other web cache engine devices in your environment where you can use them to cache the CSA software update content to save time and bandwidth for local users?
- Do you already have software distribution points deployed to most of your sites where you could preposition the software or cache it in some way to save network bandwidth?

Servers

When deploying CSA into a server environment, you need to gather several pieces of data for use in the later phases of your project and pilot planning. Start with the operating systems in your environment and what operating systems CSA currently supports.

Reading the CSA 4.5.1 documentation, you see that CSA currently supports the following server operating systems for the end agents:

- Sun Solaris 8 (2.8) 64-bit 12/02 edition or later (corresponds to kernel Generic_108528-18 or higher), with SUNWlibCx libraries, and UltraSPARC single, dual, and quad processor systems
- Microsoft Windows NT 4.0 (Service Pack 6a only—earlier service pack versions no longer have support)
- Microsoft Windows 2000 (Server, Advanced Server) with Service Pack 0, 1, 2, 3, or 4
- Microsoft Windows 2003 Server Standard, Enterprise, Web, or Small Business Edition including Service Pack 1
- RedHat Enterprise Linux (RHEL) 3.0 Advanced or Enterprise Server

For the latest on what operating systems Cisco supports for CSA, see the release notes for the version of CSA you are getting ready to test or install.

Make a list of the operating systems you need to cover in your pilots and ensure you are supported. You might also decide to break up your pilot and rollout into phases that include the systems you can cover now and keep working with Cisco in the interim to develop support for the other operating systems you need.

All the operating systems listed previously are supported at approximately the same level. However, you should note that there is no graphical user interface to CSA on Solaris 8. All the others have the same look and feel to the user interface as their desktop equivalents.

In a server environment, you probably do not have as many applications as you do in a typical desktop environment, but those applications are no less critical (sometimes more critical) to the operation of your business.

To be prepared, ask yourself the following questions:

- What are the issues you currently encounter in this server environment that you can correct with CSA? For example, are viruses your biggest issue? Are unauthorized access problems causing you headaches? What about users installing applications not properly reviewed for security vulnerabilities? Is patching in a timely fashion an issue?
- Do you have a central build or default build for the servers or do server administrators build their servers however they like?
- What are your standard applications in your server environment?
- What do you want to include in your server policies to ensure appropriate protection? For example, do you want to protect web or database content from unauthorized modification? Do you want to stop application owners from modifying system software or stop application owners from installing new, unauthorized, or unreviewed applications?

The answers to those questions vary, but it is important that you have the answers for two reasons. You need to make sure you have a clear understanding of how to use the policies and capabilities of CSA, and you need to think about issues to examine.

Desktops/Laptops

Many companies consider servers to be their most important assets, but there is just as much (if not more) sensitive information on the desktops and laptops that the user community uses on a daily basis.

In some cases, users of desktops and laptops have more freedom to install software to decide what information is processed on them, and where they can be placed to allow the business to operate.

By their nature, desktops and laptops are also more vulnerable to attacks because of this flexibility and mobility, whether the attacks are web-based, application-based, or network-based. More users browse to malicious sites or run applications on their laptops or desktops than they would ever browse to from a server. In addition, the mobility of laptops makes them dangerous. Laptops can be moved into hostile environments, become infected, and then bring that infection back into your internal corporate environment where your typical protection methods are inadequate to stop that imported infection.

These possibilities cause the potential for damage both to the local machine and any other machine that a desktop or laptop can reach via the network.

CSA can help you with all these attacks both in detection and prevention (depending on the configuration of the policies) and allow you to have a measure of control over the activities that might cause damage to your environment.

Desktop/Laptop Operating System Support

The CSA 4.5.1 documentation outlines current support for CSA use by Cisco on the following desktop operating systems:

- Microsoft Windows 2000 Professional with Service Pack 0, 1, 2, 3, or 4
- Microsoft Windows XP (Professional or Home Edition) Service Pack 0, 1, or 2
- RedHat Enterprise Linux (RHEL) 3.0 Workstation

You need to be aware of what desktop and laptop operating systems you have and take that into account in your pilot and project planning.

To learn the latest information on the operating systems Cisco supports in the CSA, see the release notes for the version of CSA you are getting ready to test or install.

NOTE Solaris 8 is not listed here as a desktop operating system, although it can be used for either server or desktop environments. This is because CSA for Solaris 8 does not include a graphical user interface at this time. You can use CSA on any of the operating systems listed in the servers section, but you should be aware of this difference.

NOTE All the supported Windows operating systems listed in this section are the U.S. English version. Refer to the latest release notes for the version of CSA that you have to ensure compatibility with any internationalized versions of Microsoft Windows. With CSA 4.5 and later, certain internationalized versions of Windows are supported and internationalization (translation) of the base CSA user interface messages, events, and the help system. As of the CSA 4.5 release notes, this included running CSA on internationalized versions of Microsoft Windows and having a localized (translated) version of the agent messages and user interface for French, German, and Japanese (Kanji). CSA does not support international languages that display characters right-to-left (Arabic or Hebrew) at this time. The CSA MC user interface is always in U.S. English.

Applications

You need to ask several questions about the existing application environment on your desktops/laptops. Many of these questions are similar to those listed for servers.

- How are your desktops/laptops built?
- Does everyone start with a standard "image" or build?
- What standard (centrally or IT-supplied) applications do all users have or need to use?
- What are the most business critical applications?
- What other security applications exist in your environment already? (For example, spyware, anti-virus, and so on.)
- Are users allowed to install software?
- What nonstandard (or non-IT supplied) applications do most users install? What are the most popular?
- Are users local administrators (Windows) or "root" (Linux) on their desktops and laptops?
- What applications do you use remotely to manage or distribute software to desktops and laptops? (For example, Altiris, Radia, SMS, Bigfix, and so on.)
- If you decide to use the personal firewall policies in CSA, what ports (TCP/UDP) do your applications use, and in which direction must they be allowed to enable the applications to continue working?

The list of applications does not have to be exhaustive. You should, however, have a good idea of classes of applications, so that you can make some informed security policy decisions about what you want to protect. CSA has analysis tools that can help you better understand your environment and the applications you run in it. You can use that knowledge to apply appropriate security policies and minimize impact.

For example, if you have an internally developed application that every user runs every day to do financials, you might want to think about developing a policy for that application to protect it from damage and the data it writes. When developing such a policy, you should consider where the application is allowed to write—on a local disk, on removable media, on a network share?

The following list outlines specific applications to pay attention to in your planning processes if you have them in your environment:

- **Software applications that closely protect their licensing (for example, AutoCAD, MacroMedia Fireworks MX, SAS, Zuken Visual CAD, HyperSnap DX, and so on)**—Each copy of these applications tends to be expensive or has a fairly secure piece of code that watches the operating system closely to prevent licensing fraud or piracy. To these applications, CSA can, at times, look like a debugger trying to interfere with the licensing code; therefore, the application can exit without completing a run or in some cases crash. You can work around this situation by implementing a simple policy change that adds the application in question to the builtin CSA application class called **<Processes Requiring Kernel Only Protection>**. Subsequent runs of that application do not trigger this particular issue, and the application is allowed to run correctly.

- **Web-based applications that download code (for example, QuickTest Pro, Lotus Sametime Web Collaboration Software, WebEx, and so on) or execute command shells**—You might want to adjust your CSA policies to allow these applications to work properly without being denied or querying users too many times. For example, you would not want to allow a web browser to download and run any content from the network, but maybe this is acceptable from certain IP addresses. CSA allows you to make these decisions and easily adjust policies to cover these situations.
- **Applications that distribute software, patches, or make changes to the desktop/laptop system from a centralized point (for example, Microsoft SMS, Radia, Altiris, Bigfix, and so on)**— Policies in CSA 4.5 or later cover several of these "mass deployment" software packages; however, you might want to make additional adjustments for the environment to meet your requirements for distributing software, patches, or making other changes to end hosts.

You also need to understand how your applications and systems are used on a day-to-day basis. CSA can help with this when you deploy it in a pilot. For more information, see Chapter 4, "Project Implementation Plan."

Beyond Known Applications

CSA is capable of both analysis and protection in all the environments discussed in this chapter (desktops, laptops and servers). This section discusses CSA's analysis capability so that you have this information as a foundation when you read the section on "Application Deployment Investigation" in Chapter 9, "Custom Policies."

You probably like to think you understand all the operations of your environment:

- What software is out there (for example, Microsoft Office)?
- What versions of that software exist (for example, you no longer have Internet Explorer 4.0)?
- What software do users typically download and use on a day-to-day basis?
- Do you understand from your vendor documentation how your applications operate?
- Do you know if anyone is violating your security or ethics policies and running software they should not be using or are not properly licensed for?
- Are you sure that application owners are not installing software on servers that has not been authorized? (For example, do you have a server that was supposed to be a web server, and is it authorized to have an unpatched SQL 2000 database server on it as well?)

During the testing, rollout, and implementation of CSA, you will discover many things about your environment. Be prepared for this and do a little bit of homework ahead of time to lessen the impact or pain.

You should not, however, be afraid of these discoveries. You do not need to make a policy for every application on your system, nor do you need to know about every possible application a user might download and run. This is the power of behavioral policies, or policies that take action based on the behavior of an application or system rather than based on solely what version runs or which particular executable tries to perform a function.

The existing policies included with your CSA take into account many typical application actions and only query the user or deny an action if it is suspicious or known to be clearly dangerous.

Imagine, for example, that you open Microsoft Word to read a document. No actions needed. Then you use a function in Word to pull down a template from the Internet, and that copy of Word you have running continues to operate as before, but is also tagged by CSA as a **<Network Application>** and watched closely. If Word then attempts to do something suspicious, such as writing over a system executable, the user can be queried or the action denied to prevent damage to the system. None of these functions, however, required a rule that applied specifically to Microsoft Word. Instead, any application performing these actions would get similar treatment.

Cisco, fortunately, has done most of the hard work for you by developing those policies that bring a system to a known, secure state. Cisco includes policies that allow for the normal operation of each of the supported operating systems, expected behaviors of many major applications, and expected network communications between your system and other systems on the network.

This does not mean that system applications, for example, are always given a free ride. Instead, they are allowed to perform functions that have been tested and verified as reasonably safe without querying the user.

Important Individuals

By this point in the deployment, you have assembled a good deal of important information on your computing environment. Now it is time to gather the important individuals necessary to support a successful pilot and rollout of CSA.

These people should be familiar to you if you rolled out software in your company before, but this section examines each group or individual and discusses why they are particularly important to this testing and rollout process.

Project Team

You should gather a small team of individuals to be your core project team. Depending on the size of your company, IT department, and security teams, this can range from one person (you are it!) to a team of eight to ten people for a large enterprise. You might want representation from teams that perform the following functions in your company:

- **Team responsible for desktop/laptop (or server) software support**—Obviously, team members must be aware of their responsibilities.
- **Team responsible for quality assurance (for example, the testing of software for stability and usability in your environment)** —They need to be aware of CSA being a part of the standard environment in which they must test all new software packages. This could include both the IT Quality Assurance functions which most companies have, as well as the Engineering Quality Assurance functions if CSA might impact their software development or testing environments.
- **Team responsible for frontline or phone support for your organization**—The folks who answer the phone when someone calls Tech Support need to have Frequently Asked Questions (FAQs) and other documentation at hand and should be able to handle the majority of end-user concerns and questions.
- **Team responsible for corporate information security**—Depending on your environment this might be one team or multiple teams that can assist in the analysis and development of a security policy across your network.
- **Team responsible for internal corporate communications**—As much as systems administrators have joked for decades about how nice the computing environment would be without the users, you do need to keep the user base informed of what is coming, and most importantly *why.*

Executive Sponsor

The number of roles played by the executive sponsor depends on your company. The sponsor might be the person who signs off on the eventual purchase orders to buy CSA, or it might be the person who is there to help with political roadblocks if the project team encounters any in the testing or deployment. This person should be at a high enough level to provide that support and step in to correct anything blocking the project from becoming a success.

Project Manager

This person pulls together your project team and keeps things on track for testing, documentation, and notes. Otherwise, you might be so excited to try this product that you skip some important step in the process and cause yourself grief later in the deployment. Pick someone who is not afraid to document everything and keep the team on track but also has the team's support for that work. You should make sure that the project manager reads this section to gain familiarity with CSA and understand what information makes this project move more smoothly.

Support Team

For ongoing support of CSA, you need some percentage of time from a few people, depending on the complexity of your deployment and their comfort level and experience with the product.

As an example, the following is a breakdown of typical resources used at numerous large enterprise customers that have deployed CSA:

- **CSA administrators**—One FTE (Full Time Equivalent), meaning full-time employee. Generally the work is shared by at least two people, sometimes three people out of the organization that uses CSA, whether that be the desktop or server system administration teams. Responsibilities can include: policy changes, development, and escalations from a front-line support organization. These are usually the people in your team that end up contacting the Cisco Technical Assistance Center (TAC) for support if it is necessary.
- **Front-line support: negligible**—This really depends on whether or not you have a dedicated front-line support staff. If you do, supporting CSA is generally no worse than supporting any other deployed application and is often less painful than most Office applications. In either case, training the support staff and users and making documentation easily available to both groups helps to minimize any CSA impacts.
- **Host support**—The extent of support depends on how many CSA Management Centers you deploy in your environment, but in most medium to large environments this is no more than three to five servers. Therefore, support is generally not a huge burden. The group needs minimal work from the host support side (such as backups, hardware failure resolution, and so on).
- **Desktop or server software quality assurance team**—This is the same group you use to test software, patches, and so on before release to the general user population. In a small company, this might be the same people as the CSA administrators or it could be a dedicated team. In either case, they need to be trained to be aware of the possible changes to their testing caused by CSA. For example, when testing Microsoft Word Patch#1234, there were issues with saving files. Do we need, therefore, to try disabling CSA temporarily to see if the problems are caused by Microsoft Word or by our CSA policies?

You might need a few or all of these roles depending on the size of your organization and how you typically release software into your environment. Deployment of CSA might be easier for companies that have restrictive environments in which all software must be released from a central point than for companies in which everyone can install anything they want at any time. However, securing either environment with CSA is achievable.

Always keep the goal in sight: You are trying to save your organization money. Whether you calculate that money to include time, personnel, security incidents, cleanup time, or other issues, this book helps you to use what we are building on to start building return on investment scenarios you can use to validate your work.

Summary

We hope this chapter helped to better understand the information you need to make your deployment of CSA a success. From the network, to your servers and desktops and your applications, and even to the formation of a project team—all these things help you develop an appropriate plan for deploying CSA and getting what you expect from that deployment.

Next we help you develop a CSA project implementation plan and help justify the returns that a deployment of CSA can provide your enterprise.

CHAPTER 4

Project Implementation Plan

Now that you have most of the information needed to understand your environment from the guide in Chapter 3, "Information Gathering," this chapter puts it all together in the Project Implementation Plan.

This chapter explores:

- Timelines for testing, evaluation, and deployment of Cisco Security Agent (CSA)
- Selection of contributors to the Project Implementation Plan
- Deciding how success is defined for this project
- Metrics (statistics) on timelines and helpdesk trouble tickets
- Return on Investment (ROI) ideas and suggestions to help kickstart the discussions
- Training your team, helpdesk staff, and users
- Exploring scenarios of how to run a pilot
- Documentation suggestions to help you focus on critical areas
- The level of ongoing support needed for CSA after deployment

Thinking about all these tasks and steps at this stage helps you move toward a well-planned, staged, and documented rollout that maximizes savings for your organization.

Timeline

No one timeline can fit every organization's needs, but this section explores some possible scenarios to give you ideas on how to effectively build a timeline that fits your needs.

When getting ready to pilot and deploy CSA, you need to answer some questions about your environment that help determine how the timeline is laid out.

The following list summarizes some useful questions to ask yourself:

- How urgent is the need to deploy CSA to your environment? Is management demanding immediate relief or do you have some time to take measured steps?

If you have some time to take gradual steps, you have the flexibility to carefully plan a deployment of CSA. In case you do not have this luxury, this section points out possibilities that you can use to shortcut or speed up your deployment.

- From the data you gathered from the guides in the last chapter (Chapter 3), can you describe your deployment environment?
  - If you install CSA on desktop computers, do users typically have local administrator rights (Windows) or "root" privileges (UNIX) to install software whenever they want? Or is all software distributed in the initial install of their machines?

    If all software is centrally distributed and users do not have access to install their own software, then adjusting the CSA policies is fairly straightforward, depending on the mechanisms you use to distribute software.

    If users are able to install their own software whenever they want, and central control is only what you wish you had (maybe you get away with central control and distribution of key packages, such as antivirus and security patches), then you want to allocate more time to adjust policies during the pilot stages. We point out some ideas, however, that should save you considerable time.
  - If you install CSA on servers, do they all start with a common operating system image when they are set up, or are they all uniquely configured?

    As with desktops, if you start with a common image, then the configuration of a "base" policy set for CSA is straightforward. If you configure each server differently (for the base applications), then it will take slightly longer but again, we point out some well-tested shortcuts along the way to help you save time.
- How long does the process take for a new software package to be distributed in your environment? How much time is typically needed for testing, evaluation, quality assurance, interoperability testing, and deployment? Do you have centralized mechanisms to speed software deployment (such as Altiris, SMS, Radia, and so on)?

  You should be able to treat CSA deployment like any other security software deployment—the same processes, same background work for support and testing.
- How long does it take to order equipment, get funding for software licenses, and so on? This also affects your timeline.

These are a few issues you should consider when preparing a project timeline.

The next section explores a few possible timeline examples.

Example 1: The "Not in a Hurry" Deployment Timeline

For an environment where you are not in a rush to deploy, plan to schedule the following:

- A week or so for testing within your project team.
- A month for a full pilot. Use a good crosssection of individuals across your user base, such as engineering, sales, marketing, IT, management, and administrative staff. You should also use a good cross section of the equipment that your user base uses on a daily basis.
- A couple weeks for postpilot to analyze the results, make necessary policy changes, and then finalize the deployment plans.
- As short as one week or as long as three to four weeks to distribute software, depending on how you distribute it. Again, treat this in the same way you treat other packages.
- One to two weeks post deployment to make policy changes for things not caught in pilot, and update documentation for ongoing self-help user support or helpdesk documentation.

The steps outlined in this example take between 45–60 days depending on how fast the steps can be completed in your current environment. This example maximizes the testing time. In addition, the approach minimizes the impact on the people who use the deployment after the pilot. This approach has the drawback of taking the most time to deploy to your entire organization because of the extended pilot time.

Example 2: The "How Fast Can We See This Work" Timeline

For an environment where you do not have the luxury of a full-blown pilot and testing setup, and you want your project to start showing results as soon as possible, plan on the following:

- Schedule a day or two for initial testing within your project team.
- Roll out the initial CSA kits to all users in a data-gathering mode to collect information about your environment.
- Apply the information from the data-gathering mode to create policies to cover the core operating system and critical applications first (about one to two weeks).
- Apply those policies in test mode to all workstations and monitor events for a few days to see if they perform as expected.
- Activate the policies (take them out of test mode) and move on to less critical applications. Perform the same steps for these less critical applications by testing them and applying them

In this example, you see results from your purchase of CSA within weeks rather than months; however, you might have some impact that could have been caught in a smaller but longer pilot. If viruses and worms are widespread and you cannot patch fast enough to keep up, stabilizing your environment might be your top priority.

You need to judge, based on your environment, which of these examples (or parts of these examples) apply best to your environment. The later sections in this chapter to discuss what data-gathering mode and test mode mean in more detail, and how you can best use them to your benefit.

Contributors

Chapter 3 described the important individuals to include in the deployment planning of CSA in your environment.

An executive sponsor, project manager, project team, and support team are all part of a successful CSA project. They should have input to the project implementation plan, whether they are executive sponsors advising on expected timelines for deployment or support teams preparing documentation and information for users and support staff before deployment.

As we go through some background on metrics and ROI measurements, keep your project team in the loop and discuss these items in detail with them. The decisions you make concerning measures of success and returns on this investment of time and money should be understood and documented.

If you are not completely sure you understand all the uses that your users put their computers to each day for business, you might include a few select individual users in your discussions to get their input on how to best communicate the future changes to their environment.

Pre-Planning

This section looks into how to define some success criteria for the CSA pilot and deployment. It examines how to define metrics to prove that success, your ROI information gathering, and what sort of training your staff and users might need to help them.

What Is Success?

This is a huge question, but what in the space of bringing CSA into your desktop or server environments defines success?

Many different factors can define success in your environment, such as:

- Measurable reduction (through either objective or subjective methods) in time spent on handling security issues in your environment (virus, worm, malicious code, and so on).
- Measurable reduction in support cases for security issues in your environment (reimaging or reinstalling machines because of damage from odd behavior calls because of spyware, and so on).
- Installation of CSA with minimal user complaints during initial rollout.
- Users learning and being more aware of security issues because CSA stops particular attacks or notifies the end user or the administrator of attempted attacks.
- Users not noticing a significant slowdown or impact to their daily work.

Who Defines Success?

When you define the success of this project, the definition process should follow basic, well-accepted project management guidelines just as with any other product you might deploy in your environment.

Use your pilot group to grow a set of success metrics both for the pilot and the final implementation. During the process of defining metrics, continually ask yourself questions that define what both customers want. Think of your customers in these terms:

- You as a customer who wants a more stable and secure computing environment, among other desires
- Your end users as customers who want everything to run perfectly all the time, no interruptions, and nothing ever changing

You cannot please everyone all the time. However, you need to put yourself in the shoes of your users during this evaluation and design phase. For example, you might think about the following questions:

- What will change in their normal environment?
- Why is it changing?
- What resources are available to help them resolve an issue? No matter what the technical level of computer users, they always appreciate avoiding long waits on the phone or sorting through thousands of pages of documentation to look for resolutions to day-to-day issues.

Ask yourself these questions throughout this process, and try to make things as unobtrusive and clear as possible. Realize however that this *is* a change to the environment, and it *will* impact the end users. The most significant success metric to achieve is to make the impact of deploying and installing CSA as invisible as possible to your end-user community. Try to avoid the inconvenience to users that occurs when you must clean up after a virus or worm. The clean up process could be as simple as performing a few steps to remove a virus or worm, or as complicated as completely reimaging a computer hard drive and recovering from lost of data.

Defining Metrics

The following section examines ways to design some metrics now and gives you useful ideas to make this documentation process easier. This section considers metrics for project timelines, deployment scopes, helpdesk tickets and time to resolve them, and user interaction issues.

Implementation Timeline

As discussed earlier in this chapter, your timeline for implementation and deployment of CSA depends somewhat on how urgent your situation is. For example, how much pressure are you getting from your upper management ranks to "just fix it?"

When looking at metrics for implementing CSA, take into account the following:

- The time it takes to deploy an 8-MB software package to your machines.

  If necessary, break this down to determine how long it takes to deploy to one machine and multiply that out to get some estimates of the time needed.

- How aggressive do you want to be?

  Do you need to see some improvement in your base-security situation today? Next week? Next month? What is acceptable to you and your staff?

  If you need to see improvements today, set your timelines short for piloting and initial testing and speed up the basic implementation (meaning, CSA in **TESTMODE** or with minimal policies) to get that improvement.

- How will you deploy the system? How will you get the initial CSA installation kits onto your users' machines and installed? After CSA is on a machine, it is easy to update using the builtin mechanisms on the Management Center. However, you need to use one of a wide range of methods to get CSA onto the users' machines initially (for example, Altiris, SMS, Radia, PSEXEC, or a CD by mail).

Number of Hosts

The number of hosts you have in your environments obviously affects how you want to set expectations and metrics for your CSA deployment.

Unless immediate enterprise domination is on your list of requirements, you should consider splitting your deployments up into achievable, supportable sections. Perhaps a successful deployment to 500 hosts a week would be a good metric with which to start. This gives you a chance to see the effects of your deployment on a manageable numbers of hosts, and resolve issues early before CSA makes it onto your entire enterprise.

As mentioned previously, during the CSA installation process, you will discover new issues in the environment. Therefore, you should install CSA, but do it in chunks that you can support. Your helpdesk staff will appreciate you too!

Helpdesk Tickets

Most enterprise IT departments seem to guide the success metrics for any software deployment by how their helpdesk staff lives through the exercise.

You want them to appreciate you, so include them not only in pilot teams, but include some success metrics for the number and type of tickets you expect them to handle and still call this deployment a success.

Consider the following categories of trouble tickets as examples (with accompanying possibilities for metrics on each and estimated time to resolve):

- Conflict with other software
  - Metric: Medium caseload.
  - Average time to resolve: Short (depending on complexity of policy changes needed to resolve issue).
  - What is this: This could be as simple as a query that CSA presents to users when they start their software packages, or as complex as a conflict between another software package and CSA. This conflict could arise when CSA or the software package presents an error or does not start (although the latter is rare, it does happen but there are ways to quickly work around it).
- Feature Request
  - Metric: Low caseload.
  - Average time to resolve: Short-to-long (short for simple policy updates or changes to your deployment, long for product suggestions that need development time from Cisco).
  - What is this: Everyone has their own opinions on how software should look, react, and behave in this environment. Set aside something to gather up requests for changes to your deployment of CSA, or to the product itself, and handle them appropriately.
- Policy Modification Request
  - Metric: High caseload in the beginning, lowering over time as things settle in.
  - Average time to resolve: The time is usually brief but it depends, of course, on the complexity of the change requested, and the level of CSA policy development understanding by the administrator. It could be long if you end up arguing over the business versus nonbusiness aspects. Or the time could

be too long, in which case you should help yourself and your helpdesk staff. Have good definitions of what software is required for business in contrast to software used for nonbusiness (personal) purposes. You should then set your users' expectations accordingly, based on those definitions—how long can they expect to wait for an answer to a question about business software issues versus personal software issues?

– What is this: This is the bucket for all requests for changes to your CSA policies whether the request is due to conflicts that cause undue headaches or just changes to make things run more smoothly. Expect quite a few of these up front if your environment is diverse, but they will settle over a short period of time as users become accustomed to your policies.

NOTE To save the time of you and your helpdesk, you might want to categorize policy modification requests as business-related and nonbusiness-related. Just be sure to clearly define what you mean by business and nonbusiness-related. For example, is Microsoft Word business-related? Are computer games business-related? You might wish to define Service Level Agreements (SLA) with your users up front to set expectations on how often business or nonbusiness policy-related changes occur.

The following looks at an example to clarify the preceding discussion. You could define rules for handling business-related changes as follows:

- Impacting changes (meaning changes that stop the business from operating normally) are analyzed and handled within one business day of receipt.
- Normal business-related policy changes that do not immediately impact users but are perhaps annoying are analyzed and handled within one week.
- Nonbusiness-related policy changes within one business quarter (they do deserve an answer eventually).

- CSA Questions
  – Metric: High caseload in the beginning, lowering over time as users become accustomed to the presence of CSA.
  – Average time to resolve: Very short—*if* you do your homework ahead of time and write up those frequently asked questions for your staff and the helpdesk groups.
  – What is this: At first glance, this seems to be a catch-all category. However, the better you write your documentation and train your staff before the deployment, the quicker they can answer questions and cases in this category.

NOTE Frequently Asked Questions (FAQ) web pages or e-mailed documentation can help the most. Users who work with CSA for the first time need to understand why you are installing it. They ask themselves this question: What benefits do I get as a user for the pleasure of installing another software package on my desktop? They also need to be aware that in most configurations, they will see popup queries and messages from CSA. The more prepared they are for these popups and messages and the better they understand how to use CSA to secure their machines in the most unintrusive way, the happier they are.

- Installation/Uninstallation Questions
  - Metric: Shoot for a low caseload in this category, although installation at most sites proves to amount to medium caseloads.
  - Average time to resolve: Medium to long. These issues usually are not resolved in five minutes. It takes a bit of log file reading, and perhaps some reading of CSA documentation ahead of time to help develop instructions on how to resolve these issues. They are handled quicker over time as your helpdesk staff becomes more comfortable with issues and possible resolutions. Again, develop documentation early in the process and keep it up-to-date as you discover new things in your pilot.
  - What is this: This is the category for all installation and uninstallation questions about CSA (yes, sometimes users have an issue and need to uninstall or reinstall). Hopefully, with good piloting and quality assurance testing, this category will have a low caseload. Good documentation for your helpdesk and technical staff is the key to keeping this as straightforward as possible. Cisco has documentation available on http://www.cisco.com that can assist you in developing break-fix documentation, which outlines what happens when there are problems with the installation programs and you need to manually uninstall CSA. The document outlines the steps you need to take.

The preceding list has outlined nurmerous possible categories to help you develop topics for both helpdesk cases and metrics to measure them by. You need to decide what makes sense for your environment as far as an acceptable SLA for each of these categories. If you have a medium-to-large site, you likely have similar categories worked out for other software packages and do not have to reinvent the wheel here. In this case, you can use the preceding list as primary categories to work from and develop your categories and metrics based on them. The better you develop these categories ahead of time, the easier it is to develop case metrics to measure the comparative difficulty of installing and operating various software packages.

Typically, customers who install CSA in their enterprise have found graphics and office document-handling packages to be more helpdesk-intensive than CSA.

User Interaction and Queries

What do computer users hate the most? Interuptions. Whether it is a virus, spyware, web browser-based scripting (JavaScript, VBScript, and so on), or security programs themselves, users hate popup messages that interrupt their work.

The following are some definitions you should understand:

- CSA Query Message—Often referred to as a popup because that is what it does. CSA opens a window in the middle of your screen with a question that you must answer before proceeding. Figure 4-1 illustrates an example of this. Some messages might also include a secondary challenge—a series of letters you must enter to ensure for sensitive operations that there is a human in front of the machine (and not something just clicking Yes for you). Figure 4-2 displays an example of this.

Figure 4-1 *A Standard Cisco Security Agent Version 4.5 Query*

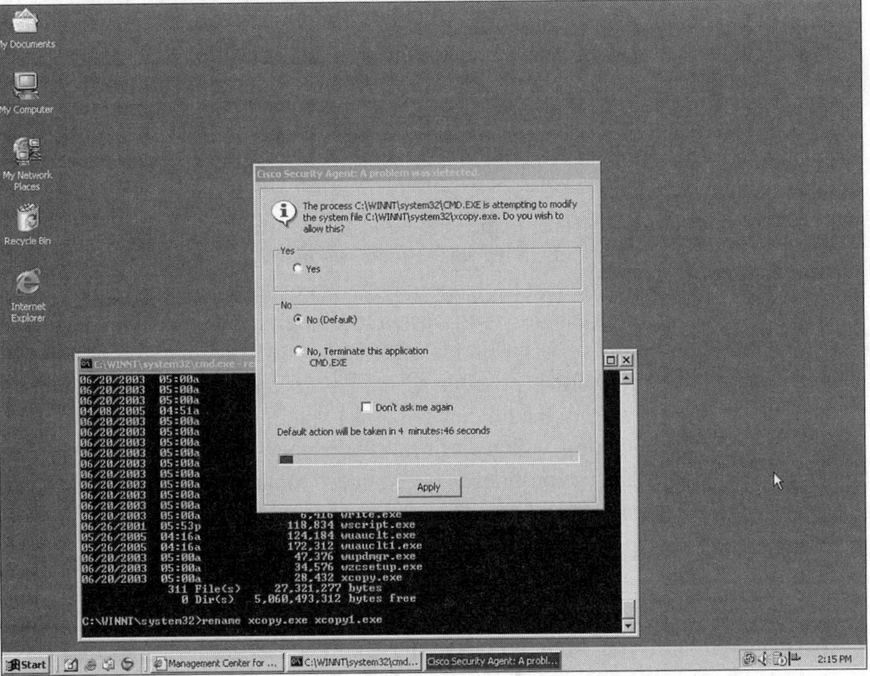

Figure 4-2 *A Standard Cisco Security Agent Version 4.5 Query with a Challenge*

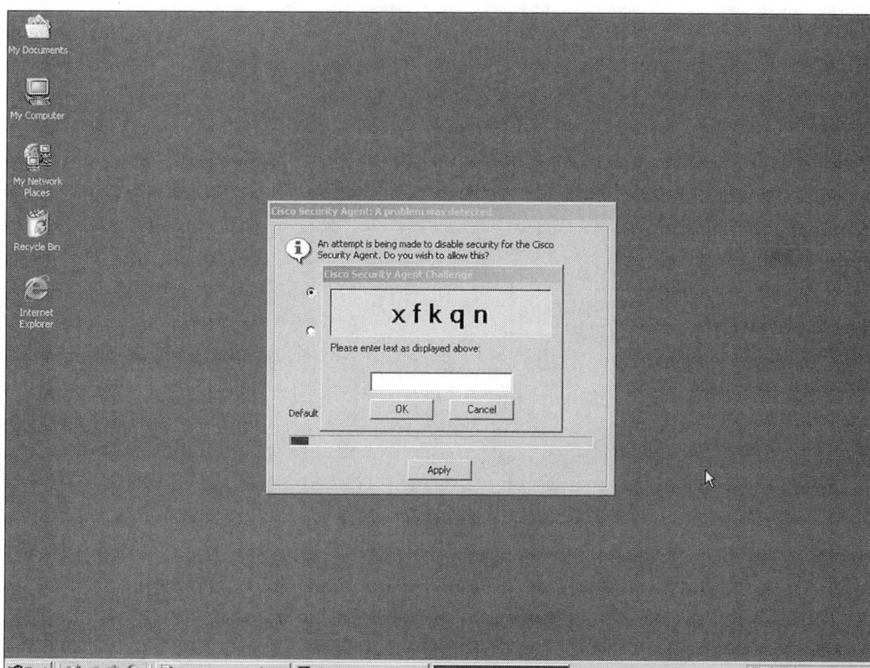

- CSA Balloon Message—these are messages that appear as a little balloon above the Cisco Security Agent red flag in your taskbar. Figure 4-3 displays an example of a balloon message. They do not require any interaction and can be silenced by the user if they become annoying via the CSA menu on the user's machine.

Figure 4-3 *A Standard Cisco Security Agent Version 4.5 Balloon Message*

With these factors in mind, what can you do to define some metrics for how you want your users to interact with CSA?

- You can take a simple approach and set the **No User Interaction** checkbox, which disables all popup messages and queries—in fact it removes the CSA flag and user interface completely from the user's sight. CSA still operates normally; however, *any* query message that would have appeared to the user takes the default answer instead of giving the user a choice.

  This is a bit severe—make sure you understand what sort of environment you are deploying this option to, and test it well for the side effects of not giving the user any choice.

- You can test these metrics for the number of query messages in a pilot and in various stages throughout your pilot. Poll your pilot users for feedback on the numbers of query messages they see during their daily activities to come up with changes to the CSA policy that you need to make. You can also poll users to develop a metric of what are acceptable query levels.

This is an example of the thought process for the number of acceptable queries to see: Are three queries a day an acceptable metric for your users as an end goal? Are 20 queries a day acceptable?

- How can users use the **Don't ask again** checkbox to save time and queries in the future? You should take a look at the rules that you develop (and the policies provided by Cisco) and see what makes sense for your organization. Remember that as the CSA administrator, you can decide what answers to what questions that appear can be saved. You can also change that decision later with a simple policy change. This can be useful, especially if you make a decision based on the information you have at the time, and then later discover that you would like to change your mind and not allow users to save a particular answer to a particular query based on some new information.

Many companies are able to reduce their events and queries to reasonable numbers, and this book helps you along that path, but user environments differ greatly and it is hard to recommend one number over another. You need to keep your query messages to a minimum if at all possible, so that:

- Your users actually read what is on the screen in front of them when a query displays, and then they take appropriate action.
- Your users do not become annoyed by too many query messages and get in the habit of clicking Yes to anything that pops up on the screen (definitely a *bad* habit).

During your project planning, remember that your CSA policies reflect your security policy. However, to successfully deploy any security package, you must make tradeoffs between security and usability.

ROI

ROI is the ultimate measure of success for a good project. This needs to be researched and typically documented to explain the reasoning behind the project.

If you are lucky and plan so well that you have extra time and money to invest in deploying CSA to all your machines, you can have a preventative measure in place *before* an attack happens. This is the best possible situation. However, most people come looking for security software not because they have unlimited time or resources to deploy it, but because their network and hosts have suffered a meltdown (perhaps for the second or third time) and they urgently need help.

However, help or mitigation against future attacks implies cost in manpower (people/time), capital expenses (equipment deployed—in this case, Management Center), and operating costs (software purchases, on-going time and effort, and support). Whenever cost is involved, most organizations want to have proof of a return on that investment.

In this case, several categories can be tracked to calculate a return on your investment in the purchase, deployment, and ongoing support of CSA. The following defines a set of them and gives you some examples on how to do this:

- Cost of an incident
  - Define what an incident is to you and your organization. This can be something as simple as one attack or infection, or it can be the percentage of your organization that is affected by a particular security issue during a specified time.
  - Do not overcomplicate things. For your organization, just figure out how much a minor versus a major incident costs you *per* occurrence.

    Major can be defined as a certain number of hours spent by a specified number of staff members or the number of machines affected (or infected as the case may be).

    Minor can be defined as everything that falls under the major threshold, but guard against including insignificant instances; for example, an employee brings a virus into the workplace, it affects only his machine, and is detected and cleaned by the antivirus. Such an incident probably does not qualify for a huge expense line or significant tracking.
  - Start tracking the time spent on these incidents *before* you deploy CSA if at all possible. It is difficult to get numbers out of people after an incident, as they are usually exhausted and either under- or over-estimate the time actually spent.
  - Track all costs associated with an incident that it is reasonable to track and track them as quickly as possible:

    Did you have to take down a portion of production networking? What was the lost time (man-hours) because of this (to both those infected and not infected)?

    Did you have to recover and reimage users' workstations because of malicious code or other infections that were not cleanable through traditional methods (antivirus, cleaning programs, and so on).

    Was travel required to mobilize a remote work force to address issues at remote locations?

    How long were users unable to work? (This can be hard to track, but it is worth trying to estimate.)
- Calculate the number of incidents you have in a typical year.
  - You do not generally gain much by measuring less than a year (such as measuring a quarter or month), because you are trying to define a general figure to work with.

  - Separate your list of incidents based on the criteria you came up with in the preceding "Cost of an Incident" section (criteria such as cost or severity of the incident). Use the major and minor criteria examples (or your own definitions) to break the list up into those two groups. Go back as far as you can track these incidents to give yourself a good base from which to work. If you do not have that base to work from, start the tracking methods to gather this information, so you are in the habit of collecting the appropriate information *as it happens*.
- Gather the number of total machines you expect to deploy CSA to, and negotiate at least a starting point quote for what your cost of CSA will be (from the software perspective).
  - If you already purchased CSA, this is the easy part.
  - If you have not purchased CSA, contact your account manager or reseller and get at least a ballpark number to work with.
- Do your best to split the numbers you have from the earlier items in this list to operating expenses and capital expenses.

Now that you understand what information you need to gather, you might ask yourself what you expect to gain from it.

To help you answer that question, Table 4-1 outlines a quick formula.

Table 4-1 *Example Incident Cost Chart*

Year	Cost	Frequency	Event Cost	Total Cost	
2004	$200,000 minor	4	$800,000.00		
	$2.5 million major	2	$5,000,000.00	$5,800,000.00	OPERATING EXPENSE
2005	$200,000 minor	4	$800,000.00		
	$2.5 million major	2	$5,000,000.00	$5,800,000.00	OPERATING EXPENSE

In this chart, we determined that a minor virus, worm, or malicious code incident typically costs 200,000 dollars. This figure is calculated from the average wages per hour across all employees typically involved in handling an incident and lost time (users, production networks, and so on) caused by the incident. The major incident that is shown in the example costs roughly 2.5 million dollars. We then track back and agree that we had four minor and two major incidents in the 2004 calendar year, and the same in 2005.

This brings us to a rough total of approximately 5.8 million dollars spent each year in time and effort just to combat incidents that should be preventable with the help of CSA. This calculation is based on our knowledge of what CSA is capable of doing and stopping.

Although those numbers might seem enormous, think carefully about the last major virus or worm issue you had in your company, and what you lost because of it. Actually, we consider these numbers to be fairly conservative for most medium to large businesses.

So in this example case, as long as the capital and operating expenses to deploy CSA cost *less* than 5.8 million dollars, then you received a return on your investment.

What should you expect to see? After deploying CSA, you should hope to see most of those major events go away, and the number of minor incidents minimized. For those incidents that do occur post-CSA rollout, they should be contained to a small base of users as opposed to a large group that needs remediation. In addition, the effects of the incident on user computers should be so minimal that users can continue working.

In the preceding example, if you get rid of the major incidents and contain your issues to minor incidents in the first year, you would save five million dollars.

What about the incidentals? In a large enterprise, there is typically a limited security and operations staff available to investigate, track down, and remediate machines inflected by a virus or malicious code. We all want to have staff available to dispatch at the first sign of a security issue. However, most companies cannot afford that. On the other hand, think of the amount of time it takes just to add up to the five million dollars in the example. If you can get all that time (or most of it) back and dedicate it to working on other security issues, what is that worth, and how can you represent it as a return on this investment?

At this point, it might be useful for you to review the information covered in this section, and go back and look at some previous incidents you experienced. Try to fill in the blanks and gather information to then compare to your post-CSA deployment information. It will be invaluable in proving your case later on.

Phased Approach

You now know the details of your environment, including the following: the machines you have; what you want to deploy CSA to; what information you want to gather for an effective pilot and deployment; and perhaps out of the metrics and return on investment work, you have an idea of where you want to install CSA first. This section looks at the rationale for using a phased approach.

A phased approach is important to a successful deployment of CSA because unless you have done this many times before, you learn things during deployment that you did not understand or think to cover in your project planning and pilots.

Because of this, you should plan where and how much you deploy during this planning phase. You can then have the pilot and deployment phases cover the information you need to properly develop your policies. In addition, you can also get the biggest return for your investment up front and move a step ahead of the remediation/cleanup never-ending loop.

Look carefully at your environment and choose some areas in which you can be successful in small chunks first (such as a small group of desktop users, or a certain set of servers that are all running the same software, such as a web server or SQL server). After you tackle those through the appropriate pilot and deployment rollout phases, move on to more complicated environments.

Training Requirements

The following section describes an important part of the CSA deployment processes: training.

As with almost any new software deployment, you should develop training for the following groups:

- Administrators—This can include desktop administrators, server administrators, and application administrators.
- Support staff—This might encompass everyone in a fully stratified model of helpdesk support: front-line people who answer the phones, second-line support, and escalation support. On the other hand, support staff can merely encompass a simple support staff structure that can be a single person.
- Users—It is gratifying to see users actually use the tools available to them, and most users do end up feeling more empowered if they have tools to resolve problems themselves rather than waiting on a helpdesk call for hours.

What Does Training Encompass?

Training for CSA takes on a wide range of possible forms depending on your environment. However, here are some examples that apply to most environments:

- Administrators
- System managers of the Management Center

  Read the CSA documentation (at least the installation and release notes).

  Some portion of the administration staff should attend a CSA training class if possible to get professional hands-on training, even if it is a train-the-trainer situation.
- Administrators (of desktops, servers, applications, and so on) in the environments you deploy to

Simple documentation and training on what users need to be aware of when CSA is installed and operating, including the following:

  — What tools or software should you (as an administrator) expect to become nonfunctional?
  — Where do you look at log messages to find out if CSA is breaks something?
  — How do you debug an issue to figure out if CSA causes the problem or if some other application causes it?
  — What logs do you need to provide the escalation staff in your company if you need more help? Or if you are the escalation staff, what sort of information does Cisco TAC need to properly debug an issue?
  — What sorts of messages can you expect to see on you screen, and how should you handle them? What should you report to security?
  — How are policy changes handled?

- Support staff

  All the things in the previous section (administrators) plus:

  — What sorts of problems should the support staff expect to see on a regular basis and how are they handled?
  — What can go wrong with an installation of CSA?
  — How do you manually uninstall CSA if needed?
  — What is a business policy change versus a personal policy change? For example, Oracle having an issue would likely be a business policy change and therefore a higher priority; Kazaa being broken would likely be a personal policy change and therefore be a lower priority.
  — What are the expected SLAs for the pilot and for final rollout (and for any changes needed)?

- Users

  — A "what should users expect from CSA" e-mail or web discussion.
  — Include screenshots of the agent-user interface with a description of the various options and what they do.

NOTE Do not forget that you can turn various options on or off in the user interface via an Agent UI Control Rule from the CSA MC. This changes what your users see.

- Explain the Security Level slider under the System Security menu. Does it make a difference (between Low, Medium, High)? This depends on your policies and settings.
- Are users allowed to set the Security Level to Off temporarily? Do end users need to remember to turn it back on?
- What is Network Lock?
- How do you erase a saved user query response? How do you list the saved user query responses?

These are all examples to get you thinking.

Good communication (whether a voice mail broadcast, Video on Demand presentation, all-hands meetings, or e-mail) is key to a successful deployment of CSA.

The last thing you want is users who are unaware of what CSA is, why it pops up on their screens, and why it is important to the security of the enterprise. If users do not know the answers to these questions, the CSA is the first thing they try to disable or remove from their systems. If successful, this serves to lessen the overall security infrastructure you are working to build.

Pilot

In this section, you have the opportunity to try CSA.

Now that you have collected all this information and started a plan for the eventual rollout of CSA, you need to get your pilot going. The following sections look at the overall process:

- Setting up a successful CSA pilot
- Supporting your pilot users well
- Exploring some common mistakes that you can avoid when setting up a CSA pilot
- Testing CSA
- Establishing success criteria for your pilot

Defining Inclusion

Everyone wants to try the new toy. This happens in any environment as you would discover if you ask any Cisco employee how many pilots they try to sign up for a month. You are actually try to gain something from this pilot though; you are not just giving users a new thing to play with.

Any good pilot begins with the definition of what you want to accomplish and what user communities you want to cover.

For example, you want to consider which of the following communities you have in your company that you want to cover:

- System administrators —This is a good group to be sure because these individuals are generally experienced in the operation of a computer-operating system. However, system administrators are not always the best evaluators for user-interface work. For example, they might not see anything wrong with a command line having 420 options.
- Programmers—This set of users often stretch their machines to the limit as far as CPU and memory (and sometimes creative coding techniques), so they are often a good set to test with. However, they often have interesting ideas about what constitutes a good user interaction. They might not realize that four point type for an error message or 300 button selections presented to a novice user are not acceptable.
- Administrative staff—It is always good to include administrative staff. (Administrative in this section means support staff for management and executives.) They are usually quite demanding and do not necessarily understand all the underpinnings of the operating system they are using. Their input is useful for developing FAQ documentation for later use. If you can make them happy with the documentation and information available, you are well on your way.
- Sales and marketing staff—Because this group is mobile, demanding, and often operating in hazardous environments, it represents a good mix for testing out CSA and how it operates in a multitude of environments.
- Mobile or remote workers —Mobility usually means connecting a variety of ways (wireless, wired, home network, VPN, DSL, cable modem, ISDN, dialup, and so on). These are good things to test.

After you select some areas to target for your testing, you need to define your expectations for the pilot.

As described previously, many users want to "play with the new gadget;" however, you need results, too. Make sure you have a clear set of guidelines for your pilot users that encompass the following, at a minimum:

- Expected participation level
  - Can they install it and never report back? (Answer: Of course not.) They must participate in whatever forum and manner you define.
  - Establish an e-mail list or web-based location in your existing environment where you and your pilot users can communicate on a regular basis about things they discover.
  - Keep copies of all communications during the pilot (announcements, pilot user discussions, and feedback). It will prove invaluable later.
  - Establish penalties for not keeping up. You are likely to ask them to try uninstalling and reinstalling various installation kits you build along the way. They must be able to keep up and do it on time. If not, they need to be taken off the pilot (or perhaps not temporarily allowed on future pilots).

- Willingness to test security software that can break the normal operation of their machine
  - Users must keep good backups of their data and applications, but be willing to keep up with various policy changes or setting changes you require throughout the pilot.
  - Obviously you hope nothing severe happens, but users are quite creative—they always discover new bugs or issues in software that you did not expect. Be prepared for this by making sure they have good backups and know how to use the pilot support team for help.

You will add more items specific to your environment to this list; however, these are some items that you should make sure to cover to avoid difficulties down the road.

Support Model

Every good pilot deserves good support. However, users need to have some tools up front for self-support, and more need to be developed during the pilot to prepare you for the full rollout of CSA across your environment.

Self-support can be as easy as a quick web page, an e-mail list for communicating questions and answers, or a dynamic FAQ website that has an initial set of questions and answers. Users can help you build the list of FAQs to develop a set that meets everyone's needs.

The following are some pilot support expectations:

- Expected support channels

  Make users aware of how they can get support through the pilot.

  - Do you have an e-mail list for pilot users to discuss and resolve issues?
  - Do you have an FAQ e-mail or website to start users with some initial information?
  - What are users expected to report to the list?

    Any installation/uninstall issues?

    CSA queries or popup messages that occur too often for a normal task?

    Applications that users know are disabled by CSA?
  - Do all the users know how to eliminate CSA as the cause of a problem? For example, you might want to train users to suspend the agent, try the action again and see if it works better, or uninstall the agent to see if the issue recurs.

  If your organization is a typical medium-to-large environment, you likely need support for your pilot that is separate from your normal helpdesk processes. Have your helpdesk supply a representative, however, to the pilot-support process to gather information along the way to allow you to transition the support to your standard processes later. After all, you do not want to personally support this forever, unless you are the only person on the support staff.

- Supported platforms during the pilot

  Supported platforms include more than just what the CSA supports. It means what will you cover in your pilot? All Windows desktops? All Windows XP SP1, but not SP2 desktops? All RedHat Enterprise Linux desktops?

  Depending on your environment, you might *support* only the Windows 2003 Server, but there are numerous Windows NT 4 and Windows 2000 servers still around. Will you support the pilot on those machines as well?

- How to get emergency help
  - Do all pilot users know how to disable CSA? (This includes using the Off security level setting and stopping the agent service.)
  - If an application worked before installing CSA and does not work now, and stopping the agent does not help, do users know how to uninstall and reinstall the security agent to see if CSA is really the issue?
  - Do users have the instructions available to them to remove CSA manually if for some reason the installation becomes corrupted? Corruption in this case could be caused by hard drive problems, partial installs, or power issues. Do they know how to boot into Safe mode for Windows or single-user for Linux/Solaris, and do they have administrative access (administrator or root) to their pilot machine?
  - Have you identified someone in the pilot support team who has the appropriate contact information for your Cisco SE or Cisco TAC support in case you need more help?

Remember, your pilot group should be drawn from people across your user base, and if the pilot goes well, they will be your advocates to other users in their environments when it comes time for the larger rollout. Useful and well documented support plans mean happier users in the end.

Common Mistakes

The next section covers a few common mistakes that pilots encounter and how you can avoid them.

Policies Not Matching a Well-Defined Security Policy or Plan

There is nothing more irritating to you and your users than a CSA policy that is so restrictive and secured that employees cannot complete their work.

To avoid this problem, plan out your needs and desires for this pilot and rollout carefully, paying attention to what affects your environment most.

Do not try to tackle all your environment's security problems at once. Remember, CSA is modular and flexible, and because of this, you can take your time and test various policies *before* you inflict them on an entire environment.

By comparing policy modules to your security plans or needs, you make sure you receive a return for this investment right away. To better understand how this works, consider the following sample scenario: You do not have many problems with Windows viruses, but web browser-based malicious code and spyware are driving your systems into the ground. Install the modules that cover these areas and do not plug in other modules that you don not need for now.

TIP Take the time to read through the default modules supplied by Cisco for the environment you are deploying. There are some modules you cannot do without, for example, anything in the <All Windows>, <All Solaris>, or <All Linux> group. Many other things can fail if you remove any of those policies.

Not Using the "Application Deployment Investigation" Features

Use the tools available to you. If you do not have another method to gather this information on your applications and their usage, use CSA to help you profile your environment.

Collect information before you activate your policies (meaning before you take them out of **TESTMODE**) so you can make some policy changes before the pilot users even see it.

The following are two examples of what you can look into with the help of application deployment investigation:

- Find out what web browsers people use in your company and make sure they are covered in the appropriate application class for web browsers, so that their content is handled.
- Find out what applications actively talk on the network and make sure they are covered to work (or not) in the policies.

Not Using TESTMODE to Your Advantage

TESTMODE is one of the most useful features of CSA policies. With version 4.5 and later, you can now put individual rule modules and entire groups into **TESTMODE**.

TESTMODE allows you to try new policies before you enable them. Then you can see the queries that would have been generated to each user and what sort of log messages you would see, and you can tune appropriately to minimize errors or conflicts.

Use **TESTMODE** on a builtin rule module that you do not currently have to see what effect it would have.

The following scenario shows effective use of TESTMODE: Cisco IP Softphone Module is not attached to any default policies, but perhaps you want to try it out. Attach it to one of your policies and turn it on in TESTMODE. After you are comfortable with the effect it has on your environment, turn off the TESTMODE checkbox and regenerate your rules—all deployed!

Not Sizing Hardware Appropriately for the Pilot/Deployment

Many things can affect how hardware should be sized for a CSA pilot; however, there are a few key things to remember (in addition to the guides mentioned in the CSA documentation and release notes for the version you are using):

- The CSA MC and the VMS software suite that it relies on for operation is not typically memory-intensive. 6–8 GB of RAM is more than sufficient for a large (80–100,000 machines) deployment (in most cases).
- Disk space, and CPU speed (and the number of CPUs) are the limiting factors.
  - Disk space needs to accommodate the CSA database (MSDE for small deployments, SQL 2000 Standard, or Enterprise depending on the size of the deployment) and log files locally.
  - The number and speed of the CPUs needed for your deployment depend on several factors:

    Number of agents

    Polling time

    Network bandwidth (how fast the agents send up traffic)
- Most large environments or deployments (over 10,000 agents) require at least two processors over 3.0 Ghz in speed.

For a pilot or test environment (limited in number to under 500 if you use MSDE, or 5,000 if you are using a local copy of SQL 2000 Server), a fairly small machine will be sufficient to complete the pilot.

Not Documenting Policies and Rules to Allow Good Management

Some customers create separate rule modules and policies for everything they find, and this is not necessary.

Try to understand the existing policies and apply your changes under a new policy appropriately:

- Group like items together.
- Title the policies with a keyword to help you differentiate it from Cisco builtin policies.
- Try not to modify Cisco builtin policies (consider them read-only for the purpose of policy development except in the most severe circumstances). Make your own policy and rules to override the Cisco builtin ones if needed. This saves you time when you upgrade later. Otherwise, you spend considerable time merging and cleaning up policies again when upgrades happen.

Mark your policies with a version number to help track them, especially if you export them and then import them into another console. If every rule module and policy has a version number, it simplifies importing policies considerably.

Separate policies for business-critical software from personal or individually purchased software in your environment (assuming you allow users to install their own software). This is a life saver if it comes down to making critical policy choices. If one particular rule causes you issues and you do not know if it is business-critical, you might feel you must live with it rather than tune it out appropriately based on a real business need.

Not Setting Event-Log Thresholds Appropriately

Use the "Event Sets" and other event-log settings to manage your logs appropriately.

During a pilot, you really do not need events past one week. You need to be actively working on looking at events on a daily basis during the pilot to save yourself from doing it later.

Allowing logs to collect forever is bad practice for many reasons, not the least of which is a bloated database that becomes slow and difficult to search. If you want to save logs longer than a couple weeks, consider looking at an offline event storage or analysis engine (such as Cisco SIMS or MARS).

Not Backing Up the Pilot Server and Database

With CSA 4.5 and later, the database contains the most important data for recovering and restoring your CSA MC.

The database contains not only all your groups, policies, rule modules, and so on, but your software licenses, and SSL certificate keys that CSA uses to communicate with the MC.

If you have your database backups and they are good, do yourself a favor and restore them once in a while just to make sure. You can then recover your Management Center quickly.

If you lose your certificates (that is the database is destroyed and you did not back it up), your agents cannot communicate with any new Management Center you create to replace it. Therefore you need either a manual replacement of the SSL certificates on each agent, or a reinstallation of the agent itself. Neither is fun, so help yourself now and back up those databases right away before you pass out installation kits.

Testing Methods

There are many different methods you can use in your pilots to test CSA. The following cover a few to start you thinking about how you would like to test during your pilot:

- Install CSA on each type of operating system you have in a closed lab environment and attempt to attack or infect the machines with various programs or Trojan files.
- Your users can install CSA on their desktop machines and operate normally for a period of two weeks and report any issues or problems. Those normal operations should include reading e-mail, printing, moving to wireless, trying dialup, installing software, and so on. You tune the policy appropriately and report back to them on completion of any changes that will improve whatever issues they run into.
- Your users can install CSA on their machines and attempt to run every standard application they typically use. They try each function typically used (Open, Save, Print, Download, and so on), and report back any changes. You make policy changes and then they repeat the process until the major issues are resolved.
- Install CSA on one development server of each function type in your environment (such as web, application, database, and so on). Have the agent in **TESTMODE** and watch for one week during normal development and testing. Then turn on the policies after tuning out obvious issues and test again for one week.

As you can see, these cases are all different, and each covers some areas and not others. How you test CSA is highly dependent on your environment and what you want to get out of this deployment.

If you need immediate relief from viruses, worms, and so on in your environment, you likely will not do something as formal as the solution outlined in the fourth bullet in the preceding list. However, you might try to shrink the timelines for the example in the second bullet and see if that helps you meet the goal.

No testing method is wrong (aside from perhaps trying out live malicious code in your production environment). You need to take pieces of each of these suggestions and fit them to your plan.

Success Criteria

When you reach this point in the chapter, you should have a pretty good idea of what success for your pilot means to you and your organization. The following is a list of the top items to remember when you lay out the success or closure criteria for your pilot:

- How long does the pilot last?
- Do the pilot users (or a majority of them) believe they have the tools necessary to self support for most issues that might occur?
- Do the pilot users (or a majority of them) believe CSA is ready for deployment as it stands at the end of the pilot period?
- Are the support teams happy with the progress on documentation and issue resolution?
- Do you think that, based on the policies you have developed in the pilot, you can minimize impact to the user community as much as possible and receive a return on your investment in time and dollars by deploying CSA? (Hopefully the answer is yes if the testing went well.)

Production Implementation

This section describes the actual implementation or rollout of CSA.

Table 4-2 outlines a sample timeline for a medium-to-large enterprise environment that points out the key milestones to be aware of during a production implementation of CSA:

Table 4-2 *Cisco Security Agent Implementation Timeline for a Medium-to-Large Enterprise Environment*

Timeline	Tasks
Six to eight weeks before deployment (minimum, depending on your lead times to order equipment)	Order and set up your production environment equipment. Do you need one or several servers? Do you need a remote database server or just tablespace on an existing database server in your corporate environment? Do you have appropriate licenses for the products needed? Windows, SQL 2000 Standard or Enterprise, and so on, and CSA?
Two weeks before deployment	Conduct training of support and helpdesk staffs on all the issues to expect, and expected impact on business (if any in your environment). E-mail, web, or voicemail announcement to your users describing what is going to occur and when. Also direct them to a source of help online (webpage) to gather more information on what CSA is and what they should expect.

continues

Table 4-2 *Cisco Security Agent Implementation Timeline for a Medium-to-Large Enterprise*

Timeline	Tasks
One week before deployment	E-mails to the user community again reminding them about what is coming. FAQ online and available for users to self support (and for support staff as well). Installation kit ready to go from the Management Center and tested with whatever deployment method you plan to use. Small deployments can obviously let users just download the kit from the MC kits page. However, in medium and large deployments it will probably be best to use some automated method (for example, Microsoft SMS, Altiris, Radia, or in urgent situations without a better choice, SysInternals PSEXEC tool from a script—http://www.sysinternals.com).
Deployment time!	If you can, release your agents in a staged or phased manner for several reasons: This gives you time to spot issues before they become everyone's issues and make policy modifications. This lets the load grow gradually on your Management Center and allows you to watch things as they happen to correct any issues that arise. This does not mean that you need to deploy one to two per day—many companies have deployed as many as 40,000 in a five-day week globally. Tune the deployment to your needs and size of your company.
One day after deployment	Look through your events and tune whatever policies need changing to handle the things you did not catch in your pilot. Discuss helpdesk or support cases with your support team and see if a new FAQ needs to be written to minimize helpdesk requests. Also identify any issues going on that you do not see in the event logs on the MC.
After one week and one month	Check your database usage and machine load to ensure things go smoothly. Test a backup to make sure you can restore your database and system on another machine in case of disaster. Ensure that you have your Event Sets and Event Log Management settings configured appropriately. To keep your server running smoothly and sanely, try to keep the number of events under one million that you store on the server at any time. Although it is possible to store more than that (disk space is cheap), you will find searches and other processes work better when you do not over do it.

Documentation

Documentation of your project plan, pilot, and subsequent deployment and rollout of CSA is key to the success of the whole project and to any recovery you might want to perform later to resolve hardware issues, or any upgrades you want to perform in the future.

At the very least, you should gather the following documentation at the listed stages:

- Pilot Phase
  - List of initial policies and any settings you changed upon installation of CSA.
  - Known conflicts or problems in your environment that caused you issues during your pilot.
  - Documentation on any major successes (or failures) that occurred during the pilot that can assist your other efforts later.
- Production Rollout
  - Step-by-step instructions on how to get to where you are now on the Management Center (meaning how to move from the OS installation to the point when you distribute CSA kits).
  - A copy (export) of all your CSA MC settings.
  - All support and helpdesk documentation, license documentation, and offline copies of your FAQ for users.

TIP If you export the appropriate groups for your deployments, those export files will include all the dependent information needed to make it a complete export (that is, the right policies, rule modules, application classes, and so on).

Proper and up-to-date documentation is key to the day-to-day running of your CSA environment, but it is also key to helping someone else understand your environment, so that you can get the help you need when you run into issues that you cannot handle.

Ongoing Support

So you survived deployment! Now what?

For most environments, ongoing support of a CSA deployment is not too difficult (that is their intention). However, there are several things you need to do for ongoing support of your deployment that keep it running smoothly and efficiently. The next sections examine this in detail.

Backups

If you do not have good backups of your CSA databases and a good export of your policies and settings, you are asking for trouble.

To reiterate, if you do not back up the server databases (and therefore the security certificates [SSL]) that CSA uses to communicate with the MC, your agents will *not* talk to any new console you build to replace one that has damaged hardware. If you have the backups, the restore process is simple, and you can be running again quickly.

Realize that when your Management Center is down, your agents still protect the end systems. However, they cannot do several key things:

- They cannot receive new policies.
- They cannot send their events up to the Management Center (they do cache them up to a certain number of events).
- They cannot receive any event correlation data nor pass any new event correlation data back up to the MC.

Database Maintenance

You need to use the Database Maintenance menu under the MC to check on the status of your database (local or remote) and take appropriate action if any logs are nearing capacity.

CSA MC clears hosts out of its database that have not polled in a couple weeks (the expectation is that the host is no longer in service). If a host is removed from the host table and comes back later, it will simply register again and continue operating. No changes on the agent are needed. You can also use the **Search->Hosts** function on the MC to identify hosts that have not polled in a certain number of days and mark them to be removed.

VMS and CSA MC Log Maintenance

A few primary log directories contain log files for the VMS and CSA MC products. Depending on where you install the products, you will need to look for these log directories under directory names, such as:

- Program Files\CSCOpx\log
- Program Files\CSCOpx\CSAMC45\log

Normally the two products manage their own log's files, but if you find yourself out of disk space, check those directories for any old log files and archive or remove them as appropriate.

Policy Exports

It is also critical to back up policy exports. You should use the builtin Export mechanism from the CSA MC to export your groups and associated policies. Save this file to several safe locations and back it up offline.

Event Logs

Use the Event Sets and Event Log Management MC menu items to configure your CSA MC to archive or delete events after a certain period of time (or certain number of events). There are limits to the number kept for each category, but they are extremely high and designed to keep the database from getting out of control.

In most cases, notice level events can be deleted after four to five days, alert and higher level events kept for one week, and all events archived or deleted after two weeks. Depending on the size of your deployment and how many events per machine per day occur, you might need to tune this to a shorter period of time to keep things running smoothly.

Policy Updates

We cannot repeat this recommendation enough: Have a good security policy in place ahead of time to define what policy updates you will perform for users, and identify which policy updates are "best effort." In a normal environment (even a complex large enterprise), it should be normal behavior to perform one clustered policy update not more than once a month.

You should not think of doing updates during a crisis or attack—you should have the policies you need in place ahead of time for the major attack avenues.

CSA is both a defense in-depth and behavioral security program. Even if one policy experiences problems, others back it up, and as long as you have most of the major default security modules in place for your operating system, a policy should be able to react accordingly and prevent an attack from succeeding on your system. You can make CSA vulnerable if you poorly configure your policies. There is no guaranteed protection. Generally, if you use the default policies and add things to them, you do not have too many issues. However, because all policies are completely configurable, you can do anything you want (up to and including dangerous things). We discuss policy development in great detail later in this book, so please be familiar with how policies interact and work before making major sweeping policy changes.

Hopefully, the work to deploy CSA in your environment does not look too bad. Many large customers of CSA are able to operate their CSA deployments on a day-to-day basis with one FTE (Full-Time Equivalent) headcount, which is often split across several people to cover time zones or areas of the company.

Summary

Despite how complex CSA might look, we hope that after reading this chapter you have a better feel for the ease and practicality of implementing CSA. We are confident that you will see a good return on your investment for the time and effort you spend on the planning, piloting, and deployment.

Many companies approach the implementation of CSA with great concern over the imagined requirements of making thousands of policy changes and constantly performing daily tuning to make it a success. Not only are they usually pleasantly surprised by how the wizards and tuning process help them through deploying CSA in their environment, but they are happy with the investment return. Just think back to the example in this chapter—even if you halved that return, you should be able to easily deploy CSA for less than 2.5 million dollars (or less than the cost of one major incident to a large enterprise) based on those statistics in the example.

CHAPTER 5

Integration into Corporate Documentation

This chapter explores the different types of documentation needed for a successful deployment, ongoing support, and maintenance of Cisco Security Agent (CSA) within your enterprise.

This chapter covers the following topics:

- Integration with security policy documentation
- Proper use of change control for management of CSA
- Integration into quality assurance documentation and processes, including:
  - Software upgrades and new software acquisition
  - Hardware platform testing
- Documentation of support contacts and escalation procedures

No one looks forward to it, but with patience and proper documentation you can avoid common pitfalls or headaches related to the ongoing care and feeding of your CSA deployment.

Security Policy Document

In this section, we explore how to review your security policies and how to export them to a plain text file for use in the recovery process. The export process is particularly critical, so that you do not lose valuable policy information in case of a database crash or data loss.

CSA policies, when properly created and documented for your enterprise, should reflect your environment and the security policies you have written to cover that environment.

The Cisco Security Agent Management Center (CSA MC) provides assistance in documenting the CSA policies you use or design to enhance or supplement your corporate security policy. This function is called Explain rules, as highlighted in Figure 5-1.

Figure 5-1 *Host Display Screen of Cisco Security Agent Version 4.5*

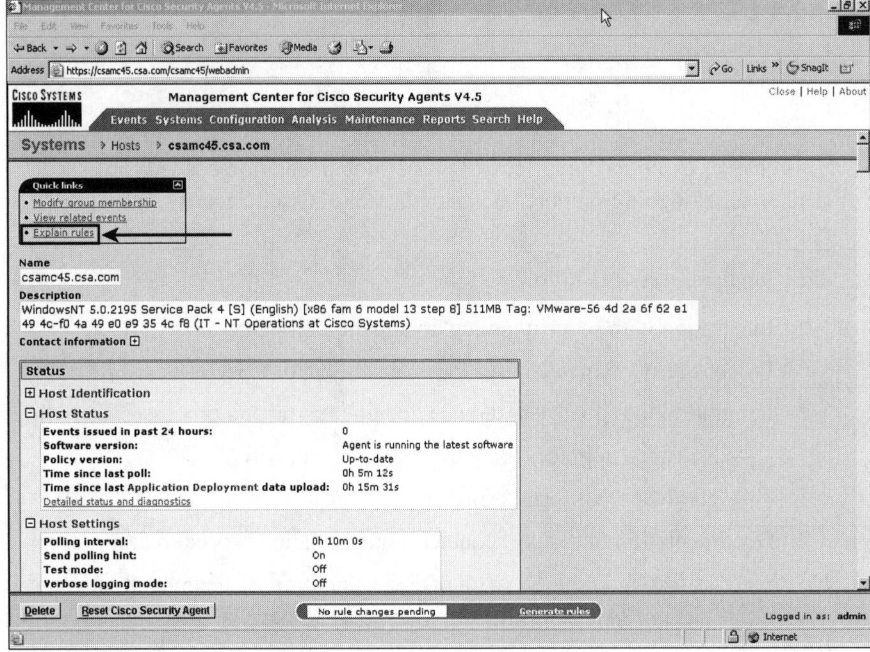

Figure 5-1 shows a typical display of a host detail screen in CSA version 4.5. You receive information about the host and about any groups and policies currently attached to this host.

As shown in Figure 5-2, if you scroll down that page, you see a list of all rules, in precedence order, that apply to this host.

Figure 5-2 *Rules List in Cisco Security Agent Version 4.5 Host Display Screen*

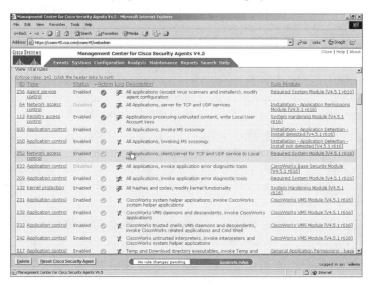

ID	Type	Status	Action	Log	Description	Rule Module
256	Agent service control	Enabled			All applications (except virus scanners and installers), modify agent configuration	Required System Module [V4.5.1 r616]
64	Network access control	Disabled			All Applications, server for TCP and UDP services	Installation - Application Permissions Module [V4.5.1 r616]
113	Registry access control	Enabled			Applications processing untrusted content, write Local User Account keys	System Hardening Module [V4.5.1 r616]
600	Application control	Enabled			All Applications, Invoke MS sysocmgr	Installation - Application Detection - Install detected [V4.5.1 r616]
160	Application control	Enabled			All Applications, Invoking MS sysocmgr	Installation - Application Detection - Install not detected [V4.5.1 r616]
252	Network access control	Enabled			All applications, client/server for TCP and UDP service to Local Host	Required System Module [V4.5.1 r616]
633	Application control	Disabled			All applications, invoke application error diagnostic tools	CiscoWorks Base Security Module [V4.5.1 r616]
269	Application control	Enabled			All applications, invoke application error diagnostic tools	Required System Module [V4.5.1 r616]
132	Kernel protection	Enabled			All hashes and codes, modify kernel functionality	System Hardening Module [V4.5.1 r616]
231	Application control	Enabled			CiscoWorks system helper applications, invoke CiscoWorks system helper applications	CiscoWorks VMS Module [V4.5.1 r616]
232	Application control	Enabled			CiscoWorks VMS daemons and descendents, invoke CiscoWorks applications	CiscoWorks VMS Module [V4.5.1 r616]
233	Application control	Enabled			CiscoWorks trusted shells, VMS daemons and descendents, invoke CiscoWorks related applications and Cmd Shell	CiscoWorks VMS Module [V4.5.1 r616]
242	Application control	Enabled			CiscoWorks untrusted interpreters, invoke interpreters and CiscoWorks system helper applications	CiscoWorks VMS Module [V4.5.1 r616]
517	Application control	Enabled			Temp and Download directory executables, invoke Temp and	General Application Permissions - base

As you can see in Figure 5-2, this is the beginning of the list of rules attached to this particular example host. You see rule ID numbers, rule types, statuses, actions that apply, and so on.

If you scroll back up to the top of your host detail screen and select the Explain rules link highlighted in Figure 5-1, you can see a list similar to the example host illustrated in Figure 5-3.

Figure 5-3 *Explain Rules List for Example Host in Cisco Security Agent Version 4.5*

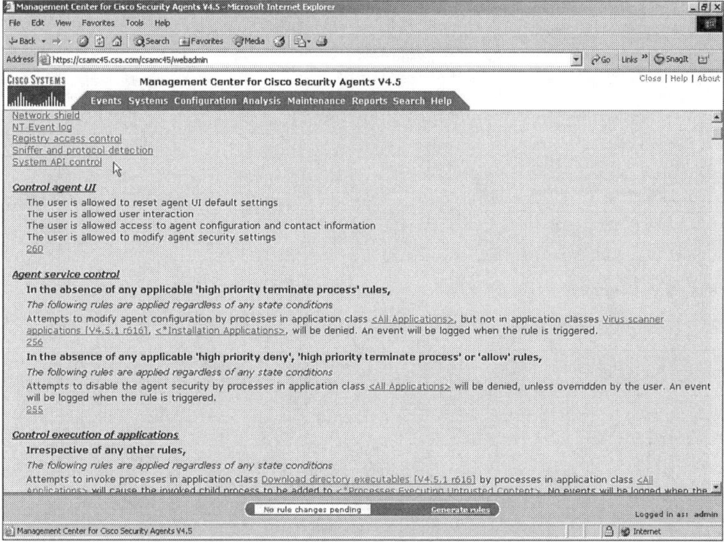

You can see that the rules have been converted into a more readable format, and the rules can be cut and pasted into a security policy documentation set. This conversion can help you document your CSA policy, so that you can confirm that it is written and operating as expected.

You can compare rules in Figure 5-2 and Figure 5-3. For example, in Figure 5-2, you can see that the first rule listed is rule ID 256, which is an Agent service control rule. It protects the CSA from modifications to its configuration. You can find that number on Figure 5-3 and see how the rule converts into a more readable format.

You can *explain* the rules for your final (or ongoing) CSA, and then print them for future reference. You should be aware, however, that the Explain rules functionality does not print out the contents of every variable and class (application, and so on) that you need for complete disaster recovery of your security policies. For a more complete set of recovery information, you also need:

- A complete, usable backup of your CSA database (the local one if you use a local SQL database or the remote database if you use the new remote database functionality in CSA version 4.5 or later).
- A complete export of your CSA groups and policies.

You can complete an export of your groups and policy information by choosing either **Export** if you have the Maintenance screen selected already or choosing **Export** from the Maintenance pop-up menu under **Export>Import**, as shown in Figure 5-4.

Figure 5-4 *Cisco Security Agent Version 4.5 Maintenance Menu—Exporting Information*

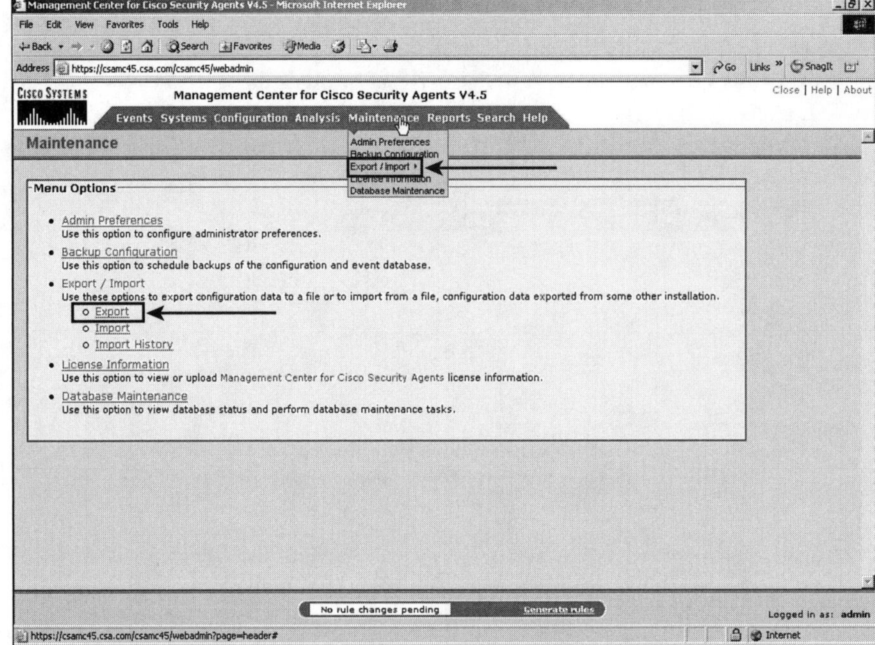

Next, select **New** at the bottom-left of the next screen, and then compare your screen to Figure 5-5.

Figure 5-5 *Cisco Security Agent Version 4.5 New Export*

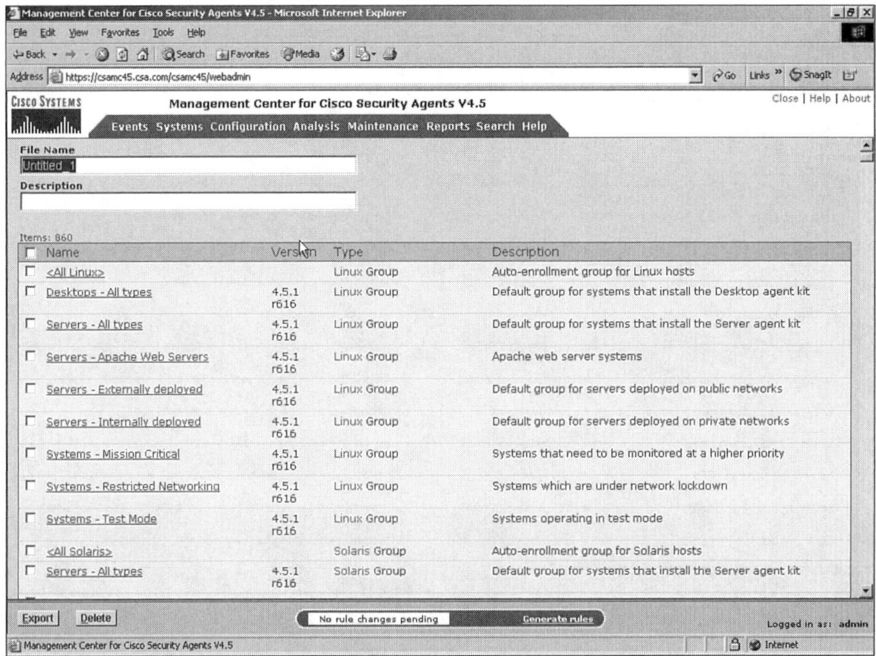

Enter a name for your export in the **File Name** field at the top, and a short description of this export; it is best to include the version number in the name of the export file. The description can include the CSA version you export from (such as 450-565) or the version of this export (for example, Pilot v1 or Production v8).

You next select the item you want to export. This can be as broad as a CSA group or as specific as one policy or application class.

When you select an item, any items in the database necessary to allow that item to be *complete* automatically export with the item you selected. Consider the following examples:

- If you select one particular CSA policy to export, the MC exports all rule modules, rules, application classes, and other variables and settings needed to make it a complete and functional import file. You can use it on another MC or the same one if you needed to recover.
- If you select one particular CSA group to export, the MC exports all related policies and other information attached to the group. You do not need to individually select every policy, rule module, application class, and so on when you perform an export.

In Figure 5-6, **Desktops—All types** has been selected to export.

Figure 5-6 *Cisco Security Agent Version 4.5 Desktops—All Types Export Selection*

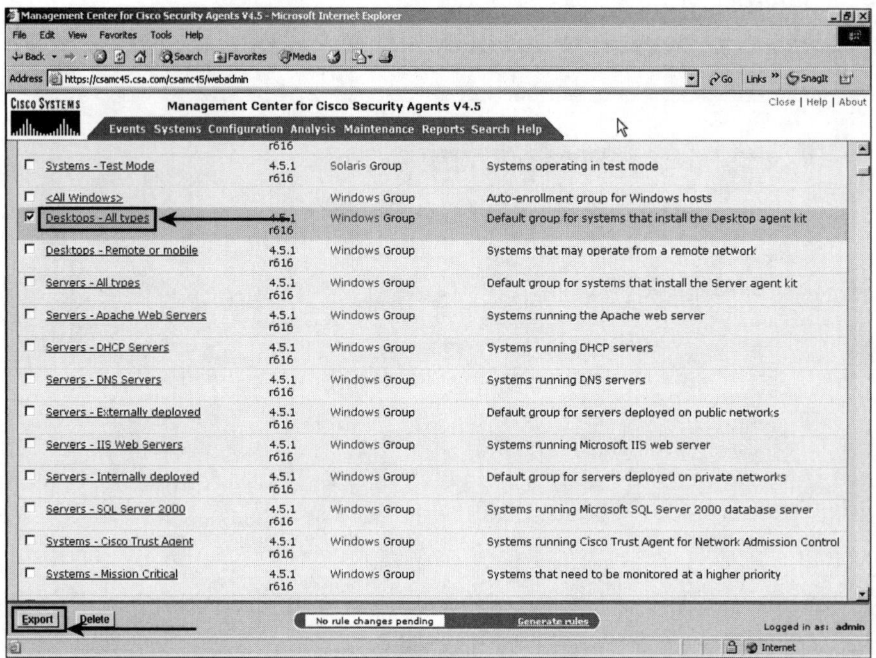

When you select all the items you want to export, click the **Export** button at the bottom left of the browser window. It prompts you to confirm you want to export the selected items. Click **OK** when you are ready, and it begins the process of exporting the selected items to an export file.

You then see the Export Progress screen (Figure 5-7) as it walks through all the areas it needs to export to complete your file.

Figure 5-7 *Cisco Security Agent Version 4.5 Export Progress Screen*

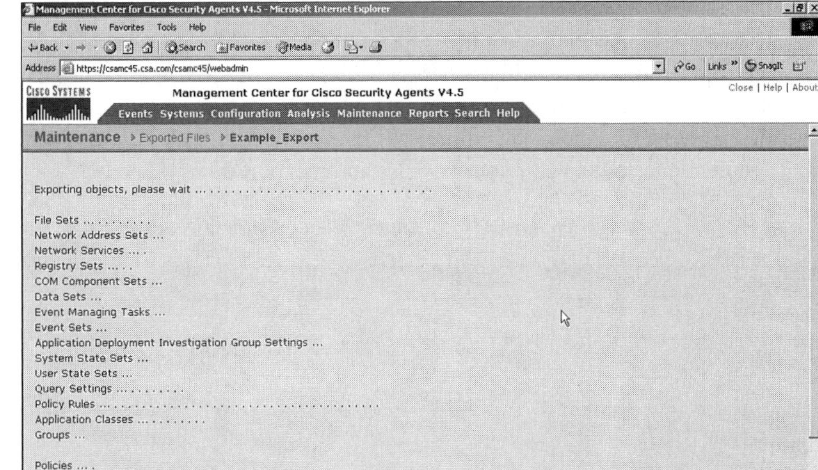

When it completes, it notifies you with a link at the bottom of the Export Progress screen, as shown in Figure 5-8.

Figure 5-8 *Cisco Security Agent Version 4.5 Export Completed—Ready to Download*

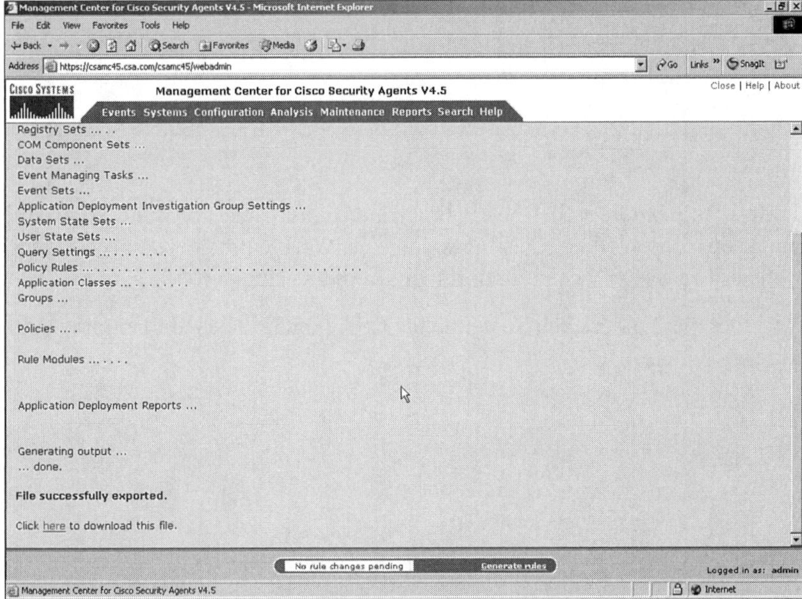

Click on the **here** link at the bottom of the Export Progress screen to download your export file. Save it to a location you can readily access (for example, the Windows Desktop).

Figure 5-9 shows that the export file is a text file in XML format; this is a common format used by applications today. Although it is readable and editable, Cisco does not recommend direct editing of the file. Because there are numerous settings and variables documented in the file that are interdependent, editing this by hand can be a challenge. Use the management interface to edit your policies and reexport them if needed.

Figure 5-9 *Cisco Security Agent Version 4.5 Example Export File in Windows Notepad Format*

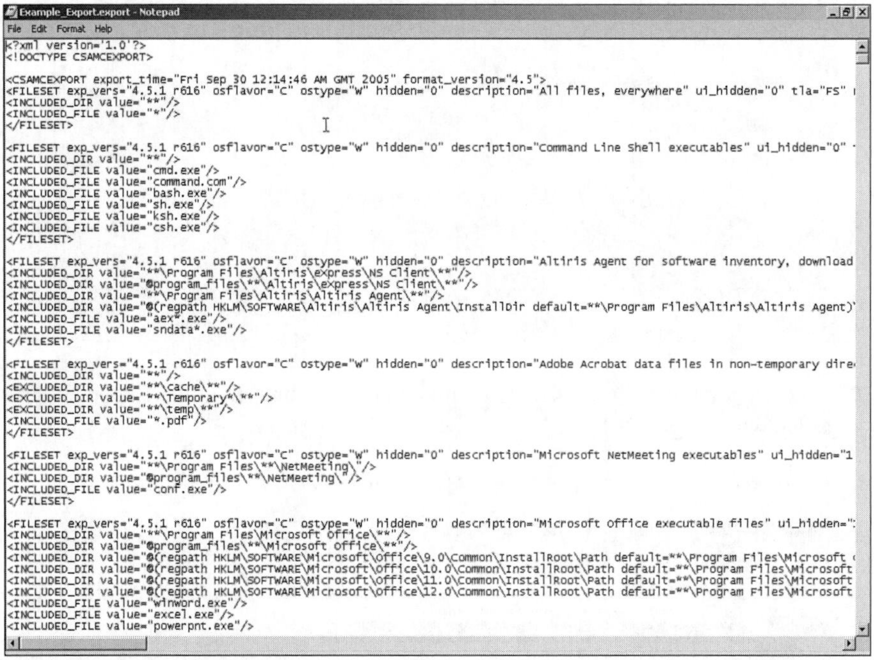

Example_Export.export - Notepad

File Edit Format Help


```
<?xml version='1.0'?>
<!DOCTYPE CSAMCEXPORT>

<CSAMCEXPORT export_time="Fri Sep 30 12:14:46 AM GMT 2005" format_version="4.5">
<FILESET exp_vers="4.5.1 r616" osflavor="C" ostype="W" hidden="0" description="All files, everywhere" ui_hidden="0" tla="FS"
<INCLUDED_DIR value="**"/>
<INCLUDED_FILE value="*"/>
</FILESET>

<FILESET exp_vers="4.5.1 r616" osflavor="C" ostype="W" hidden="0" description="Command Line Shell executables" ui_hidden="0"
<INCLUDED_DIR value="**"/>
<INCLUDED_FILE value="cmd.exe"/>
<INCLUDED_FILE value="command.com"/>
<INCLUDED_FILE value="bash.exe"/>
<INCLUDED_FILE value="sh.exe"/>
<INCLUDED_FILE value="ksh.exe"/>
<INCLUDED_FILE value="csh.exe"/>
</FILESET>

<FILESET exp_vers="4.5.1 r616" osflavor="C" ostype="W" hidden="0" description="Altiris Agent for software inventory, download
<INCLUDED_DIR value="**\Program Files\Altiris\express\NS Client\**"/>
<INCLUDED_DIR value="@program_files\**\Altiris\express\NS Client\**"/>
<INCLUDED_DIR value="**\Program Files\Altiris\Altiris Agent\**"/>
<INCLUDED_DIR value="@(regpath HKLM\SOFTWARE\Altiris\Altiris Agent\InstallDir default=**\Program Files\Altiris\Altiris Agent)'
<INCLUDED_FILE value="aex*.exe"/>
<INCLUDED_FILE value="sndata*.exe"/>
</FILESET>

<FILESET exp_vers="4.5.1 r616" osflavor="C" ostype="W" hidden="0" description="Adobe Acrobat data files in non-temporary dire
<INCLUDED_DIR value="**"/>
<EXCLUDED_DIR value="**\cache\**"/>
<EXCLUDED_DIR value="**\Temporary*\**"/>
<EXCLUDED_DIR value="**\temp\**"/>
<INCLUDED_FILE value="*.pdf"/>
</FILESET>

<FILESET exp_vers="4.5.1 r616" osflavor="C" ostype="W" hidden="0" description="Microsoft NetMeeting executables" ui_hidden="1
<INCLUDED_DIR value="**\Program Files\**\NetMeeting\"/>
<INCLUDED_DIR value="@program_files\**\NetMeeting\"/>
<INCLUDED_FILE value="conf.exe"/>
</FILESET>

<FILESET exp_vers="4.5.1 r616" osflavor="C" ostype="W" hidden="0" description="Microsoft Office executable files" ui_hidden="
<INCLUDED_DIR value="**\Program Files\Microsoft Office\**"/>
<INCLUDED_DIR value="@program_files\**\Microsoft Office\**"/>
<INCLUDED_DIR value="@(regpath HKLM\SOFTWARE\Microsoft\Office\9.0\Common\InstallRoot\Path default=**\Program Files\Microsoft
<INCLUDED_DIR value="@(regpath HKLM\SOFTWARE\Microsoft\Office\10.0\Common\InstallRoot\Path default=**\Program Files\Microsoft
<INCLUDED_DIR value="@(regpath HKLM\SOFTWARE\Microsoft\Office\11.0\Common\InstallRoot\Path default=**\Program Files\Microsoft
<INCLUDED_DIR value="@(regpath HKLM\SOFTWARE\Microsoft\Office\12.0\Common\InstallRoot\Path default=**\Program Files\Microsoft
<INCLUDED_FILE value="winword.exe"/>
<INCLUDED_FILE value="excel.exe"/>
<INCLUDED_FILE value="powerpnt.exe"/>
```


Perform this export process every time you make changes to your CSA production policies and keep a copy offline. This saves you considerable time if you need to recover your policies because you can reimport them from this simple file.

Together these pieces help to define the CSA policies needed to enforce your corporate security policies.

Change Control Documentation

Every good enterprise production computing environment has a change control process to track changes made to that environment. These days, it is not only a good idea, but it is often an auditable item for your company.

Consider your CSA MC and agents in the same way you would any other security-related environment. Handle changes to that environment as security-significant changes and control and document them appropriately.

You should use the audit capabilities within CSA to assist you in the change control processes and control changes to CSA and CSA policies by enforcing a process around by whom, how, and when changes are made.

You should also use the built-in authentication (username/password) or other authentication mechanisms (such as Lightweight Directory Access Protocol [LDAP], and so on) to maintain separate user identification for your administrators. This allows you to use the CSA audit logs more effectively because you have a particular user ID associated with an audit log entry, instead of the standard Admin account.

This section and the subsections it contains review items you should watch for when developing good change management controls for your CSA environment, including how to manage and audit those changes.

To ensure a stable and secure environment, in addition to good security policy development, you should examine the following changes for some method of control (access or process) to properly check them before they affect the production environment:

- Any changes made to the CSA MC or related machines (for example, all MC machines and remote database server[s], if used)

  Although temporary downtime does not affect the endpoint CSA on your machines in the short term, long-term downtimes create several concerns. For example, you cannot make changes to policies, agents cannot get software updates, you do not see security events, and agents cannot take advantage of the Event Correlation functionality of CSA.

- All read/write access to the CSA MC console should be carefully controlled and limited to as few personnel as needed to properly manage it in your environment.
- Policy changes:
  - Should be reviewed ahead of implementation.
  - Should be tested on a development CSA MC (or in a different group, so that they do not affect everyone until properly tested).

- Should be reviewed for their impact on the security policy currently enforced. You should question if this change is necessary to continue business, and if the answer is yes, what impact would it have on your existing security policy?
- Should be documented because you can never have too much documentation in the policies you define for your environment. CSA MC provides a place to make quick and longer, more detailed descriptions on many items. Take advantage of these up front when you write your policies and try new techniques. The people who follow you will thank you because they will not need to figure this out again.

- Carefully control when and how agent software updates happen and think about the following:
  - Will you use the built-in mechanism?
  - Will you use inline HTTP web interception, such as the Cisco Application and Content Networking Software (ACNS) product, to save bandwidth?
  - Will you use some other mass software deployment mechanism to upgrade your agent software, such as Microsoft Systems Management Server (SMS), Radia, or Altiris?

  You need to plan and implement special controls for these to avoid headaches. Consider, for example, the case of releasing an agent software update to 40,000 clients through an immediate, silent background update. Is your network ready for 40,000 * 8 MB to happen all at the same time? Control, staging, and testing are obviously important here.

Auditing Changes to Cisco Security Agent Policies

CSA provides useful mechanisms for tracking and auditing changes to the MC policies and settings.

There are two primary mechanisms available for this:

- Audit trail
- View change history

To access the audit trail history, find the **Reports** menu and select **Audit Trail**, as shown in Figure 5-10.

Figure 5-10 *Cisco Security Agent Audit Trail Menu Selection*

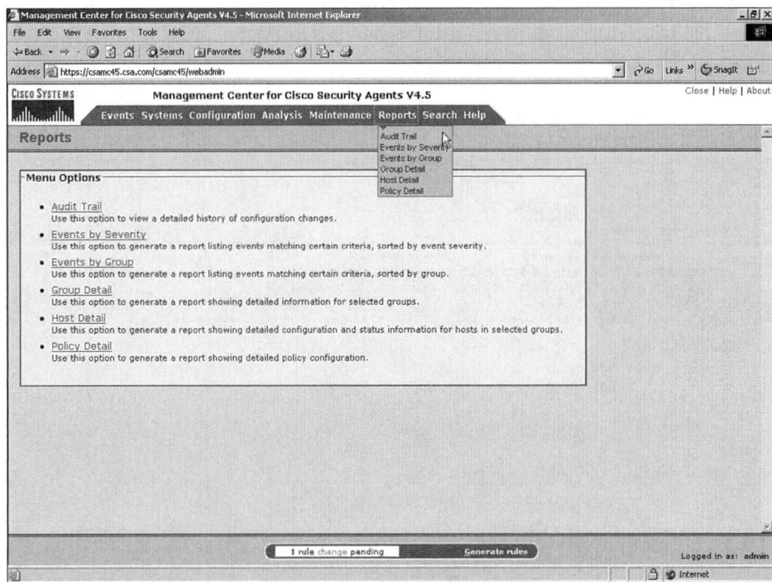

After selecting **Audit Trail**, you see a display similar to Figure 5-11. You can see that it logs the actions taken, the date and time, and the administrator who made the change. You can also filter the audit log based on the name of the administrator or the action you seek (such as **File Set** if you want to see changes made to file sets).

Figure 5-11 *Cisco Security Agent Audit Trail Logs*

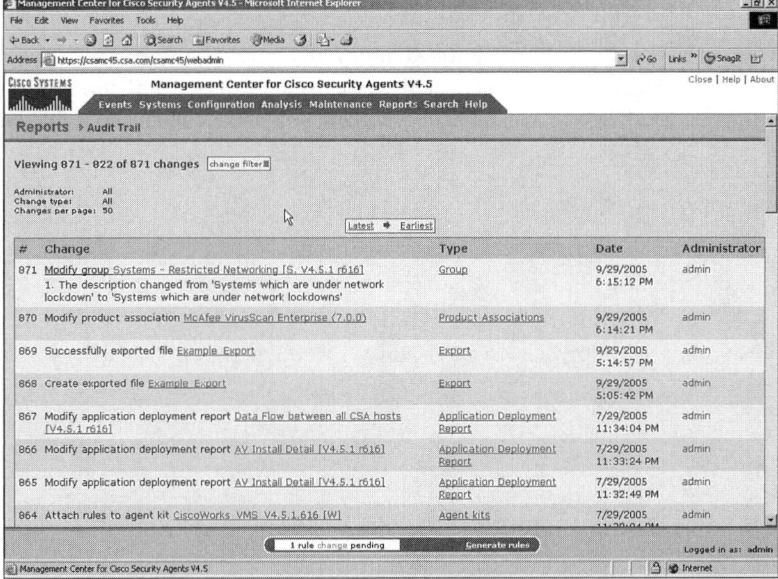

The other mechanism included to assist with change tracking in CSA is **View change history**, which is an alterable selection on most items (such as policies, rules modules, and so on). Near the top of items that have change history available, you see a **View change history** link, as shown in Figure 5-12.

Figure 5-12 *Cisco Security Agent **View Change History** Selection*

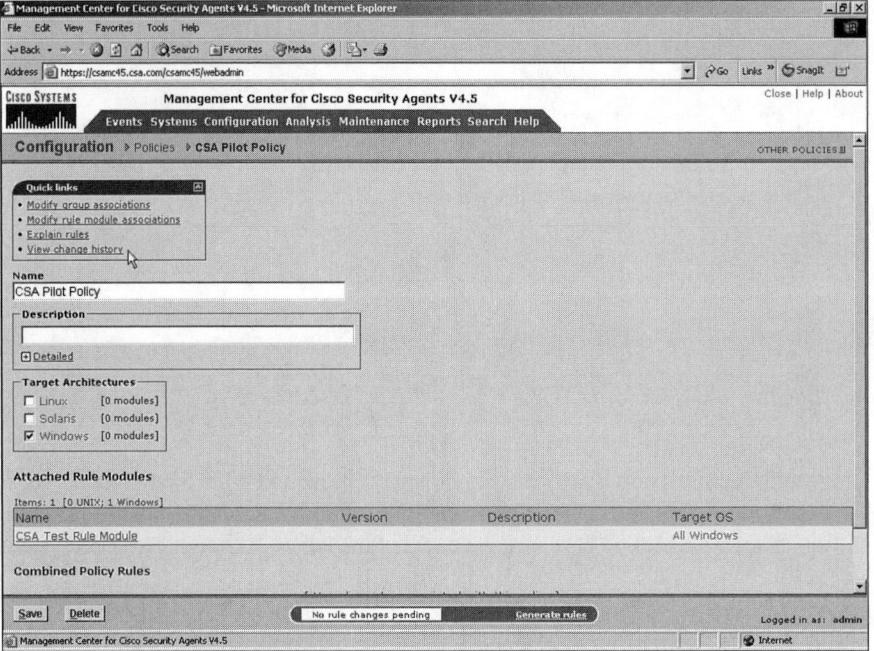

When you click on the **View change history** link, you should see a screen similar to Figure 5-13, which shows you the changes made to this item since it was created. As with the audit trail, you can filter based on several criteria if you make changes to a particular item.

Figure 5-13 *Cisco Security Agent View Change History Log*

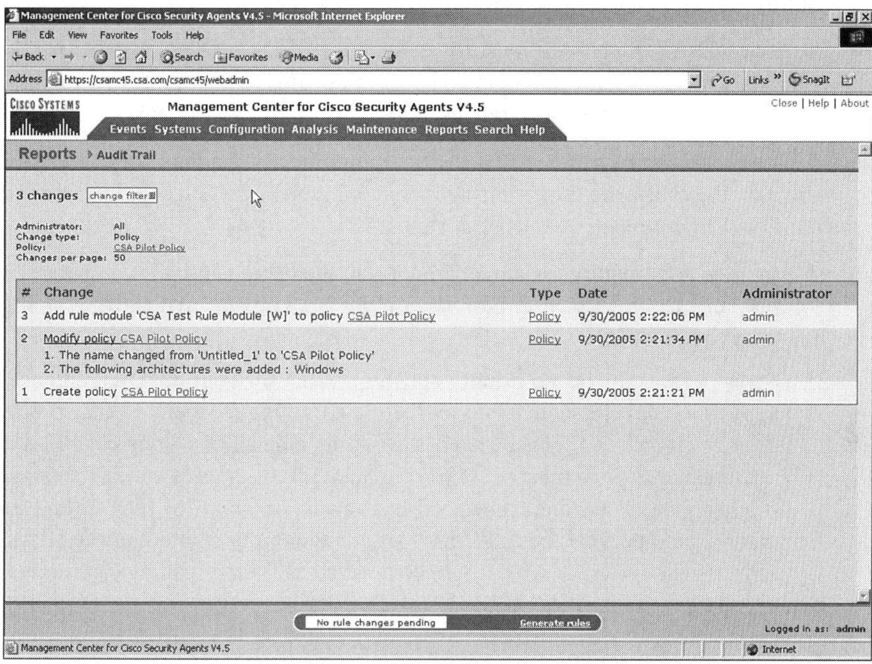

There are tools provided to assist you with auditing and tracking changes. However, you will want to supplement these with your own processes and checklists to assist in keeping your production environment stable.

NOTE You should be aware, however, that the export function for your CSA policies does not export the audit or change logs and history information. These can be restored if you do a full database backup and restore that back up after a crash. If, however, you import the policies into a new MC, you start with an empty audit log and change history (for example, the change history on each policy, rule module, and so on).

Quality Assurance

The task of quality assurance and the importance you give it directly relates to the size and complexity of your computing environment.

For example, if you have only a few hundred computers that have the same configuration, quality assurance is easy. On the other hand, if those computers manage critical financial or engineering data on a daily basis, you might want to put more work into assuring the stability and uptime of your environment.

The use of CSA (or any security software package) adds another variable into the quality assurance process for any environment, regardless of size or complexity. In this case, we examine quality assurance as it relates to your desktop or server environments.

To ensure the least frustration and best cooperation from your quality assurance groups, you should do the following things during the planning, rollout, and subsequent operation of your CSA environment:

- Include your quality assurance group(s) in the testing and pilot process as early as possible. Do this for every new version of CSA you plan to deploy, so your group can give you feedback.
- Spend a few minutes up front to document CSA for your quality assurance and application development teams and provide training for them. Doing so will save you time down the road. This does not have to include an hour-long class or a detailed document everyone must read. You can take screenshots of various messages that might pop up, make more advanced users aware of where log files are and how to look at them, and provide the full CSA documentation on an internal web site, so that anyone who looks for what might be deemed as boring reading can find it.
- For most corporations, quality assurance in the desktop or server application area includes fairly indepth and detailed testing plans, so you should work closely with those teams to develop a test plan for CSA. In addition, plan how to best integrate CSA conflict testing into the performed application testing.

What does conflict testing mean? Because CSA is capable of stopping most actions performed by a user or application on a system, there is always a chance of it stopping something you want to allow. For example, an application might be stopped from operating normally by an existing policy or something similar.

This does not mean you need to spend hours of extra time testing with every new application now that you have CSA. It means that your quality assurance staff needs to be aware of the existence of CSA as part of the application test and review process before they deploy an application to your environment, and they need to know how to properly determine whether something is a CSA or application issue.

Quality Assurance Debugging

How does your quality assurance group know if an issue that "never happened before" or "cannot possibly be this application" is related to CSA or not?

They can take a severe route, if your policy allows it, and remove CSA to see if that changes the situation. However, by now you should know that there are alternative methods to most quality assurance and testing issues. The following are suggestions your quality assurance group can use.

There are two ways to disable CSA temporarily that do not involve an uninstall/reboot:

- The first is to simply choose **Off** as the security level. You can do this either in the user interface or by right-clicking on the red CSA flag in the Windows taskbar (or Linux taskbar if you are running a Windows-based user interface), as shown in Figure 5-14. Depending on your policy, you might be asked a question or two to verify that you want to set the security level to **Off**. After this is complete, all CSA policies are in **bypass** mode except self-protection of the CSA. This means that none of your policies will trigger or affect any action that occurs on the system, unless it affects the CSA files.

Figure 5-14 *Cisco Security Agent Taskbar Flag Menu*

- The second way to disable CSA temporarily is to stop the CSA service. This is accomplished under Windows by opening a command shell (click the **Start** menu, select **Run**, and enter: **cmd** in the box that appears and click **OK**. A command window should then pop up; see Figure 5-15 for an example. Enter **net stop csagent** and press **Enter**. You are prompted (again depending on your policy settings) to confirm that you want to stop CSA. After you confirm this, you should see a confirmation that the service was stopped successfully.

  After these processes are complete, all CSA services stop. This includes self-protection of the agent and its files and settings.

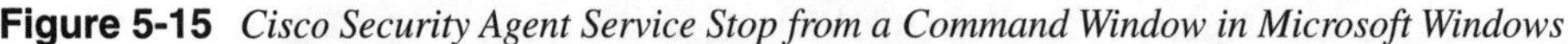

Figure 5-15 *Cisco Security Agent Service Stop from a Command Window in Microsoft Windows*

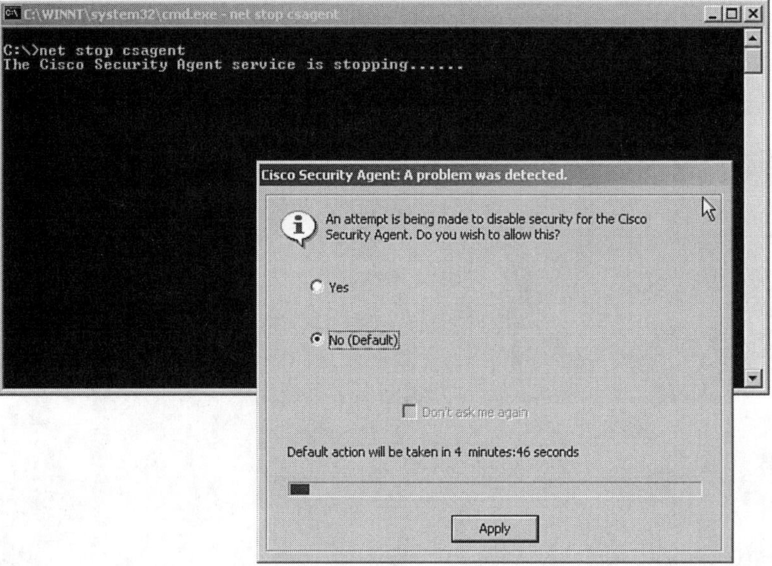

The following situation rarely occurs but you should understand it. You have an application that crashes, but it did not do this before installing CSA. However, after installing CSA (regardless of whether the agent funs or not), it crashes. This usually happens with Computer Aided Design (CAD) applications or other related applications that have extremely tight licensing code. This type of code watches for anything that looks like an operating system debugger and crashes if it thinks someone is trying to hack its licensing code. If you run into this situation and uninstalling CSA fixes the application, you can add the application in question to the built-in Cisco Security Agent application class `<Processes Requiring Kernel Only Protection>`. See Figure 5-16 for an example of an application control rule that allows an application class **AutoCAD** to run properly.

Figure 5-16 *Cisco Security Agent Application Control Rule to Add AutoCAD Application Class to <Processes Requiring Kernel Only Protection>*

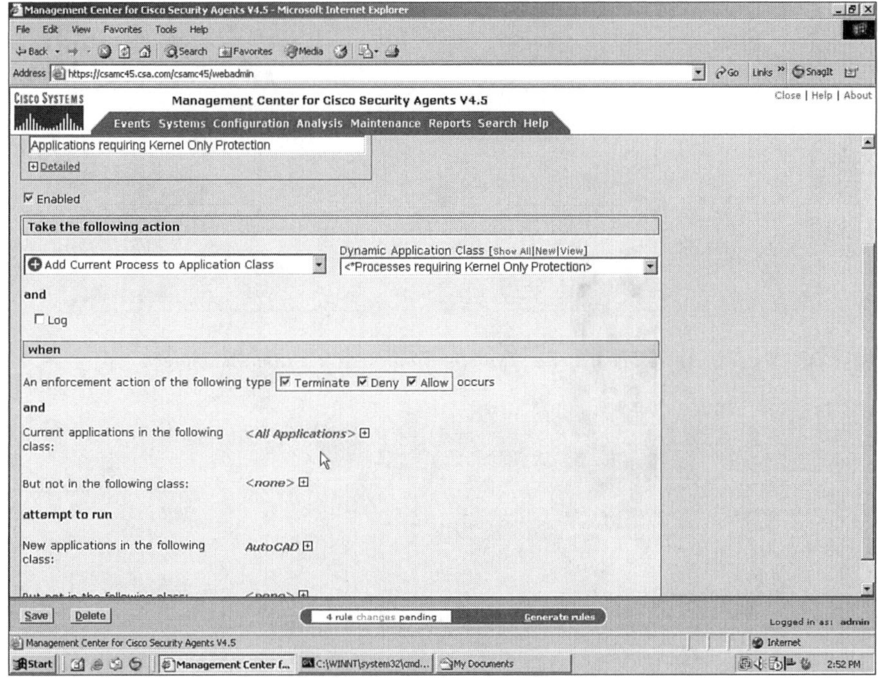

You can look at the log files for CSA through any of the following:

- Messages selection, as shown in Figure 5-17.
- The security log, as displayed in Figure 5-18.
- The endpoint log files from the log/ subdirectory of the directory you installed CSA in (usually C:\Program Files\Cisco Systems\CSAgent on Windows), as shown in Figure 5-19.

Figure 5-17 *Cisco Security Agent Messages Window*

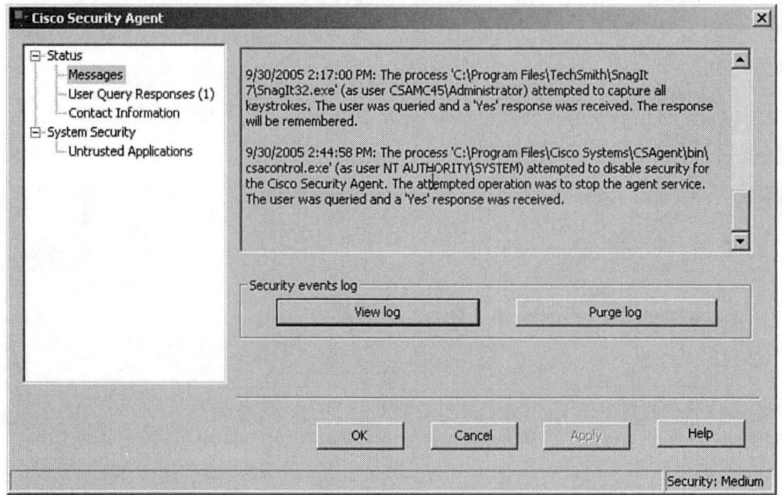

Figure 5-18 *Cisco Security Agent Security Log from the Windows User Interface Screen*

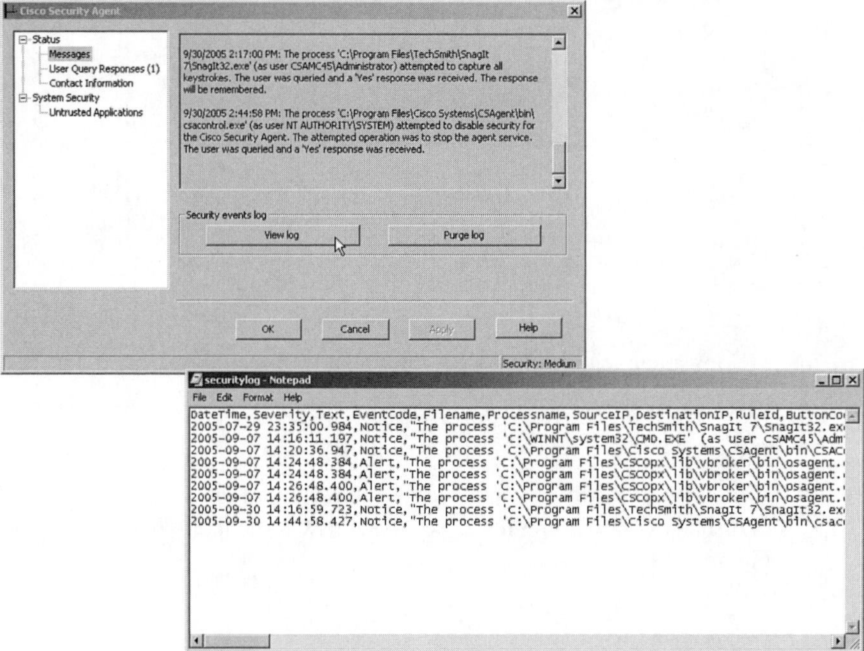

Figure 5-19 *Cisco Security Agent csalog.txt File Open in Windows Notepad Application*

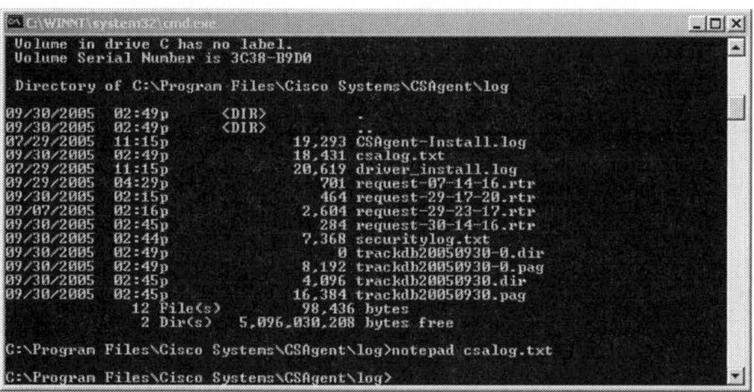

```
C:\WINNT\system32\cmd.exe
 Volume in drive C has no label.
 Volume Serial Number is 3C38-B9D0

 Directory of C:\Program Files\Cisco Systems\CSAgent\log

09/30/2005  02:49p      <DIR>          .
09/30/2005  02:49p      <DIR>          ..
07/29/2005  11:15p              19,293 CSAgent-Install.log
09/30/2005  02:49p              18,431 csalog.txt
07/29/2005  11:15p              20,619 driver_install.log
09/29/2005  04:29p                 701 request-07-14-16.rtr
09/30/2005  02:15p                 464 request-29-17-20.rtr
09/07/2005  02:16p               2,604 request-29-23-17.rtr
09/30/2005  02:45p                 284 request-30-14-16.rtr
09/30/2005  02:44p               7,368 securitylog.txt
09/30/2005  02:49p                   0 trackdb20050930-0.dir
09/30/2005  02:49p               8,192 trackdb20050930-0.pag
09/30/2005  02:45p               4,096 trackdb20050930.dir
09/30/2005  02:45p              16,384 trackdb20050930.pag
              12 File(s)         98,436 bytes
               2 Dir(s)   5,096,030,208 bytes free

C:\Program Files\Cisco Systems\CSAgent\log>notepad csalog.txt

C:\Program Files\Cisco Systems\CSAgent\log>
```

```
csalog - Notepad
File  Edit  Format  Help
[2005-09-30 14:45:01.973] [PID=4740] [csactrl]: Stopped process, leventmgr.exe pid=428
[2005-09-30 14:45:02.020] [PID=4740] [csactrl]: Service CSAgent exited (0).
[2005-09-30 14:49:13.833] [PID=400] [csactrl]: .
[2005-09-30 14:49:13.833] [PID=400] [csactrl]: Service CSAgent starting...
[2005-09-30 14:49:13.895] [PID=400] [csactrl]: Started process leventmgr.exe pid=4740
[2005-09-30 14:49:14.036] [PID=4740] [csamanager]: csamanager starting ...
[2005-09-30 14:49:14.255] [PID=4740] [csamanager]: Agent is 'managed', version=v4.5-1 build 616, os='windows 2000', os ve
[2005-09-30 14:49:14.317] [PID=4740] [csamanager]: Listening for requests on fixed channel Global\csamanager_ch_00000000
[2005-09-30 14:49:14.505] [PID=4740] [csamanager]: Initialized upload randomizer to 47
[2005-09-30 14:49:14.505] [PID=4740] [csamanager]: warning: oldest message is 252500 milliseconds old
[2005-09-30 14:49:14.505] [PID=4740] [csamanager]: UskaBoostPriority: Event handler thread priority is 15
[2005-09-30 14:49:14.552] [PID=4740] [csamanager]: Polling interval = 600 sec
[2005-09-30 14:49:14.817] [PID=4740] [csamanager]: get_system_params is unable to get DNS server list
[2005-09-30 14:49:15.130] [PID=4740] [csamanager]: load_rules: compiled runtime rule program (0) (t=250 ms)
[2005-09-30 14:49:15.192] [PID=4740] [csamanager]: COMBuildTrees: started.
[2005-09-30 14:49:15.286] [PID=4740] [csamanager]: load_rules: configured rule engine (0) (t=546 ms)
[2005-09-30 14:49:15.317] [PID=4740] [csamanager]: MC Reachability state has been set to 'Not Reachable'.
[2005-09-30 14:49:15.317] [PID=4740] [csamanager]: Agent initialization complete.
[2005-09-30 14:49:15.348] [PID=4740] [csamanager]: Start Polling.
[2005-09-30 14:49:15.583] [PID=4740] [csamanager]: COMBuildTrees: finished, elapsedTime=406 millisec
[2005-09-30 14:49:15.755] [PID=4740] [csamanager]: DoGUIDSetAssignments: COM id trees were created. Number of rcvd reques
[2005-09-30 14:49:16.786] [PID=4740] [csamanager]: Added agent UI channel-index=0 for session=0, user='Administrator', sn
[2005-09-30 14:49:18.114] [PID=4740] [csamanager]: MC Reachability state has been set to 'Reachable'.
```

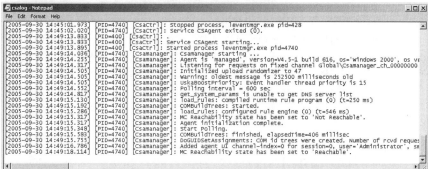

One of these preceding methods usually assists the quality assurance staff in locating and narrowing down a problem without having to uninstall and reinstall the CSA for every issue that arises.

Most software, however, works with CSA and does not cause issues or require policy changes. The default policies included with CSA are designed and tested to ensure a secure machine while treating a wide variety of actions as "normal" behaviors with no interaction or interruption.

It is important to remember that CSA is installed. Many of its actions are obvious and can be worked through in simple, easy steps or through straightforward testing and policy changes. However, using the modular and configurable features of CSA allows you to easily work through insecurely coded programs or actions.

Your quality assurance group should help you during a CSA pilot and with ongoing application deployment and provide feedback as it walks through its normal testing procedures and processes.

Hardware Platform Testing Documentation

This section examines the subject of hardware platform testing and CSA.

You probably do not expect too many issues between CSA and hardware. If Windows or Linux runs on the platform with the attached devices you want, then CSA should operate on it as well.

Although there are not many issues, the following is a list of issues to keep in mind while you choose new hardware, whether it is a new platform or a new gadget to attach to your existing platform:

- Devices for audio or video can trigger CSA policies, depending on their use. For example, you install a new camera to allow users to video conference. Depending on the software installed, you might receive a query about the software for that device attempting to monitor media devices. This is done to protect against malicious programs attaching to your computer's microphone or video camera and sending the traffic to a remote site for someone to review (yes, it has happened!).
- Although the default policies do not do anything to block the use of USB or removable devices, you can create policies to do this if your site security policy says that you should.
- As newer and newer platforms are released, new versions of Microsoft Windows or RedHat Enterprise Linux are needed to support those platforms (such as Tablet PCs, for example). This is a fairly normal expectation for any software application. However, you should check the latest release notes for the version of CSA you plan to use. Is the hardware and software combination you plan to use covered by this release? Will you need to upgrade before deployment of this new device? Will you need to contact Cisco and push to get support for a particular platform or release of Windows or Linux?
- If you have issues with testing after you install a new device, isolate that device or remove it temporarily to see if that device is causing the issue. Remember, most users believe that the last thing installed is the one causing the issue (even though they installed 12 new packages off the Internet the previous day and have not rebooted).

If a change is needed, most issues can be resolved by simple policy changes, and Cisco Security Agent's model of operation is designed to allow you to make those changes without the need for a high-touch visit to the user; for example, actually going out to a desktop to fix it.

Contacts and Support Escalation

This part is simple, right? It's just a list of support contacts you have handy, right?

You should keep a list of contacts of CSA helpers for your users and support staff and a list of other helpful support steps and information, such as:

- The phone numbers for the Cisco Technical Assistance Center (TAC) and the support contract numbers to use when calling the TAC.
- Who can escalate cases? How are cases escalated? Who can call Cisco TAC (probably not everybody)? What steps should your users and staff take locally before escalating?

To help the TAC resolve your case quickly, you should also be familiar with necessary information, such as:

- The hardware configuration of your CSA MCs.
- The version of CSA you currently run (on the CSA MCs and your end machines).
- The operating system of your CSA MC and your end machines, such as:
  - The MC can retrieve this information outlined in the three bullets above. Look under the host in question to find the operating system information for that machine.
  - Use the Application Deployment Investigation options to collect information about the applications installed on the end-user machine (desktop or server).
- The current diagnostics from CSA if you are debugging an end-user machine problem. (Hint: Select **Cisco Security Agent Diagnostics** from the Start menu to collect all the necessary logs to start them.)
- The links to the Cisco networking professional forums at http://forum.cisco.com/eforum/servlet/NetProf?page=main (or go to the main Cisco Connection Online page at http://cco.cisco.com and click on **Discussion Forums**).
- The steps necessary to test or eliminate CSA as the issue (see the "Quality Assurance" section earlier in this chapter for some ideas).
- The steps necessary to install, uninstall, and manually uninstall CSA (the latter being a document you can get from Cisco TAC or your Cisco support team because it has several steps).
- A Frequently Asked Questions (FAQ) document is generally built for your environment as you move through the pilot and discover items you think users will ask about (this list will likely grow over time).

Summary

We hope this chapter presented a few points you already knew, but also provided new information that you can use to enhance your understanding of the documentation needs of a CSA deployment in your enterprise.

Ensuring a good set of documentation on the procedures and processes of CSA is vital to smooth change control, quality assurance, and software/hardware testing. You should also see, however, that CSA is not overwhelming. You need good documentation to support your CSA deployment, and this deployment can help you with your security policy documentation—both early in your pilot and during deployment. The CSA also helps you collect information and events about your computing environment.

CSA Installation

CHAPTER 6

CSA MC Server Installation

One of the first decisions you make regarding your CSA deployment is how to architect the Cisco Security Agent Management Console (CSA MC) servers. In versions previous to Cisco Security Agent (CSA) 4.5, you were allowed to install only a single management server that handled the configuration, polling and events, and database tasks. This server also housed the database locally as either the native Microsoft Desktop Engine (MSDE) database or the upgraded Microsoft SQL database. Since the release of version 4.5, the architecture options have changed. You can now implement up to three servers and split the tasks across them for maximum performance, reliability, scalability, and better disaster recovery options. This chapter provides you with the information you need to decide which architecture is right for your deployment and also the steps necessary to implement the management server architecture. In this chapter, we explore:

- The possible CSA MC server implementation options
- Installing CSA MC servers in various configurations
- Upgrading from MSDE to Microsoft SQL 2000
- Preparing a Microsoft SQL 2000 for a CSA MC installation

Implementation Options

You can install your CSA management server software on either one, two, or three servers. Determining the number of servers is directly related to the number of agents you need to support, the amount of time you need to keep the event logs online, and the type of disaster recovery you would like to use. Your servers can have multiple roles or the roles can be split across the servers. The roles are: Event Logging and Polling, Configuration, and Database. The next section discusses the implementation options.

Option 1: Single-Server CSA MC Deployment

In a single-server deployment, you run all management functions on one server. All configuration, event reception, polling, alerting, and database interaction happen on the single server. During the default installation of the CSA MC software, the database that is installed on this server is the MSDE database. This database is sufficient for deployments smaller than 500 agents because the maximum database size for an MSDE database is only 2.0 GB. You do have the option of running Microsoft SQL 2000 on this server to house the database. To accomplish this, you either migrate the pre-installed MSDE database to SQL or implement the SQL software prior to installing the CSA MC software on the server.

It is important to understand that a single server deployment should never scale beyond 20,000 agents. The hardware requirements are listed later in this chapter in the section, "CSA MC Server Hardware Requirements." Another reason not to use a single-server deployment is that all configuration and event information is stored in the database. Therefore, you should consider the disaster recovery scenario for the server. If you were to lose this server because of software or hardware failure, you could not receive events or make policy changes to the deployed hosts. To recover from failure, you would need to restore from a backup that could be time consuming. If you want to have some level of control during a server outage, you should consider using any of the multi-server architectures listed in the next few sections.

NOTE Technically, the active servers in your deployment can exceed three if you use a SQL server redundancy scheme, such as mirroring.

Option 2: Two-Server CSA MC Deployment

In a two-server deployment, you break out some of the functions across multiple servers for greater system performance. This deployment type can scale as high as 75,000 agents. In the majority of two-server deployments, one server acts as the configuration and event and logging servers, whereas the other houses the database. Another option is to split the configuration and event and logging functions across two servers and choose one of the two to also run the SQL database. If you select the latter option, it is advisable to run the database on the Configuration server as it is the least processor-intensive and provides the most efficient use for your hardware in this type of deployment.

Option 3: Three-Server CSA MC Deployment

In a three-server deployment, you split the CSA MC software into two servers and use a third server as a dedicated database server. This type of deployment can scale as high as 100,000 agents.

NOTE The number of agents previously mentioned per deployment option is the number of agents officially supported by Cisco. To get to these numbers, you need to use hardware that meets the minimum requirements as listed in Table 6-2.

CSA MC Server Hardware Requirements

Prior to installing your CSA MC server or servers, you should verify hardware and software requirements in the release notes and installation guide of the version you are about to install. Your hardware should meet or preferably exceed the requirements. Cisco has categorized the server hardware requirements into various hardware configurations as displayed in Table 6-1. Assuming all servers you use for this deployment are identical, you should first examine the table to identify which hardware configuration you are using.

Table 6-1 *CSA MC Server Hardware Configurations*

Configuration 1	Single processor Pentium 4 (3 Ghz+) 2 GB RAM
Configuration 2	Dual processor Xeon (2.5 Ghz+) 4 GB RAM
Configuration 3	Quad processor Xeon (2.5 Ghz+) 8 GB RAM

After you identify the hardware and associate it to a configuration in Table 6-1, you can apply this information to Table 6-2 to see which options you have and how many agents you can support. In addition to having the correct hardware, you might also need to set the polling interval higher than the defaults and also use web cache engines in your network to lower the burden placed on these servers during routine operation.

Table 6-2 *CSA MC Server Architecture Options*

Configuration	# of Servers	Maximum Agents
Configuration 1	1 Server	5,000
	2 Servers	15,000
	3 Servers	20,000

continues

Table 6-2 *CSA MC Server Architecture Options (Continued)*

Configuration 2	1 Server	10,000
	2 Servers	30,000
	3 Servers	50,000
Configuration 3	1 Server	20,000
	2 Servers	75,000
	3 Servers	100,000

CSA MC Server Installation

Installing the CSA MC server is a relatively simple process, but it can become somewhat complex when you install a multiple server deployment using a remote SQL database. We walk you through a few common deployment types in the following sections. As an assumption, we expect Cisco VMS Common Services to be installed on each server that has CSA MC software loaded. We do not cover the Cisco VMS installation process in this text.

NOTE We recommend that you install only the Common Services component of CiscoWorks VMS on any server that will run CSA MC software. In addition, you want to ensure that Microsoft Terminal Services is not installed and the IIS Web server is not running prior to starting the CSA server installation process.

Single-Server Installations

When installing the CSA MC software on a single server, you have only a few options. You must first decide if you will use the default MSDE database or use Microsoft SQL 2000. You can migrate the MSDE database to a Microsoft SQL 2000 database later if you choose, but you might decide to save time in the beginning of your project by pre-installing the correct database. In the next few sections we discuss, and illustrate when necessary, the following:

- Installation of a single-server CSA MC with MSDE
- Upgrading a CSA MC MSDE installation to MS SQL 2000
- Installation of a single CSA MC with MS SQL 2000

Installation of a Single-Server CSA MC with MSDE

This type of installation is the most common and the simplest to perform as it uses the default database installation. The following steps explain this type of installation:

Step 1 Verify CiscoWorks Common Services is loaded and working correctly on your server by logging into the interface.

Step 2 Verify you have the necessary CSA licenses and software available.

Step 3 Start the CSA MC installation by launching the installer. As displayed in Figure 6-1, the Welcome screen appears.

Figure 6-1 *Installer Welcome Screen*

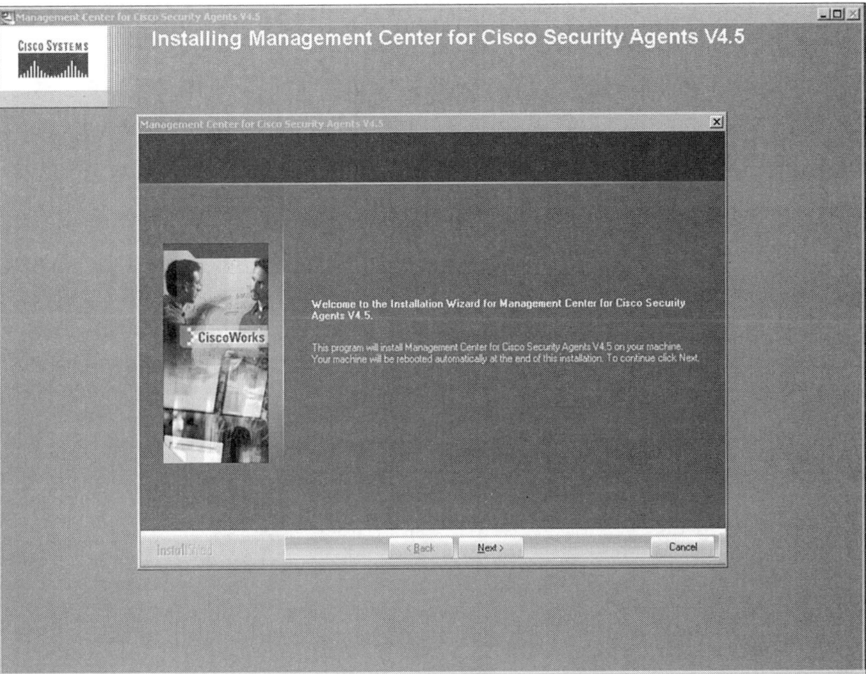

Step 4 Click **Next**.

Step 5 If your system does not meet the necessary minimum memory requirement of 1 GB, a prompt might alert you to this fact. If the prompt appears, either select **Yes** to continue anyway or **No** to stop the installation.

NOTE Although 1 GB of memory is the minimum required, you should note that the recommended amount of memory listed in Table 6-1 is actually 2GB.

Step 6 A prompt appears asking if you will use a local or remote database. Select **Local** and press **Next**, as shown in Figure 6-2.

Step 7 A local database first attempts to detect an appropriately configured MS SQL 2000 database if it has been preconfigured or falls back to installing a local MSDE database.

A remote database allows you to integrate with an SQL database on another system.

Figure 6-2 *Database Location Options*

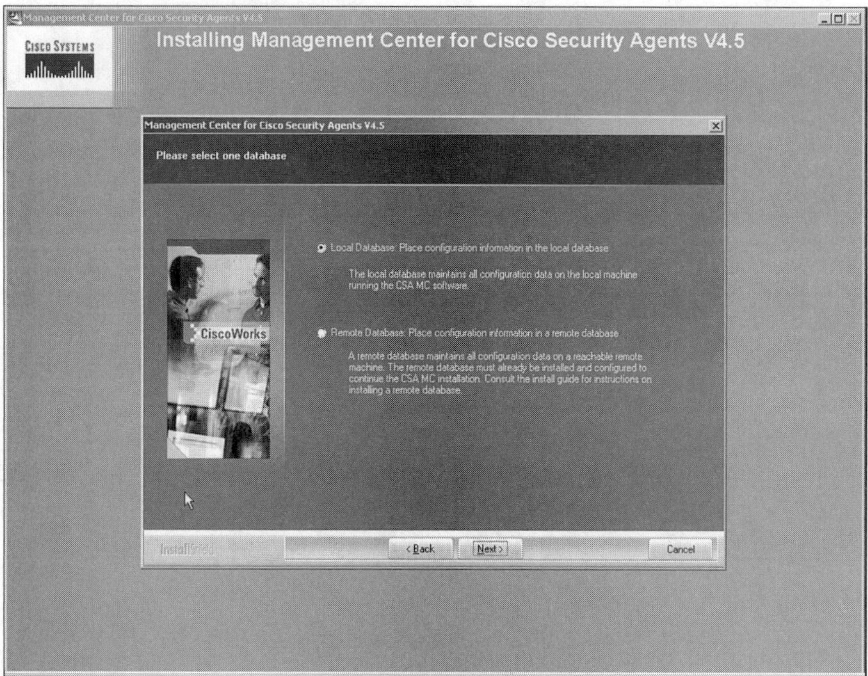

Step 8 If the installer cannot find an appropriate pre-installed database, it will inform you that it needs to install an MSDE database. Select **Yes** to continue with the MSDE installation.

Step 9 A prompt appears asking for the location in which to install the MSDE database. Click **Next** to retain the defaults if appropriate, as shown in Figure 6-3.

Figure 6-3 *MSDE Installation Location*

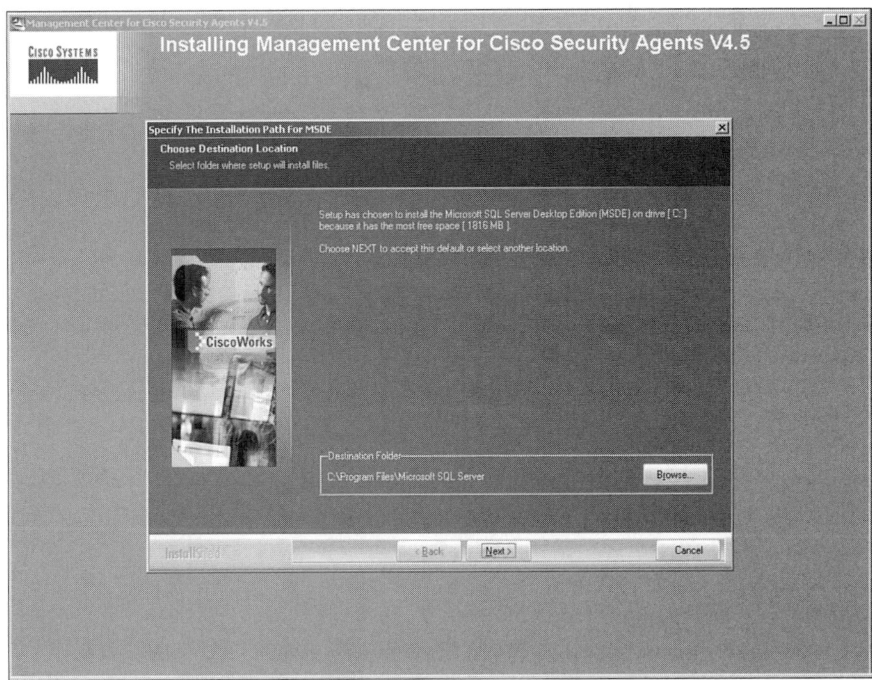

Step 10 After installation of the MSDE database, you are prompted to reboot the system, as shown in Figure 6-4.

Figure 6-4 *MSDE Required Reboot*

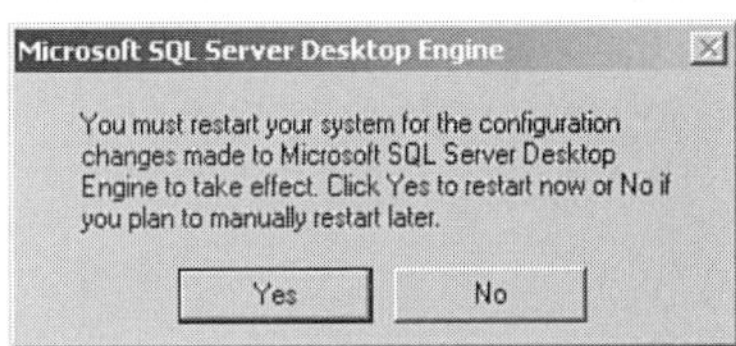

Step 11 After the system reboots, log back into the system and restart the CSA MC installation program.

Step 12 Continue through the prompts as previously explained and again select **Local Database** as the installation option.

Step 13 This time the installer detects the database and asks for a License file, as displayed in Figure 6-5.

Figure 6-5 *Installation Prompts for the CSA MC License File*

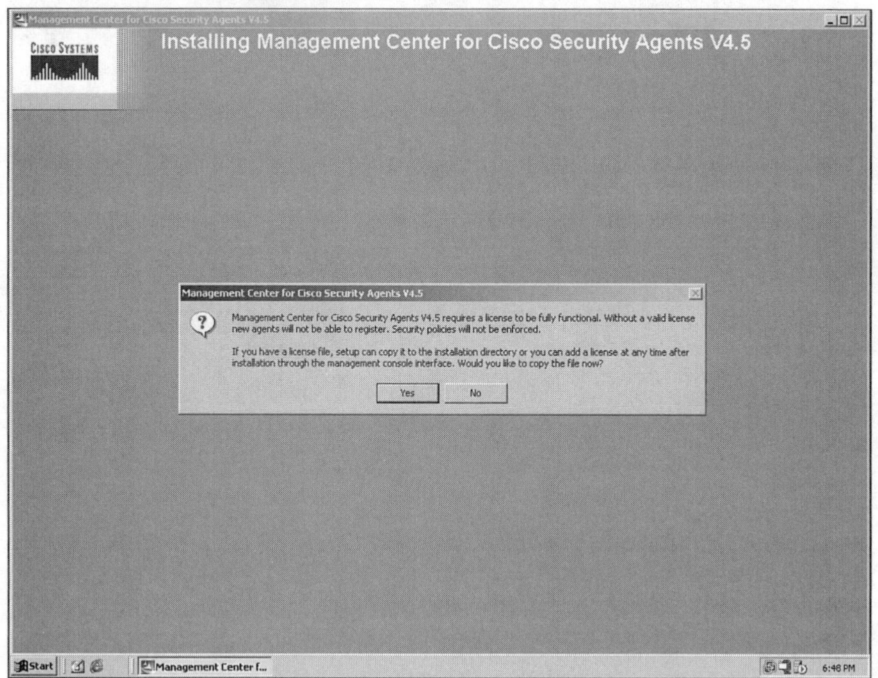

Step 14 Press the **Yes** button and navigate to the License file on your system.

Step 15 After selecting a License file, the system lets you know it is ready to begin the installation of the CSA MC software, as displayed in Figure 6-6. Press **Install** to continue.

Figure 6-6 *Ready for Install*

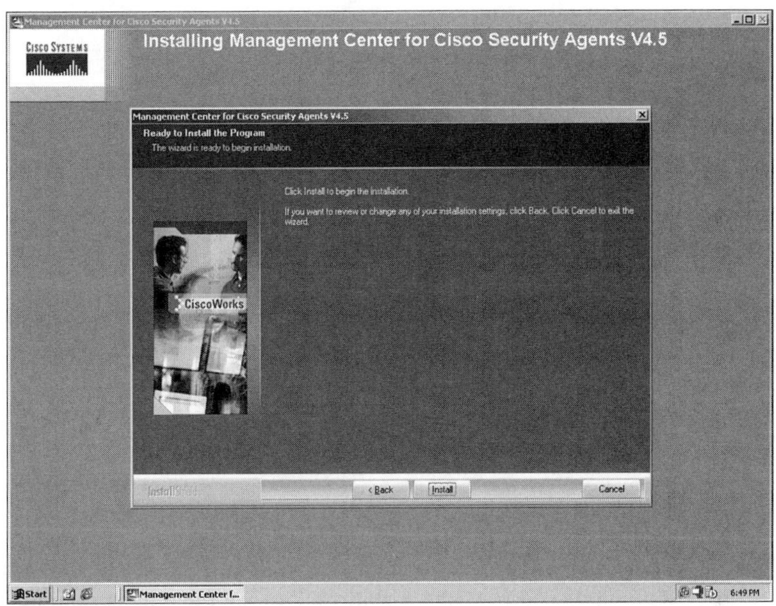

Step 16 The installer now attempts to stop running CiscoWorks VMS services and attempts to copy the necessary installation files to the appropriate location, as displayed in Figure 6-7.

Figure 6-7 *Copying the Installation Files*

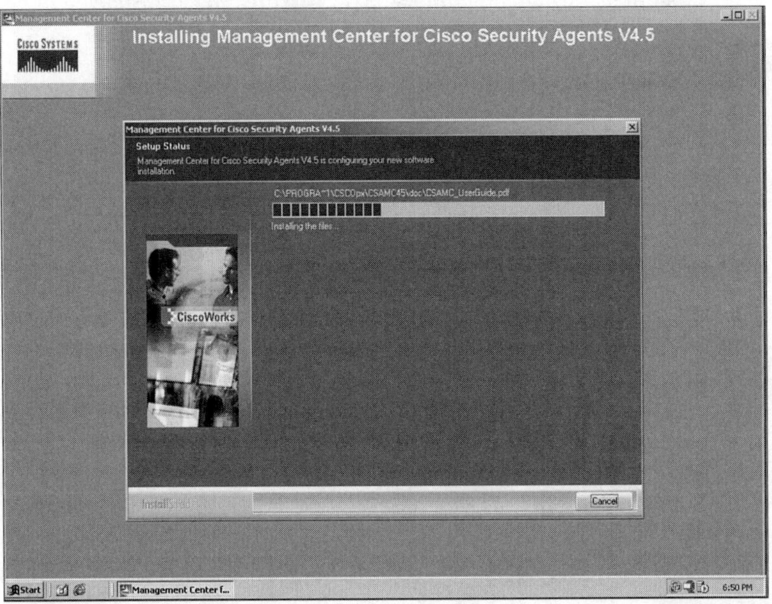

Step 17 After copying the files, the installer begins to install the necessary components and provides a status bar along the way, as shown in Figure 6-8.

Figure 6-8 *Installation Progress Screen*

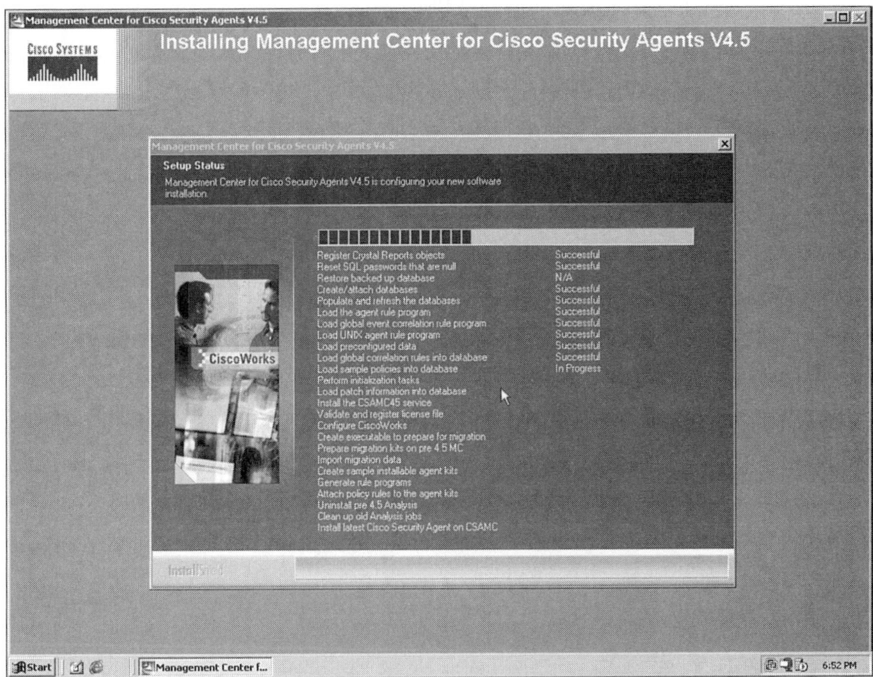

Step 18 After installing the CSA MC, the installer installs a CSA locally.

Step 19 After installing the local CSA, the installer concludes by letting you know a reboot is about to occur, as shown in Figure 6-9.

Figure 6-9 *Reboot Prompt After Installation*

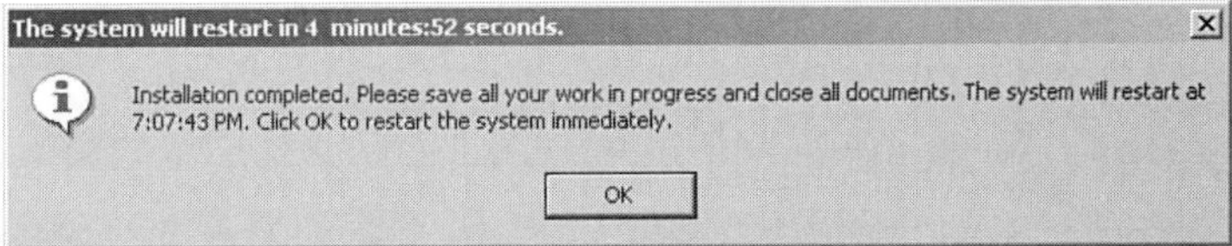

Step 20 After rebooting the system, you need to log in to the server and verify the system is functioning using the following steps:

(a) Log in to VMS and select the new **VPN/Security Management Solution** drawer

(b) Then select **Management Center** and finally select **Security Agents V4.5**. A popup window then displays the CSA MC, as shown in Figure 6-10.

(c) Alternatively, you can take a shortcut past the VMS server login screens and avoid locally loading Java by going directly to the CSA MC using https://<servername>/csamc45/webadmin. This prompts you for a login that is the same as what you would use on the VMS system. This login page is shown in Figure 6-11.

Figure 6-10 *Verify Your CSA MC Installation*

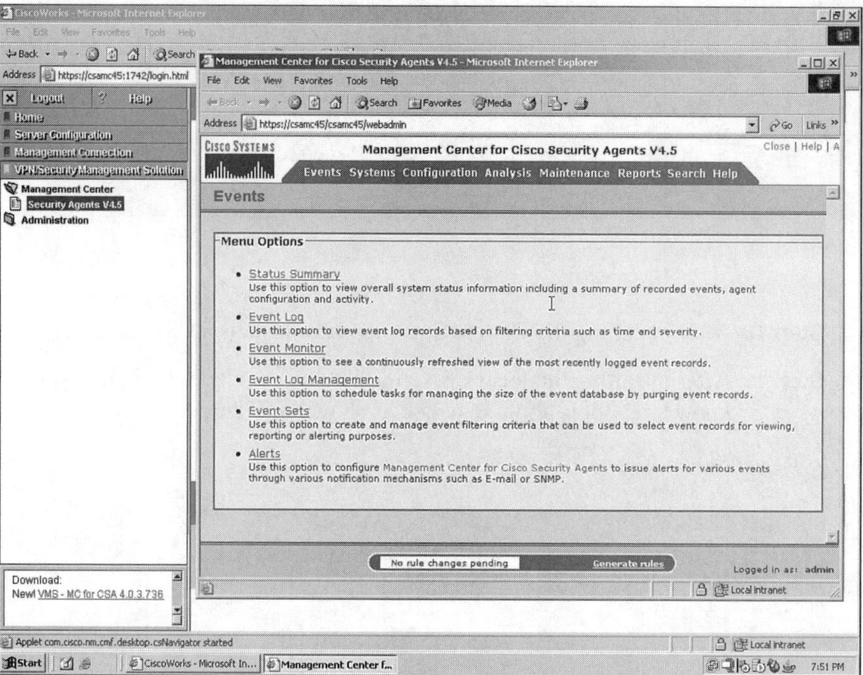

Figure 6-11 *Shortcut Login to CSA MC*

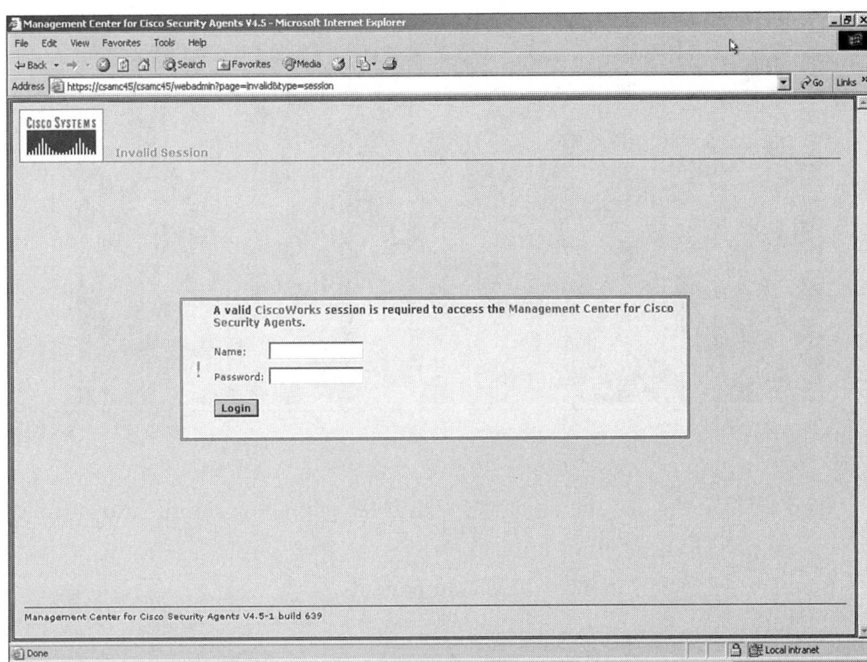

Your CSA MC installation is now complete and you can begin using the application, deploying agents, and tuning policy as necessary. If you see your deployment growing beyond the capacity of the MSDE database, you might want to upgrade to a full SQL 2000 installation. The following section explains this.

Upgrading a CSA MC MSDE Installation to MS SQL 2000

When your deployment scales beyond 500 hosts, you need to load a full copy of MS SQL 2000 because it is not included with the CSA MC product. This database includes the capability of storing more than 2 GB of data and supports the use of builtin database maintenance tools and redundancy features, such as mirroring. The following steps illustrate the upgrade process and prepare you for upgrading your own deployment if necessary.

Step 1 You must first stop the local CSA and CiscoWorks Daemon Manager. From the command line, the two commands as displayed in Figure 6-12 are:

```
net stop csagent
net stop crmdmgtd
```

Figure 6-12 *Stop the Necessary Services*

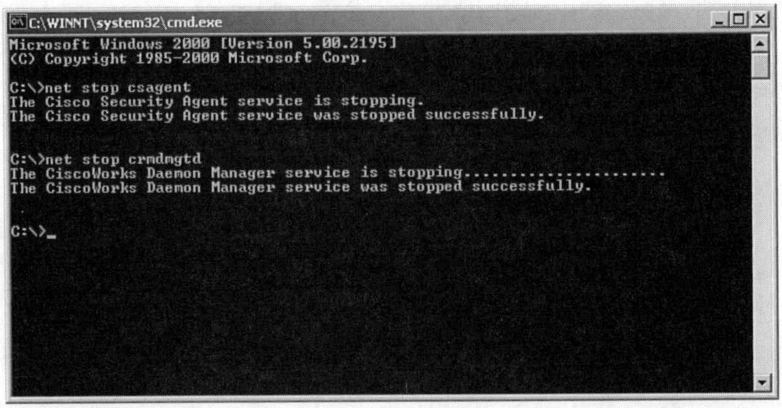

```
C:\WINNT\system32\cmd.exe
Microsoft Windows 2000 [Version 5.00.2195]
(C) Copyright 1985-2000 Microsoft Corp.

C:\>net stop csagent
The Cisco Security Agent service is stopping.
The Cisco Security Agent service was stopped successfully.

C:\>net stop crmdmgtd
The CiscoWorks Daemon Manager service is stopping.....................
The CiscoWorks Daemon Manager service was stopped successfully.

C:\>_
```

Step 2 Start the installation of MS SQL 2000 by running autorun.exe on your licensed installation CD.

Step 3 Select **SQL Server 2000 Components**.

Step 4 Select **Install Database Server**.

Step 5 The Wizard now starts, press **Next**.

Step 6 Select **Local Computer,** then press **Next**.

Step 7 Select **Upgrade**, **Remove**, or **add components to an existing instance of SQL Server**, then press **Next**.

Step 8 Leave the Default options and press **Next**.

Step 9 Select **Upgrade your existing installation** then press **Next**.

Step 10 Select the checkbox for **Yes**, **Upgrade my programs** and press **Next**.

Step 11 Select your appropriate licensing option as per your purchase of MS SQL 2000.

Step 12 A popup appears and asks if you would like to install additional components; press **Yes**.

Step 13 From the components list, select **Server Components, Management Tools, and Client Connectivity**. Also ensure that each component under those headings is selected.

Step 14 Click **Next** twice more and the installation will begin.

Step 15 When completed, press **Finish**.

Step 16 If necessary, and if your SQL installer did not include it, install SQL service pack 3a.

Step 17 Restart the server.

Step 18 Log in to the CSA MC and verify it is fully functional.

Step 19 Open the SQL Enterprise Manager application and register the CSAMC45 database if you wish to manage the database, as in Figure 6-13.

Figure 6-13 *MS SQL 2000 Enterprise Manager*

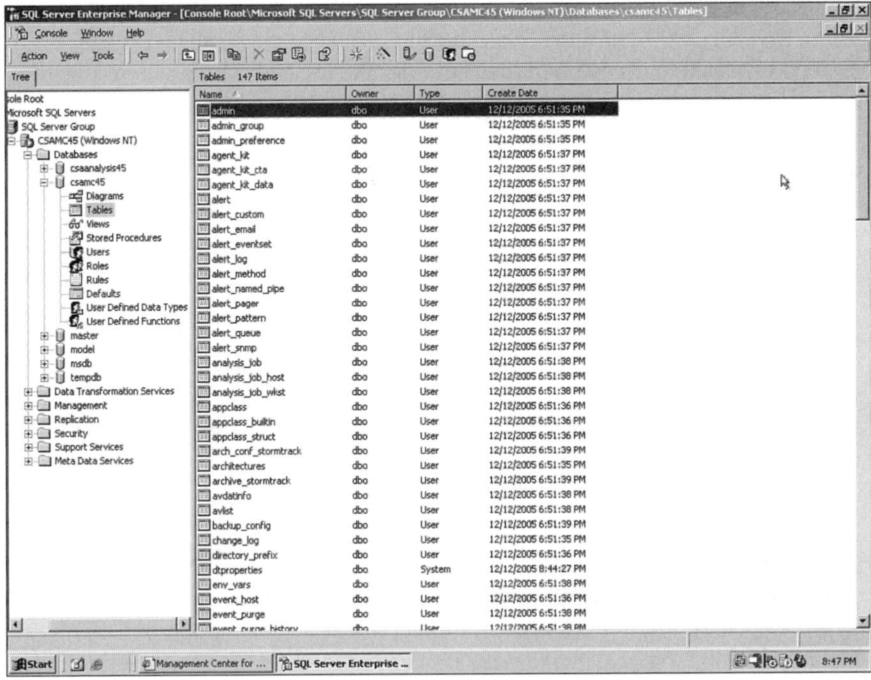

This completes the upgrade of the MSDE database to MS SQL 2000, and you should be able to manage the database just as you manage the others in your enterprise.

NOTE Cisco does not support changing CSA MC database tables and values in any way other than the way you use for the native CSA MC management interface, and you should be aware that database corruption can occur.

Installation of a Single CSA MC with MS SQL 2000

Rather than perform an upgrade from MSDE to MS SQL 2000, you might opt to pre-install MS SQL 2000 on the server prior to installing the CSA MC software. This is a common deployment configuration for smaller environments that have more than 500 hosts to manage. The installation of MS SQL 2000 and the required database setup process is not covered in this section but is discussed in the "Single CSA MC and an Additional Server for MS SQL 2000" section of this chapter. The steps are identical because the MS SQL 2000 is related to the MS SQL database installation and configuration.

Multiple Server Installations

When installing the CSA MC software on multiple servers, you must decide which components to place on which servers. There are three components to implement:

- CSA MC Configuration Graphical User Interface (GUI)
- Event and Polling Services
- MS SQL 2000 Database

You can place these components on up to three servers as necessary. The following sections cover a few of the common implementation options.

Single CSA MC and an Additional Server for MS SQL 2000

It is common for organizations to want to use existing SQL deployments with CSA or to break out the CSA SQL database to another server, so that the appropriate staff can manage and maintain it. The following steps explain the MS SQL 2000 installation and preparation that you must complete prior to installing the CSA MC components on the other server.

Step 1 Start the installation of MS SQL 2000 by running autorun.exe on your licensed installation CD.

Step 2 Select **SQL Server 2000 Components.**

Step 3 Select **Install Database Server**.

Step 4 The Wizard now starts, press **Next**.

Step 5 Select **Local Computer**, and then press **Next**.

Step 6 Select **Create a new instance of SQL Server**, or install client tools and press **Next**.

Step 7 Enter your name and company and press **Next**.

Step 8 Read and accept the license agreement.

Step 9 Select **Server and Client Tools** and press **Next**.

Step 10 Select **Default** and press **Next**.

Step 11 Select **Typical** and set the database path or leave the default and press **Next**.

Step 12 Select **Use the same account for each service**, and then provide a service account and password. Click **Next**.

Step 13 Select **Mixed Mode Authentication** and check the **Blank Password box** to leave the service account (SA) account blank and press **Next** and then press **Next** again to proceed.

Step 14 Select your appropriate license information for the SQL server.

Step 15 Setup continues and completes.

Step 16 You can now install SQL Service Pack 3a if necessary.

Make sure to ignore the security threat warning and leave the password for SA blank.

If you install SP3a, which is required, be sure to select **Upgrade MS Search and Apply SP3a**.

Step 17 After install completes, reboot the server.

Step 18 Start the SQL Enterprise Manager application from the Program Files menu.

Step 19 Right-click on the server and select **Edit SQL server registration properties**.

Step 20 Choose **SQL Server authentication** and enter **SA** or another account that has privileges on this database.

Step 21 Right-click on the Server name and select **Properties**.

Step 22 Click the large **Network Configuration** button at the bottom and verify that TCP/IP is selected and on the right side of the screen. If you need to add TCP/IP, stop and restart the SQLSERVER service.

Step 23 Right-click on databases and select **New**.

Step 24 Name the new database **CSAMC45** and press **OK**.

Step 25 Right-click the new database and select **Properties**.

Step 26 Click on the **Filegroups** tab and type **ANALYSIS** in the empty name field. Press **OK** when finished.

Step 27 Right-click the new database and select **Properties**.

Step 28 Click on the **Data files** tab. In the File Name field, add a datafile named **csamc45analysis_data**. In the space allocated field, enter **20** and in the filegroup filed, select **ANALYSIS** from the dropdown menu. Press **OK** when finished.

Step 29 Expand the Security folder under the database server.

Step 30 Right-click logins and select **New Login**.

Step 31 Create a user name such as **CSAUSER** and choose **SQL Server Authentication**. Enter a password for this user, then select the **CSAMC45 database** from the dropdown menu. Press **OK** when complete.

Step 32 Confirm the password and press **OK**.

Step 33 Click **Yes**.

Step 34 Expand the CSAMC45 database you created earlier.

Step 35 Right-click Users and select **New Database User**.

Step 36 Select the user you created earlier from the dropdown box.

Step 37 Add db_ddladmin, db_datareader, and db_datawriter Permissions, and then press **OK**.

This completes the necessary steps to install MS SQL 2000 on a remote server and also to preconfigure all components in the database necessary for you to proceed with the CSA MC installation on the other server. The first CSA MC server you install automatically becomes the Event and Polling server. It is also the Configuration GUI server until you install a second CSA MC. Then you should use the second server as the Configuration server. The following steps explain the differences in the installation of a CSA MC, which uses this remote database:

Step 1 Verify CiscoWorks Common Services is loaded and working correctly on your server by logging into the interface.

Step 2 Verify you have the necessary CSA licenses and software available.

Step 3 Follow the installation procedure outlined for installing a single CSA MC server deployment until you reach the database selection page.

Step 4 Select **Remote Database** and press **Next**.

Step 5 You must now enter the following to connect to the remote database as displayed in Figure 6-14:

- Server Name—The resolvable name of the server for the remote SQL connection
- Database Name—The name created earlier, which was CSAMC45
- User Name—The user created earlier, which was CSAUSER
- Password—The password provided for this user

Figure 6-14 *Databases Connection Information*

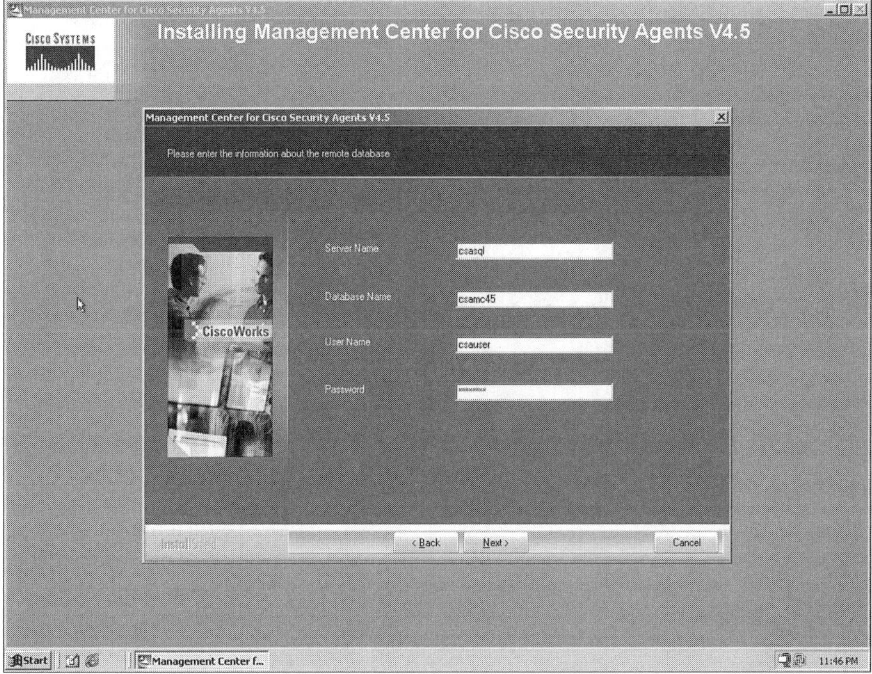

Step 6 Click **Next**.

Step 7 Continue with the installation steps you used for the single CSA MC installation. In Figure 6-15, notice that the progress bar skips many steps because the database is not local. This image is from the third server of a three-server installation. In this example, you can see that the policies were already installed in the database so there was no need to perform that action and many others.

Figure 6-15 *Installation Progress for Multi-Server*

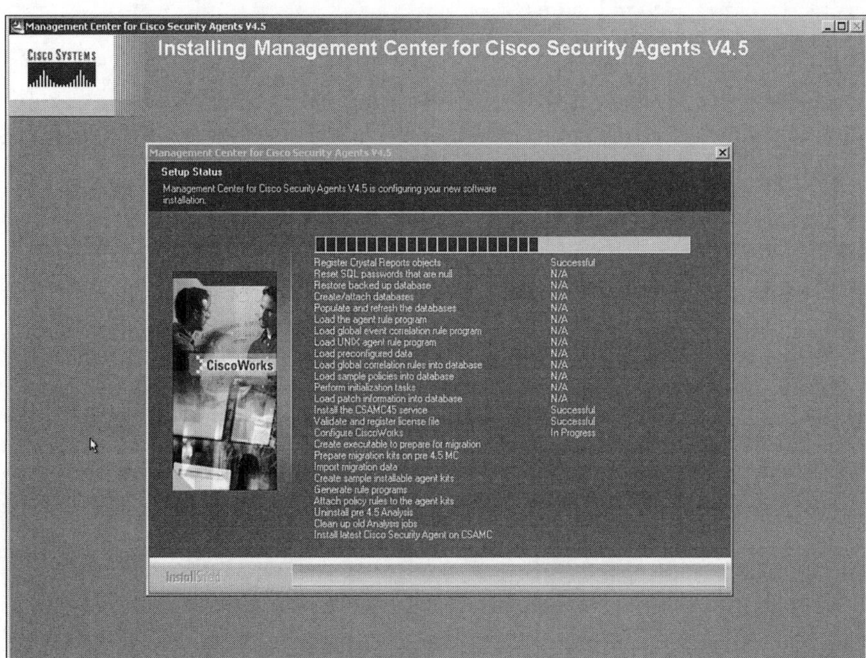

Step 8 Upon completion, look in the Windows Registry, as shown in Figure 6-16, at the keys located in HKEY_LOCAL_MACHINE\SOFTWARE\Cisco\CSAMC45. You can see that the local CSA MC is configured to use the remote server:

— DBP: Database Password

— DBU: Database User

— DSN: Database DSN referring to your SQL server

Figure 6-16 *SQL Information Listed in the Registry*

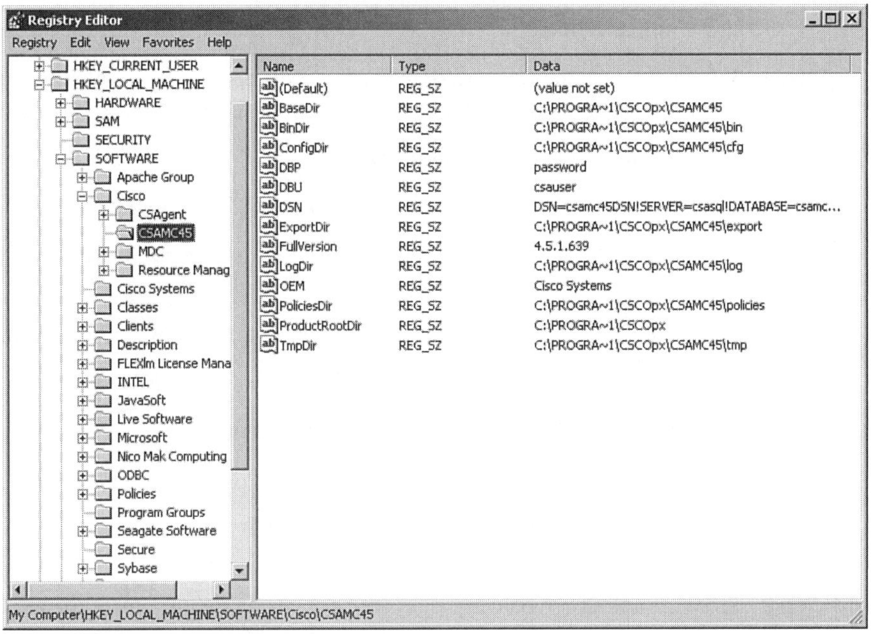
Registry Editor
Registry Edit View Favorites Help
HKEY_CURRENT_USER
HKEY_LOCAL_MACHINE
HARDWARE
SAM
SECURITY
SOFTWARE
Apache Group
Cisco
CSAgent
CSAMC45
MDC
Resource Manag
Cisco Systems
Classes
Clients
Description
FLEXlm License Mana
INTEL
JavaSoft
Live Software
Microsoft
Nico Mak Computing
ODBC
Policies
Program Groups
Seagate Software
Secure
Sybase
Name Type Data
(Default) REG_SZ (value not set)
BaseDir REG_SZ C:\PROGRA~1\CSCOpx\CSAMC45
BinDir REG_SZ C:\PROGRA~1\CSCOpx\CSAMC45\bin
ConfigDir REG_SZ C:\PROGRA~1\CSCOpx\CSAMC45\cfg
DBP REG_SZ password
DBU REG_SZ csauser
DSN REG_SZ DSN=csamc45DSN!SERVER=csasql!DATABASE=csamc...
ExportDir REG_SZ C:\PROGRA~1\CSCOpx\CSAMC45\export
FullVersion REG_SZ 4.5.1.639
LogDir REG_SZ C:\PROGRA~1\CSCOpx\CSAMC45\log
OEM REG_SZ Cisco Systems
PoliciesDir REG_SZ C:\PROGRA~1\CSCOpx\CSAMC45\policies
ProductRootDir REG_SZ C:\PROGRA~1\CSCOpx
TmpDir REG_SZ C:\PROGRA~1\CSCOpx\CSAMC45\tmp
My Computer\HKEY_LOCAL_MACHINE\SOFTWARE\Cisco\CSAMC45

You can now verify that the CSA MC is functional by logging into the system. You should notice that the installation process is not much different except for the many steps associated with installing the MS SQL 2000 server and preconfiguring the database. You should make sure you have a qualified technician perform the SQL installation if you are not confident that you can configure it and its maintenance procedures appropriately.

Two CSA MC and an Additional Server for MS SQL 2000

Installing another CSA MC server to create a three-server environment out of a two-server environment is an easy procedure. Follow these steps to accomplish this task:

Step 1 Verify CiscoWorks Common Services is loaded and working correctly on your server by logging into the interface.

Step 2 Verify that you have the necessary CSA licenses and software available.

Step 3 Connect to the first CSA MC server you installed and stop the CiscoWorks Services. This is an extremely important step, and you should always perform it before updating the CSA MC software on the servers, so you do not end up in multiple servers with multiple product versions online at the same time. Perform this by entering the following at a command-line:

Step 4 Follow the installation procedure that was outlined for installing a single CSA MC server deployment until you reach the database selection page.

Step 5 Select **Remote Database** and press **Next.**

Step 6 You must now enter the following to connect to the remote database:

- Server Name: The resolvable name of the server for the remote SQL connection
- Database Name: The name created earlier, which was **CSAMC45**
- User Name: The user created earlier, which was **CSAUSER**
- Password: The password provided for this user

Step 7 Press **Next.**

Step 8 Notice that there is less installed than previously as the database is already populated and configured.

Step 9 After completion, you can restart the services on the original CSA MC.

You now have two CSA MC servers and a dedicated database server functioning in the CSA MC architecture. To verify the installation in the SQL database, look at the mc_config table in the CSAMC45 database. You will see multiple servers listed, as shown in Figure 6-17.

Figure 6-17 *mc_config Table Displays Multiple MCs in SQL*

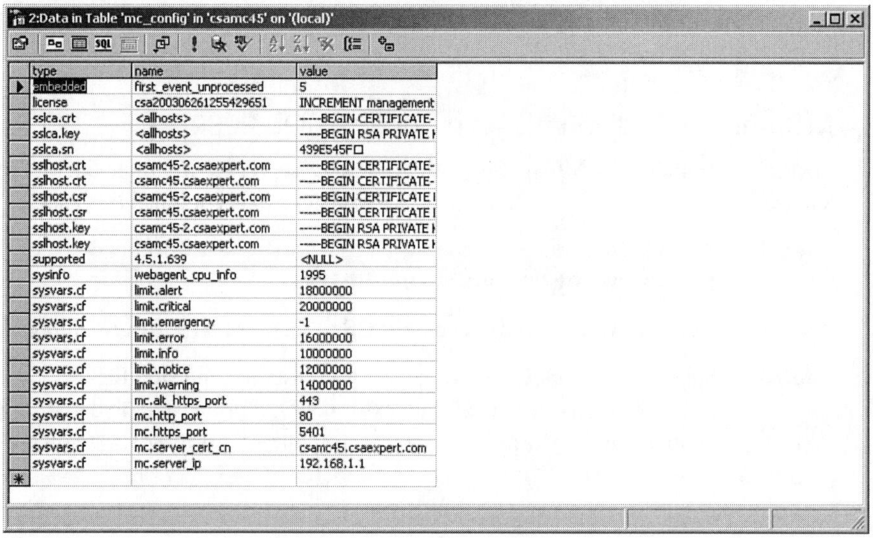

2:Data in Table 'mc_config' in 'csamc45' on '(local)'

type	name	value
embedded	first_event_unprocessed	5
license	csa200306261255429651	INCREMENT management
sslca.crt	<allhosts>	-----BEGIN CERTIFICATE-
sslca.key	<allhosts>	-----BEGIN RSA PRIVATE K
sslca.sn	<allhosts>	439E545F□
sslhost.crt	csamc45-2.csaexpert.com	-----BEGIN CERTIFICATE-
sslhost.crt	csamc45.csaexpert.com	-----BEGIN CERTIFICATE-
sslhost.csr	csamc45-2.csaexpert.com	-----BEGIN CERTIFICATE I
sslhost.csr	csamc45.csaexpert.com	-----BEGIN CERTIFICATE I
sslhost.key	csamc45-2.csaexpert.com	-----BEGIN RSA PRIVATE K
sslhost.key	csamc45.csaexpert.com	-----BEGIN RSA PRIVATE K
supported	4.5.1.639	<NULL>
sysinfo	webagent_cpu_info	1995
sysvars.cf	limit.alert	18000000
sysvars.cf	limit.critical	20000000
sysvars.cf	limit.emergency	-1
sysvars.cf	limit.error	16000000
sysvars.cf	limit.info	10000000
sysvars.cf	limit.notice	12000000
sysvars.cf	limit.warning	14000000
sysvars.cf	mc.alt_https_port	443
sysvars.cf	mc.http_port	80
sysvars.cf	mc.https_port	5401
sysvars.cf	mc.server_cert_cn	csamc45.csaexpert.com
sysvars.cf	mc.server_ip	192.168.1.1

Remember that the original CSA MC always becomes the Event and Polling server and that the second CSA MC installed becomes the Configuration GUI. This is because the original server installs all necessary components and certificates required to function without an additional server if a second is never installed. After the second server installation begins, it detects the previous configuration in the current database and assumes its role as the configuration server within the multi-server architecture.

NOTE If you use multiple servers for your deployment, all configuration and events are stored in the SQL database. This fact makes it possible to create cloned servers or images of the servers running the non-database CSA MC components, so that you could have a cold spare server ready in the case of a server failure. If you have a server failure, simply remove the failed system from the network and replace it with the cloned standby. You now have a fully functional configuration.

Summary

This chapter should prepare you for deploying the CSA MC management architecture in the hierarchy you desire. It is important that you understand the challenges and also the requirements for a multi-server deployment but also the protection it affords you. After you deploy the architecture, you are ready to proceed with your pilot, tuning, and implementation of CSA.

CHAPTER 7

CSA Deployment

After you install the Management Console (MC) servers and architect your Cisco Security Agent (CSA) groups and general policy, you need to deploy the CSA onto the systems you want to protect. These systems are likely located throughout your enterprise and are too numerous for manual installation. To efficiently install the CSAs through automated processes, you must understand the agent-build process, the contents of the agent executable, and all command-line parameters available when you attempt to script an installation package. This chapter explains these processes and the following:

- CSA installation requirements
- Creating agent kits
- Locating agent kits
- Agent kit components
- Installing agent kits from a command line

Agent Installation Requirements

Before installing the CSA software on any system in your environment, it is important to understand the required operating system levels allowed. Table 7-1 through Table 7-3 specify the installation requirements for the CSA as of version 4.5.1(639).

Table 7-1 *Windows Agent Requirements*

System Component	Requirement
Processor	Intel Pentium 200 MHz or higher **Note**: Uni/Dual/Quad processors are supported.
Operating Systems	Windows 2003 (Standard, Enterprise, Web, or Small Business) • Windows XP (Professional or Home) with Service Pack 0, 1, or 2

continues

Table 7-1 *Windows Agent Requirements (Continued)*

System Component	Requirement
Operating Systems	• Windows 2000 (Professional, Server, or Advanced Server) with Service Pack 0, 1, 2, 3, or 4 • Windows NT (Workstation, Server, or Enterprise Server) with Service Pack 6a • Requires Internet Explorer 4.0 or higher **Note**: Citrix Metaframe and Citrix XP are supported. Terminal Services are supported on XP and Windows 2000/2003. (Terminal Services are not supported on Windows NT.)
Memory	128 MB minimum
Hard Drive Space	15 MB or higher
Network	Ethernet or dial-up **Note**: Maximum of 64 IP addresses supported on a single system.

NOTE In addition to simply checking the operating system requirements, you should verify the language requirements as specified within the release notes.

Table 7-2 *Solaris Agent Requirements*

System Component	Requirement
Processor	UltraSPARC 400 MHz or higher **Note:** Uni/Dual/Quad processors are supported.
Operating Systems	Solaris 8, 64-bit 12/02 edition or higher **Note**: Solaris minimum Core Installation is not sufficient. You must also install the SUNWlibCx library.
Memory	256 MB minimum
Hard Drive Space	15 MB or higher
Network	Ethernet **Note**: Maximum of 64 IP addresses supported on a single system.

Table 7-3 *Linux Agent Requirements*

System Component	Requirement
Processor	500 MHz or higher x86 processor **Note**: Uni/Dual/Quad processors are supported.
Operating Systems	RedHat Enterprise Linux 3.0 ES, AS, or WS
Memory	256 MB minimum
Hard Drive Space	15 MB or higher
Network	Ethernet **Note**: Maximum of 64 IP addresses supported on a single system.

NOTE To check the appropriate operating system requirements for the specific version of CSA you are attempting to install, check the release notes that accompany the Cisco Security Agent Management Console (CSA MC) software, which are also available at Cisco.com.

Agent Installer

The CSA installation software is not a separate package available for download from the Cisco website. The Agent installer, known as the Agent Kit, is built on your specific CSA MC implementation to include precise information about your environment. This information includes items such as the Fully Qualified Domain Name (FQDN) of the CSA MC server and an initial protective policy. The initial policy included within each and every Agent Kit executable is the most up-to-date ruleset available at the time of Agent Kit creation. The next sections illustrate how to create an Agent Kit for your specific environment and also dissect the components of the Agent Kit.

Creating an Agent Kit

When you are ready to create an Agent Kit, follow these steps:

Step 1 Select **Systems>Agent Kits** from the top navigation bar. This will present you with a screen of currently available Agent Kits that are ready to use. Figure 7-1 shows a sample screen illustrating the many Agent Kits available. You can see that it includes information about the software revision and the target architecture.

Figure 7-1 *Agent Kits within the CSA MC GUI*

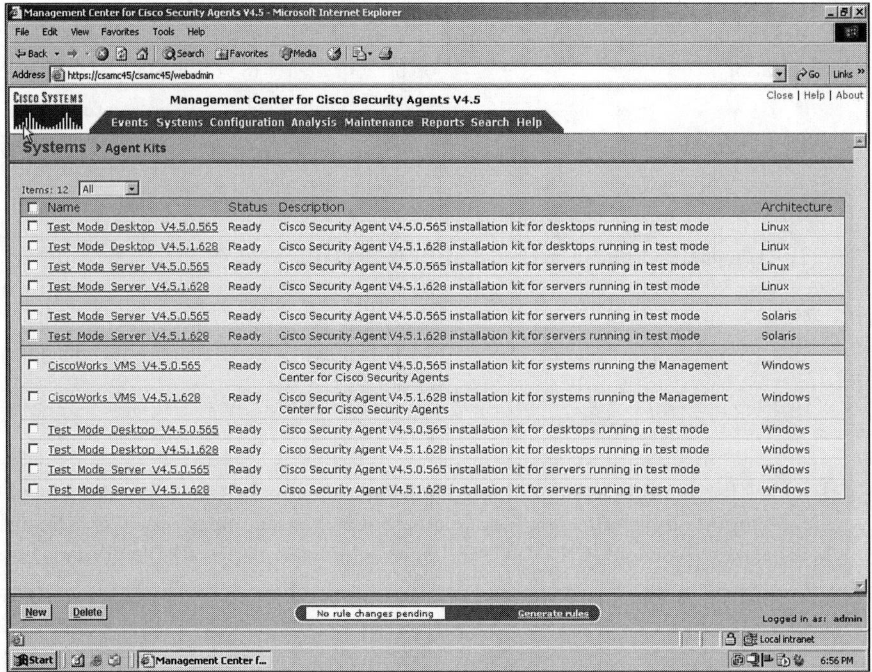

Step 2 Press the **New** button at the bottom-left corner of the interface to create a new kit. Alternatively, to view the settings you can select the clickable link associated with any of the previously created kits.

Step 3 A popup window should appear allowing you to select the correct operating system for your Agent Kit. In this example, select **Windows**. Figure 7-2 displays this.

Figure 7-2 *Selection of an Agent Kit Operating System*

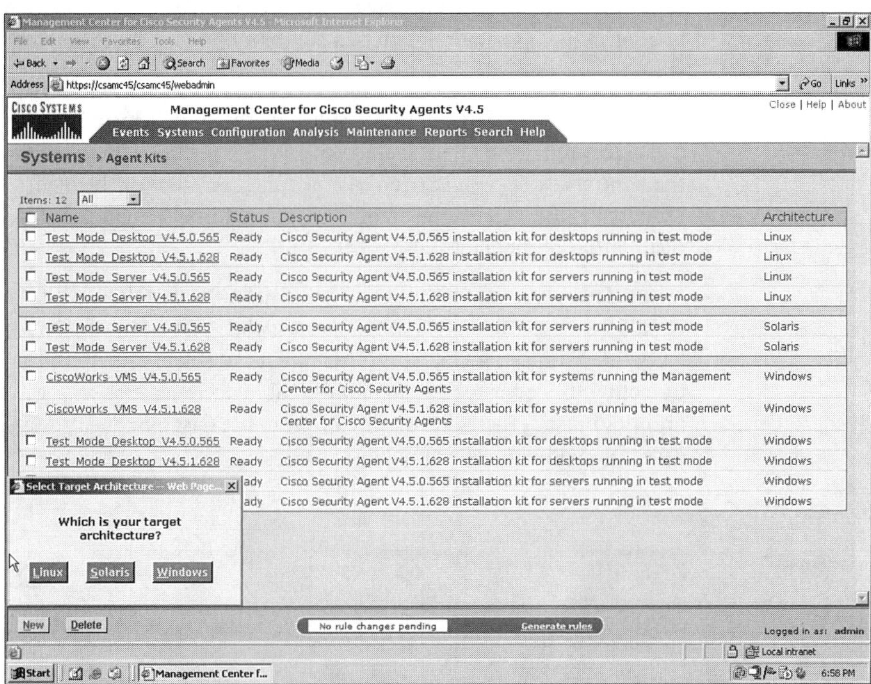

Step 4 You now must configure the Agent Kit parameters per your needs. The following list describes the settings and their uses. Figure 7-3 shows the configurable options.

- **Name**—This is part of the name of the installer file and cannot include spaces or special characters that would make it an invalid file name within some operating systems.
- **Description**—Insert a description of the purpose of this specific Agent Kit, so that other administrators can choose the appropriate kit at installation time.
- **Groups**—Select all groups to which any system that installs this specific kit should initially belong. Upon installation, the system is automatically placed in these groups.
- **Force reboot**—The installation kit can force an automatic reboot if required.

— **Quiet install**—If the installer should not ask any questions of the user, select this option. Otherwise, the user is given both the option to control the installation path and the option to install the network shim.

— **Network shim**—If this option is selected, the shim is installed. You can select this for a silent install only, which occurs when you, as the administrator, would need to make the decision for the user. Otherwise, the user is presented the option during a manual installation of the agent.

— **Cisco Trust Agent**—If you would like the CSA installer to also install the Cisco Trust Agent (CTA), which is part of the Cisco Network Admission Control (NAC) solution, select this option. Selecting this gives you other configurable options, such as the ability to install the NAC certificate from the Cisco Security ACS server and other CTA parameters.

Figure 7-3 *Agent Kit Configuration*

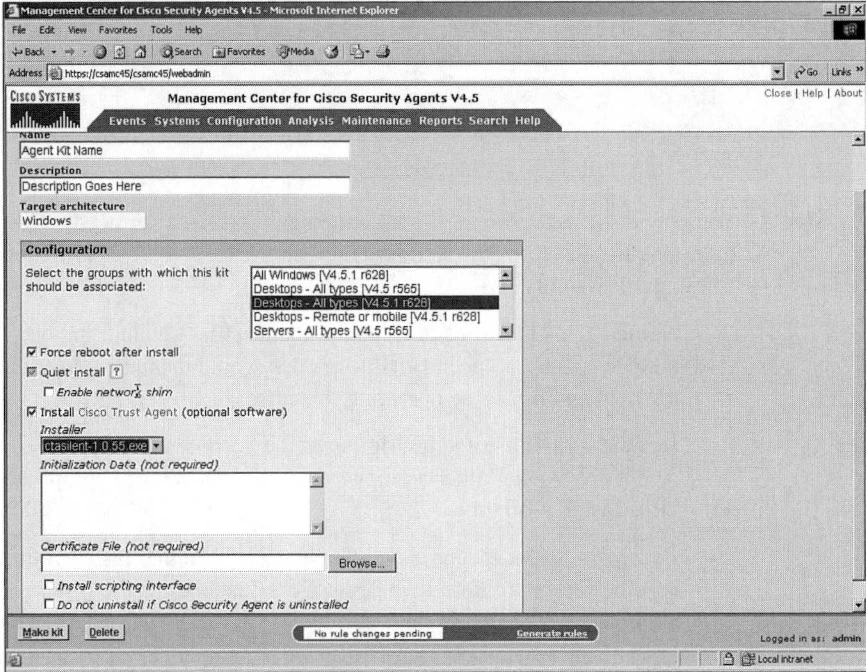

Step 5 After selecting the appropriate options for this kit, press **Make kit** to continue.

Step 6 Finally, a screen displays the options selected and affirms the creation of the Agent Kit. You can always change the group assignments and, therefore, the initial policy for this kit, but you cannot edit the other parameters without recreating the kit entirely. Figure 7-4 displays the final screen.

Figure 7-4 *Agent Kit Completion*

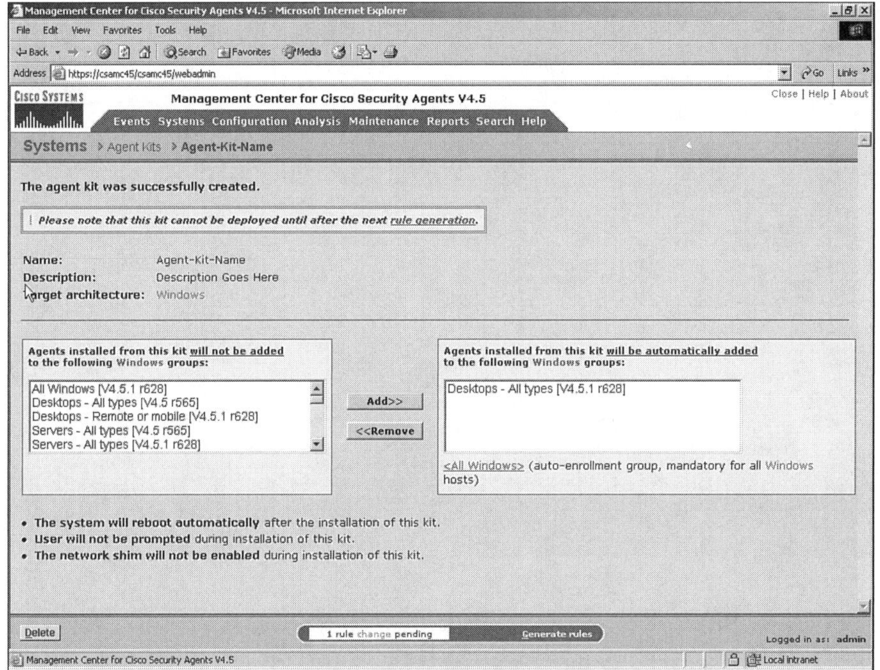

NOTE It is important to note that this newly created kit cannot be used until the next rule generation is completed.

Agent Kit Retrieval

There are multiple methods used to retrieve Agent Kits. You can obtain an Agent Kit directly from the **Systems>Agent Kits** page of the CSA MC GUI, as displayed previously in Figure 7-1. Additionally, you can obtain the Agent Kit from the URL specific to the

Agent Kit you need by opening the Agent Kit from **Systems>Agent Kits**. This URL looks something like: https://csamc45/csamc45/webadmin?page=dwnl_agent_kit&id=13. Another method of retrieval is via a URL protected by a Secure Sockets Layer (SSL) that does not require authentication. This allows remote systems that do not have management credentials to pull the kit to their system for installation. The URL you would use in the remote web browser is https://CSA_MC_NAME/csamc45/kits. This URL redirects your browser to a web page with access to all current kits, as displayed in Figure 7-5.

Figure 7-5 *Remote Access to Agent Kits via URL*

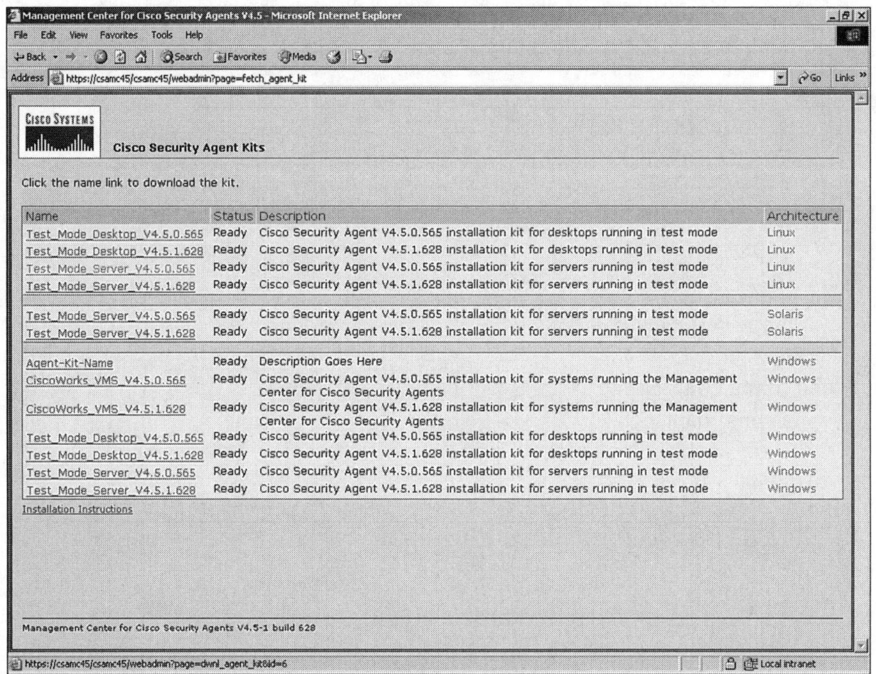

You can also retrieve the URL directly from the folder on the local CSA MC itself. The folder location is <Program_Files>\CSCOpx\CSAMC45\bin\webserver\htdocs\deploy_kits. In Figure 7-6, you can see all the kits located in this directory; this is how you would see them on your own MC.

Figure 7-6 *Directory Access to Agent Kits on the CSA MC*

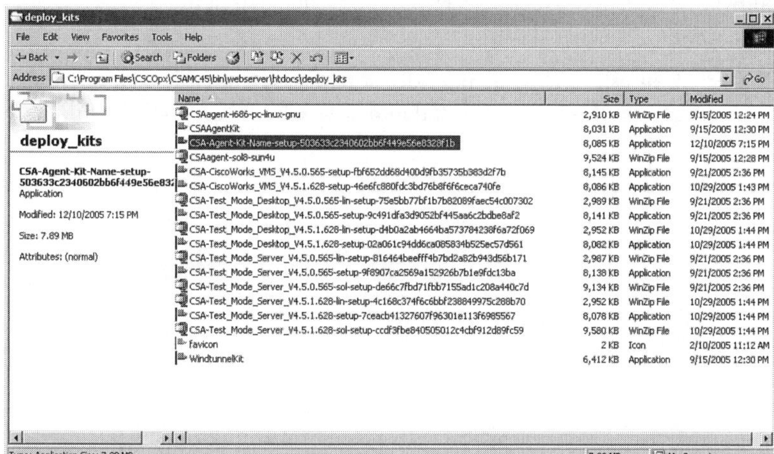

Agent Kit Dissection

After you retrieve an Agent Kit, you can install it on the system. The executable file is nothing more than a self-extracting zipped file that contains all the installation components and initial configuration settings required. Double clicking this file starts the installation, which this chapter later discusses. First, you need to open the executable in WinZip to view the files and learn more about what makes up an installer. This allows you to create scripted installers you can use in login scripts and other distribution mechanisms, such as software distribution products from BigFix (www.BigFix.com) and Microsoft (www.Microsoft.com).

Use any of the previously mentioned methods to retrieve an agent-installation executable and open the file in WinZip. You will see a set of files similar to the files shown in Figure 7-7.

Figure 7-7 *Agent Installer Contents as Viewed by WinZip*

WinZip - CSA-Agent-Kit-Name-setup-503633c2340602bb6f449e56e8328f1b.exe

File Actions Options Help

New Open Favorites Add Extract Encrypt View Install Wizard

Name	Type	Modified	Size	Ratio	Packed	Path
data1.cab	WinZip File	9/15/2005 1:30 PM	1,458,005	0%	1,456,405	
data1.hdr	HDR File	9/15/2005 1:29 PM	31,279	69%	9,825	
data2.cab	WinZip File	9/15/2005 1:30 PM	5,464,134	0%	5,462,074	
engine32.cab	WinZip File	12/15/2003 4:13 PM	459,544	0%	459,595	
layout.bin	BIN File	9/15/2005 1:30 PM	455	71%	133	
setup.exe	Install Application	11/10/2003 8:55 PM	116,880	50%	58,095	
setup.ibt	IBT File	9/15/2005 1:29 PM	449,909	4%	432,752	
setup.ini	Configuration Settings	9/15/2005 1:29 PM	572	32%	389	
setup.inx	INX File	9/15/2005 1:29 PM	348,120	33%	234,302	
Setup.iss	ISS File	2/2/2005 3:17 PM	1,518	70%	459	
agent.bundle	BUNDLE File	12/10/2005 7:15 PM	200	22%	157	
agent.rul	RUL File	12/10/2005 7:15 PM	62,108	24%	47,177	
agent.var	VAR File	12/10/2005 7:15 PM	34,569	79%	7,120	
sslca.crt	Security Certificate	10/29/2005 1:41 PM	891	25%	665	

Selected 0 files, 0 bytes Total 14 files, 8,231KB

After you extract the files to a local folder, you can view the contents of most files. The following list provides the names of the files included in the installer, a brief description, and a screenshot when applicable:

- **agent.bundle**—This file provides software version information, registration ID (ties the agent to this specific installation kit), CSA MC FQDN and IP address, and also ports used for communication.

Figure 7-8 *Contents of agent.bundle File*

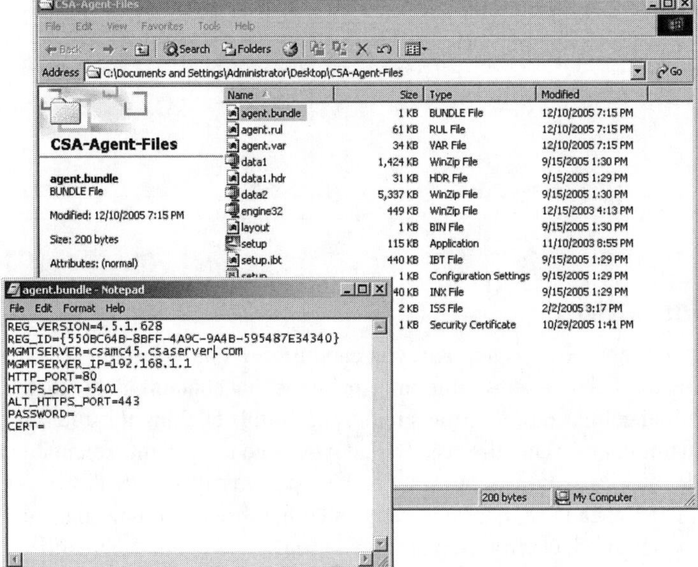

- **agent.rul**—This file provides the agent with the initial combined ruleset valid and current at the time the Agent Kit was last updated during the most recent Generate rules prior to downloading. This file is not in a readable format.
- **agent.var**—This file provides several variables the agent reads into its configuration. Many of the variables relate to query messages, but there are also variables that relate to protocol detection. Figure 7-9 displays a sample.

Figure 7-9 *Contents of agent.var File*

- **data1.zip, data2.zip, and data1.hdr**—These files contain binary installation portions of the agent and should not be opened.
- **engine32.zip**—This file contains primarily required DLL files for installation on the system.
- **layout.bin**—This is another binary component used by the installer.
- **setup.exe**—This file is the installation executable used to install the Agent Kit on the system. This file and its command-line parameters are discussed later in this chapter when you look at scripting an installation.
- **setup.ibt**—This is a configuration file for installation that does need not to be opened.
- **setup.ini, setup.inx, and setup.iss**—These files provide setup.exe and the included installshield installer parameters it needs to complete installation on the system.
- **sslca.cer**—This is the self-signed root CA (Certificate Authority) certificate used to secure communication to and from the CSA MC from the agents, and it also ensures that the agent communicates with the correct CSA MC server and not an impostor.

Figure 7-10 *sslca.cer Certificate from the CSA MC Contents*

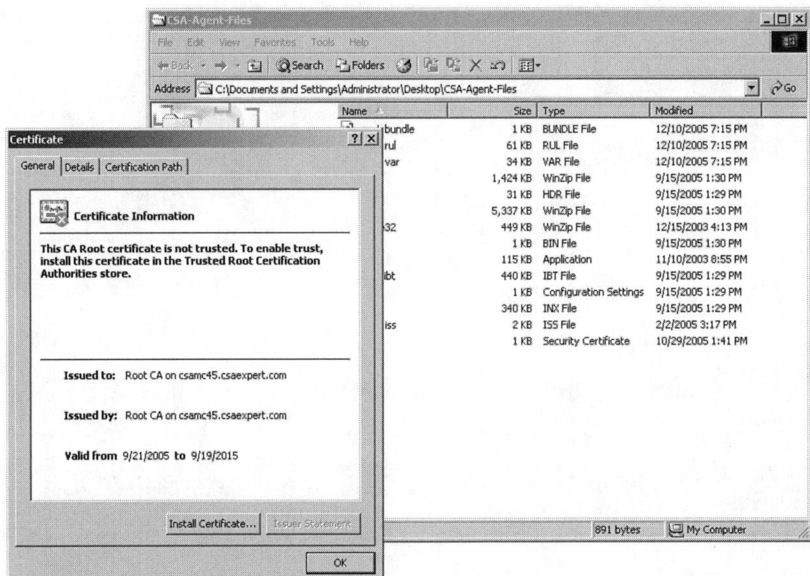

When creating installers for your enterprise, you can extract the files in the previous list to a network location and use them in login scripts, other custom scripts, or software-distribution systems. The next section discusses the command-line parameters available to setup.exe that prove useful in many environments.

Installation Parameters and Examples for SETUP.EXE

When you created the original installation kit for the Agent Kit specified earlier in this chapter, you had the option to configure many settings, such as silent installation and the network shim. If you choose to install the Agent Kit using the original self-extracting zip executable, your parameters remain intact, but they are never truly silent because the installer still launches a few graphic popups. It is a noninteractive installer and does not require user input, but it is not hidden from the user's view during installation.

If you want to script a silent installer, you need to extract the Agent Kit files and place them in an accessible location. After you extract them, you can call the setup.exe installer with added command-line parameters to add numerous settings to the installer. The next sections explain the available command-line options for setup.exe and also provide some examples using the executable in real-world deployments.

Command-Line Parameters

The setup.exe included in the zip file retrieved from the MC can use a few command-line parameters that you should be familiar with before attempting to write a scripted install. The majority of the following options all use settings of 0, which relates to disabled, and 1, which relates to enabled.

- **/s**—Specifies a silent installation.
- **autolevel=X**—Specifies the amount of interaction. Here X should be replaced by 0, 1, 2, or 3.
  - 0 = This is the default and does not need specification. All errors, messages, questions, and warnings are displayed to the user. This is a fully interactive installation.
  - 1 = No confirmations and no prompts for confirmations. Always take default actions.
  - 2 = No warnings are displayed.
  - 3 = Suppresses all warnings and errors but still shows status boxes to the user.
- **nshim=X**—Specifies if the network shim should be installed. Here X should be set to 1 to enable the network shim.
- **install_cta=X**—Specifies if the Trust Agent should be installed. Here X should be 1 to install the CTA installer packaged with the Agent Kit.
- **leave_cta=X**—Controls whether or not the Trust agent should be uninstalled when the CSA software is uninstalled. Here X should be 1 if you will not uninstall the CTA when the Agent Kit is uninstalled.
- **reboot=X**—Specifies if an automatic reboot should occur after installation completes. If X is set to 1, a reboot occurs.
- **rebootdelay=X**—Specifies the amount of time before the automatic reboot occurs if reboot=1, as previously discussed. The reboot occurs in X seconds with a default of 300 seconds if not specified.
- **mt=removeall**—Specifies that a complete uninstall should occur. This option removes the Agent Kit from the system. You must ensure that the user running the setup file can stop the agent service for a successful uninstallation.

The preceding switches are passed at the command line to the setup.exe installer with leading – to denote each individual switch except for the silent install switch with is **/s**. The following section illustrates some examples.

Command-Line Installation Examples

Using command-line parameters, you can script many types of agent installations. The following are a few examples:

- Install the Agent Kit silently with no prompts and an automatic reboot. These are common installation options for mass deployment mechanisms. The only popup displayed is related to the fact that the agent is installing.

```
setup.exe /s --autolevel=3 --reboot=1
```

- Install the Agent Kit silently with no prompts, an automatic reboot after 15 seconds, and CTA installation without removal at CSA uninstall time.

```
setup.exe /s --autolevel=3 --reboot=1 --rebootdelay=15 --
install_cta=1 --leave_cta=1
```

- Uninstall the Agent Kit silently with no prompts.

```
setup.exe /s --mt=removeall --autolevel=3
```

NOTE During scripted uninstallation, there might still be CSA query prompts for the user to turn off the agent service and run installation programs.

Allowing Scripted Uninterrupted Uninstall

When you attempt to run a silent command-line uninstallation, you often run into issues when the currently installed CSA policy queries prompt the user. These queries are typically related to stopping the agent service and running installation programs. You can circumvent these issues through CSA policy implementation and a tool like SysInternals PSEXEC, which allows you to run commands on local and remote systems as another user.

To accomplish this, follow a few simple steps to make an additional policy that allows you to perform the unattended uninstallation without prompts.

Step 1 Create two rule modules called Unattended CSA Uninstallation Rule Module and Unattended CSA Uninstallation Rule Module 2.

Step 2 Set these rule modules to be enforced only when a User/Group state set is active.

For our example, use the Administrator state set for Unattended CSA Uninstallation Rule Module and System Account state set for Unattended CSA Uninstallation Rule Module 2. Figure 7-11 shows an example of setting the state set.

Figure 7-11 *New Rule Module with State Set Applied*

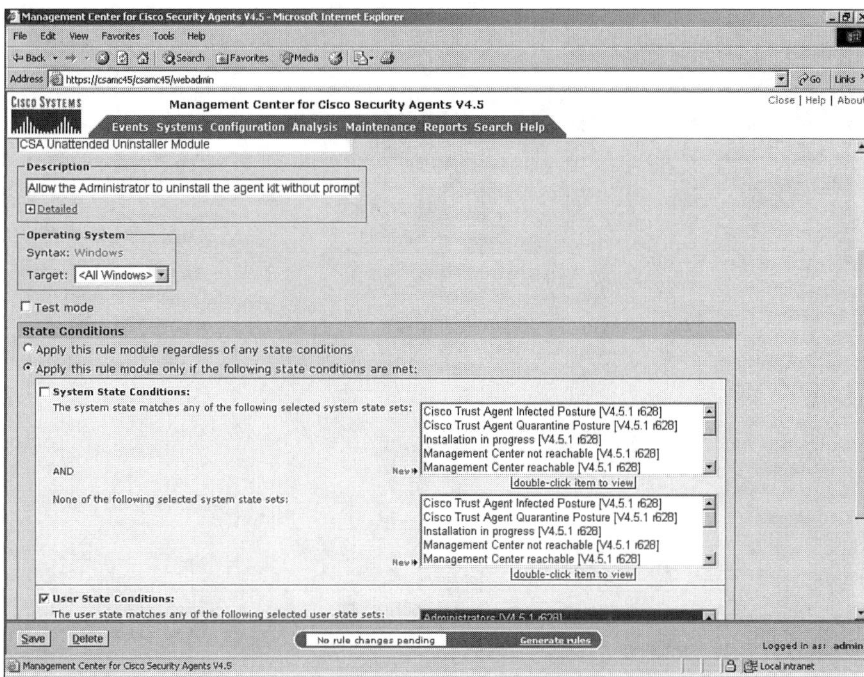

Step 3 Create a new policy called Unattended CSA Uninstallation Policy and associate the previously created rule modules from step 1 to this policy.

Step 4 Add the necessary rules to the new rule modules:

(a) Add an Agent Service Control rule to the Unattended CSA Uninstallation Rule Module, which will ***Allow*** **<All Applications>** (or specifically the csacontrol.exe application) to disable the Agent Service.

(b) Add an Application Control rule to allow SVCHOST.EXE to run SETUP.EXE in the specified agent installer path in the Unattended CSA Uninstallation Rule Module 2.

(c) Add any other rules necessary per your own testing and currently deployed policy. You can see the rules in the sample rule modules in Figures 7-12 and 7-13.

Figure 7-12 *Rules Applied when Administrator State Set Matches*

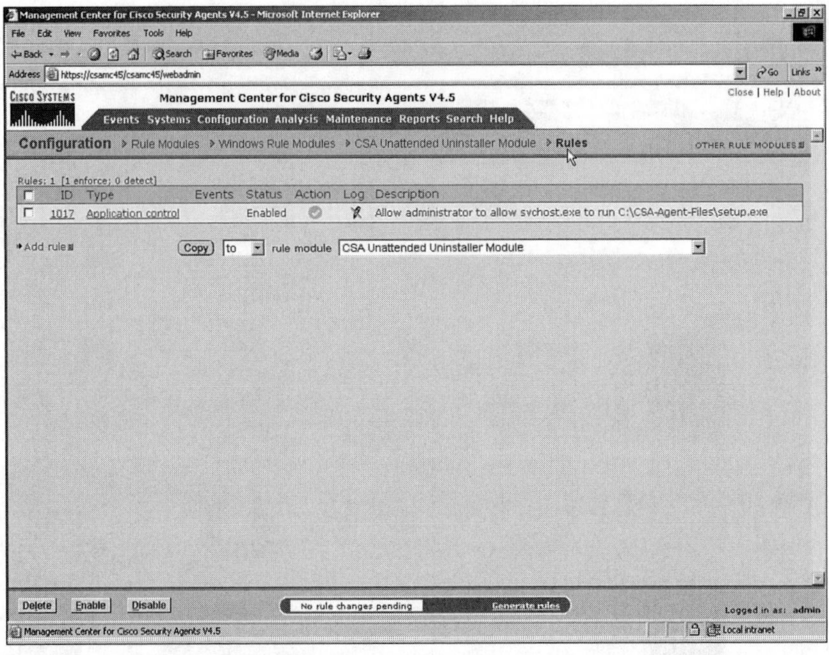

Figure 7-13 *Rules Applied when System User State Set Matches*

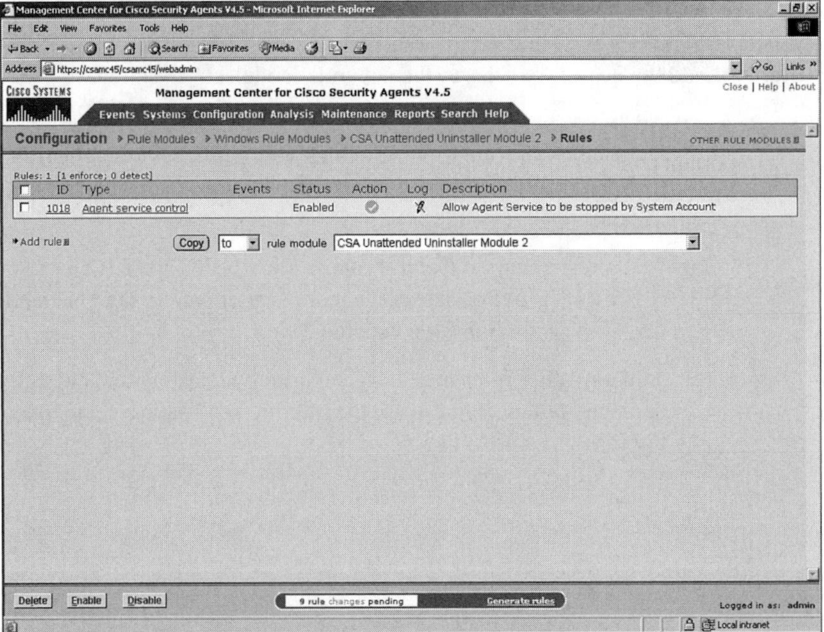

Step 5 Add your new policy to the appropriate groups to propagate the policy as necessary.

Step 6 Change your command line to use the SysInternals psexec tool that allows specification of the user that should run the command on the system as displayed in the DOS command that follows and also in Figure 7-14.

```
psexec -u administrator -p cisco123 setup.exe /s --mt=removeall --
autolevel=3
```

Figure 7-14 *PSEXEC Uninstalling the Agent as Administrator*

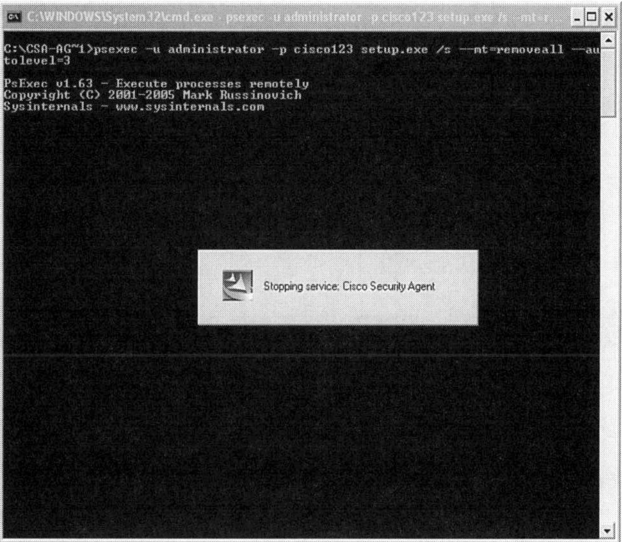

It is important to note that this succeeded because of the use of state sets. If you need to see the active state sets on a system from the CSA MC console, simply navigate to the specific agent page and select Detailed Status and Diagnostics. You can see from Figure 7-15 that the test system did in fact have the local Administrator account logged in, which allowed completion of the uninstallation without CSA queries.

Figure 7-15 *Diagnostics Displays Current State Sets*

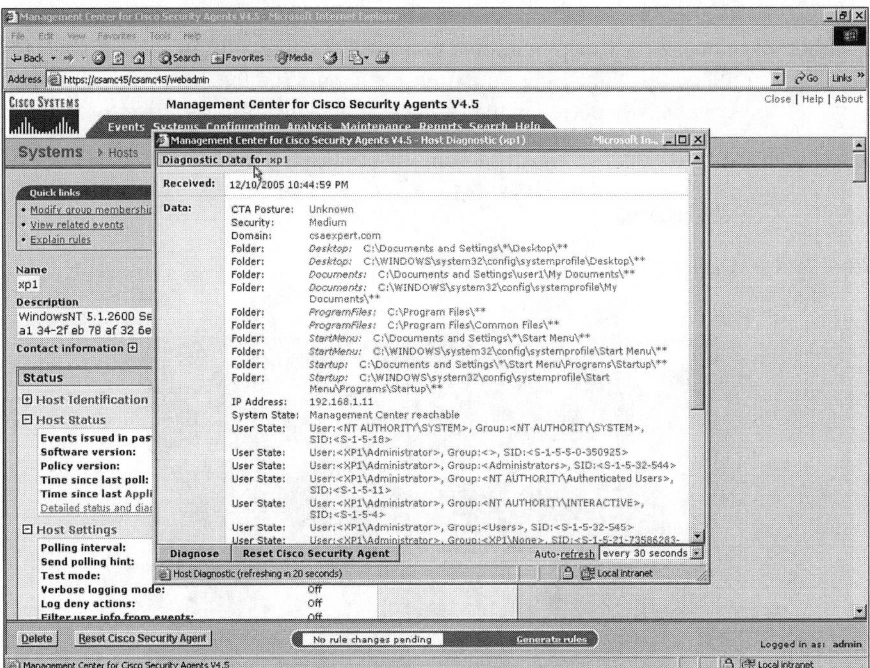

NOTE The CSA product is extremely flexible. The use of devices, such as state sets and dynamic application classes, allow you to create policies that are granular and secure without opening permanent security holes in your systems.

Summary

The CSA installation kit is a simple installer that runs directly or extracted and scripted using command-line parameters for automated installations. When combined with login scripts and software distribution systems available from companies such as BigFix and Microsoft, you can expect an efficient and effective implementation of this product throughout your enterprise.

PART IV

CSA Policy

CHAPTER **8**

Basic Policy

To most organizations, the security policy is a document that outlines how information and systems should be protected, but the policy is rarely enforced or even enforceable. The security policy as a document is valuable for several reasons including regulatory and audit requirements. However, ignorance of the policy guidelines (or even ignorance of the policy's existence) puts organizations at risk. The security policy is a high-level document made up of other policies and procedures that protect specific information and systems.

This chapter covers the following topics:

- Need for a security policy
- Components of a security policy
- Policy application in Cisco Security Agent (CSA)
- Policies included for basic operating system functions
- Builtin application-specific policies

CSA allows you to specify and enforce a security policy on the network endpoints that closely follows the documented security policy of your organization. The rules used in CSA policies directly correlate to the procedures and planks of the information security policy.

Policy Requirements

Security policies do not state only what can and cannot be done, but they give a framework for handling every aspect of information security at your organization. This policy must include sections and procedures on data and system classification, malicious software, incident response, and system documentation. Vigilant policies include a section on the protections that are given to the policy itself because that can contain sensitive information.

The goal of any good security policy is to ensure confidentiality, integrity, and availability of computer systems. The three principles of confidentiality, integrity, and availability (CIA) are called the CIA Triad and form the foundation of every good security policy. The CIA Triad also describes the goals of security policy in the simplest terms. Information must be kept confidential, data integrity should be maintained, and access to systems and information should always be available.

A good security policy addresses the confidentiality of the informational assets an organization uses and is responsible for. Customer records, employee personal information, and trade secrets must be accessed only by those with proper authorization. Not too long ago, the penalties for a breach of confidentiality were limited to bad press and possibly a loss of competitive advantage. With the recent adoption of the Health Insurance and Portability and Accountability Act of 1996 (HIPAA) and Sarbanes-Oxley (SOX), large fines and even prison sentences have become the consequences of failure to maintain information confidentiality. Maintain confidentiality by allowing only authorized personnel or processes the minimum level of access needed to specific information and keeping a log of each time that information is accessed.

Data integrity must be maintained so that valid information is used for processing and decision making. If an organization does not have data it can trust to use as the basis for making decisions, then that organization is at risk. Even worse is an organization that trusts data that has been compromised, because it does not even understand that it is at risk. To maintain the integrity of information, you must ensure that data is modified only by those with proper authorization and maintain metadata including the data and file versions and modification times.

Finally, authorized systems and users must have access to information assets and computing resources. Data or computing resources that cannot be accessed by authorized users have no value to your organization. How much money does your organization lose when the network or a critical server is down? Do times become stressful when your e-mail server is down?

CSA gives you the ability to effectively enforce your organization's information security policy. We create rules in CSA that support a specific part or line of the policy. The rules are members of rule modules. *Modules* are groups of rules that are related to protecting a certain piece of information or network infrastructure under certain conditions. Rule modules are then grouped into CSA policies. CSA policies have the purpose of protecting information or systems under all conditions at a high level.

Purpose of Policy

Good security policies have several clear purposes serving various needs. The main overriding purpose of the policy is to ensure that the principles of the CIA Triad are maintained at all times. The CSA policies applied to a machine have the sole purpose of supporting the organization's written security policy. The purposes listed in this section all support the goal of the security policy and should be applied in a clear and measured manner.

Make sure that any rules or specifications of the policy have a definite reason and be certain that the rules of the policy are easily explained. Simply creating a security policy that has no purpose, vision, or measure of reason alienates you from your users and makes enforcement of the policy much harder. Be sure to educate the user population affected by the policy so that they do not think that the policy is there only to "oppress the masses." Any security implementation is easier once the users are convinced it makes things better for them, rather than simply stopping them from doing certain things on the workstations that they probably think of as their own.

The following sections look more closely at the purposes of the policy. The list that follows is not all-inclusive and your organization might have other valid purposes for implementing a security policy. Comprehensive security policies include sections dealing with:

- Audit trails
- Acceptable use policy
- Protecting computing resources from users
- Protecting systems from vulnerabilities

Audit Trail

Comprehensive security policies address auditing access of systems and data. A log of "who did what" on the network is necessary so that a record of normal and abnormal activity is available for later review to determine if there were any attempts to access sensitive data and further determine if any of those attempts succeeded.

Audit trails are required by law for some types of information. Medical records are subject to special regulations under HIPAA. Given the corporate accounting scandals of the last few years, certain types of financial reports fall under regulatory audit controls.

CSA allows you to audit all attempted access of a resource, successful or not. It is also possible to log events of permitted actions or receive an alert when a certain permitted event occurs. An example of an instance of auditing and logging is monitoring access to payroll information on a Human Resources application server. Most machines that attempt to access the data on this server would be denied by a rule that you create. The CSA policy allows authorized machines to access the data but logs the event so that there is a record of the data access kept in the CSA logs and the Human Resources server audit log.

Acceptable Use Policy/Security and Best Practice Enforcement

As a security practitioner, you want to make sure that only actions needed to support business operations take place on systems you protect. The policy specifies what actions should and should not take place. The following is an example of a line from a security policy: Users can listen to music CDs using a standard media player, but they cannot rip music to mp3 format and save it on the local machine or a network server.

The enforcement part of the written security policy is largely done by the end user. Many organizations that still use "the honor system" of security policy enforcement know that it does not work well. The end user is a poor enforcer of security policies. Some users are sophisticated or malicious (or both), whereas others are simply ignorant of the meaning of policies and how they apply to them or their actions. Either way, you cannot trust the users to enforce the security policy themselves. CSA is designed to be the enforcement mechanism for the written security policy. The rules and modules of CSA match up to the lines and sections of the written policy.

CSA is flexible in the way that policies are implemented and enforced. Using the preceding example, you can perform the following functions:

- Prevent any application from writing mp3 files to any location.
- Specify all music file types and not just mp3 files.
- Prevent only certain applications from writing those files, so that the media player cannot rip music CDs, but the user can still copy and save an audio presentation in mp3 format from a file server.

Protection from Local and Remote User

The written security policy must address any processes that affect the stability or operation of any system or the availability of data initiated by any user, local or remote. The local user logged on to the machine as an administrator can do anything, even format the machine or willingly or unwillingly make the machine unusable. Even users who are not administrators can make a system unusable. Using the preceding mp3 example, a user can fill the hard drive of the local machine (or even a file server) with mp3 files, so that there is no available space for saving business data.

Remote users can also be troublesome for system availability. Remote users with credentials to log onto a machine can perform many tasks on that machine as if they were local. Sometimes remote users access a machine through a service that runs as the system process, which has unrestricted access to the system.

CSA protects the machine from users, even administrators, by querying the logged-in local users when they try to run a suspicious process. It also outright prevents actions that are almost always known to be malicious, such as modifying the CSA agent files themselves or deleting files in the Windows/system32 or /etc directories.

Protecting Systems and Information from Application/System Vulnerability

You must pay careful attention to vulnerable components of a system. An attack is likely to be launched from a compromised vulnerable system or process. The compromises often succeed because of a lack of enforcement mechanisms. Closely monitor these systems and processes for anomalous behavior, and put rules in place to guard against known malicious behaviors.

CSA can use Application Execution Control rules to protect vulnerable components. Using the Sasser Worm as an example, CSA prevents a known system vulnerability from leading to a system compromise in several ways, but the method we focus on is what happens right after the buffer overflow attack occurs. The lsass.exe process attempts to open a command prompt on the system. CSA, by default, allows only certain applications to open command shells and lsass.exe is not one of them. There is no good reason for that process to ever attempt to open a command prompt, and rules explicitly deny most applications from opening command prompts. Therefore, the attack fails and the vulnerability is not successfully exploited.

Protection of Application or System Vulnerability from Exploitation

The best way to prevent a system or application vulnerability from being exploited is to protect the vulnerability from attack in the first place. Guard weak systems or processes so that any known vulnerability cannot be exploited. This applies to any process that is high risk as well, such as those that run with root or system privileges.

A good example of a high-risk service that has great potential for attack is Microsoft IIS. The web publishing service runs as the system account and is often exposed to the Internet for public access. Many high-risk vulnerabilities have been released for IIS over the last few years, and the popularity of the application means that more are sure to follow. CSA has several protection mechanisms for this example. Data filters prevent the processing of certain query strings and URL components. Service restart rules can be used if a Denial of Service (DoS) attack is launched against the service.

Policy Application and Association

As stated earlier, CSA hosts are members of groups, and policies are applied to those groups. Each policy is associated to one or more rule modules that contain the actual rules. The effective CSA security policy that is applied to a host is the result of the combination of all rules associated with all the policies connected with the host's member groups. Some of the rules in different policies are directly contradictory, such as the rules both allowing and denying applications to act as network servers. In many cases, contradictory rules are applied to the same host. The rule that has the highest action priority takes precedence in those cases.

For example, rules in the Windows Required System Module allow all applications to act as servers for basic services, such as FTP, HTTP, and DNS. The Personal Firewall Module contains a rule that prevents any application from becoming a server for any TCP or UDP service, including those just mentioned. The combination of these rules tells the agent to allow all applications to act as servers for basic services, but prevent applications from acting as servers for all other services. Basic services are allowed because allow has a higher action priority than deny.

Table 8-1 and Table 8-2 show Windows and Linux default policy associations by groups. The resultant combination of all policies associated with groups that the machine is a member of is the effective policy of that machine.

Table 8-1 *Combination of Policies to Make Effective Policy for Windows Hosts*

Policy	Associated Groups		
	All Windows	**Desktops—All Types**	**Servers—All Types**
Application Classification	Yes	Yes	Yes
Operating Systems—Base Permissions—Windows	Yes	Yes	Yes
General Application—Basic Security—Windows	No	Yes	Yes
Installation Applications—Windows	No	Yes	Yes
Operating Systems—Base Protection—Windows	No	Yes	Yes
Virus Scanner Windows	No	Yes	Yes
Document Security—Windows	No	Yes	No
E-mail Client—Basic Security—Windows	No	Yes	No
IP Stack—Internal Network Security	No	Yes	No
Network Personal Firewall	No	Yes	No

Table 8-2 *Combination of Policies to Make Effective Policy for Linux Hosts*

Policy	Associated Groups		
	All Linux	Desktops—All Types	Servers—All Types
Application Classification	Yes	Yes	Yes
Operating Systems—Base Permissions—Linux	Yes	Yes	Yes
General Application—Basic Security—Linux	No	Yes	Yes
Installation Applications—Linux	No	Yes	Yes
Operating Systems—Base Protection—Linux	No	Yes	Yes
Virus Scanner Windows	No	Yes	Yes
Web browser—Linux	No	Yes	Yes
IP Stack—Internal Network Security	No	Yes	No
Network Personal Firewall	No	Yes	No

Builtin Policy Details

CSA has many default policies that provide a baseline for commonly configured operating systems and applications. Although it is almost a certainty that policy and rule tweaking will be required to make CSA work in your environment, these policies are a great place to start. The default policies are also good models to use to educate on what can be done with CSA rules and how they are applied to protect systems and information.

NOTE Regardless of any rules, CSA protects itself from modification by any application. This functionality cannot be changed unless the agent is manually disabled. Attempts by certain application classes to modify the agent might not be logged, such as the case with virus scanner applications, but the attempts still fail.

Policies are included for base protection of workstations, servers, and specific services or applications. Workstations typically act as clients for network services and servers, as the name implies, accept connections, and provide network services. CSA policies are tailored for the two usage profiles, and along with specific application policies, make sure that critical services are permitted to perform their assigned duties while the system and data is still protected in accordance with the written security policy.

As we discuss these policies, we discuss the combinations of policies assigned to different builtin groups. This gives us a better idea of what the policies actually do and puts things in a broader context. Remember that groups are specific to each operating system type or target; however, policies can be applied across operating system types to groups of each kind. Figure 8-1 shows us the application classification policy applied to all three target operating system groups.

Figure 8-1 *Example of a Policy Applied Across Multiple Operating Systems*

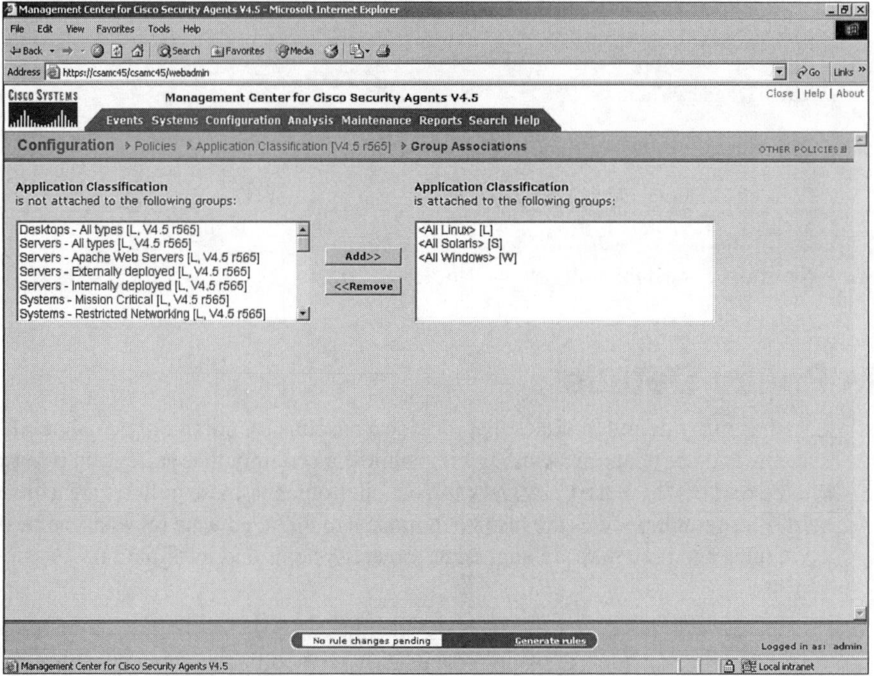

Automatically Applied Builtin Applied Policies

Each type of operating system supported by CSA has an auto-enrollment group that contains all machines running that operating system type. All Windows machines belong to the **<All Windows>** group, all Linux machines belong to the **<All Linux>** group, and so on. Policies that would apply to every machine running that operating system are attached to these groups. For example, all applications must be able to read system libraries, drivers, and driver data files on all Windows machines, whether the machine is a desktop or a server.

Policies applied to the auto-enrollment groups are generally necessary for the normal operation of the operating system and standard applications that present little or no risk to the system. These include functions such as allowing Adobe Acrobat Reader to run, allowing any application to act as a client or server to the local host, and notifying the user if an application tries to disable CSA.

Whenever there is a question about what the policy actually does, simply click **Explain Rules**. This gives you an easy-to-understand interpretation of the rules on the screen and an example is seen in Figure 8-2.

Figure 8-2 *Explain Rules Screen*

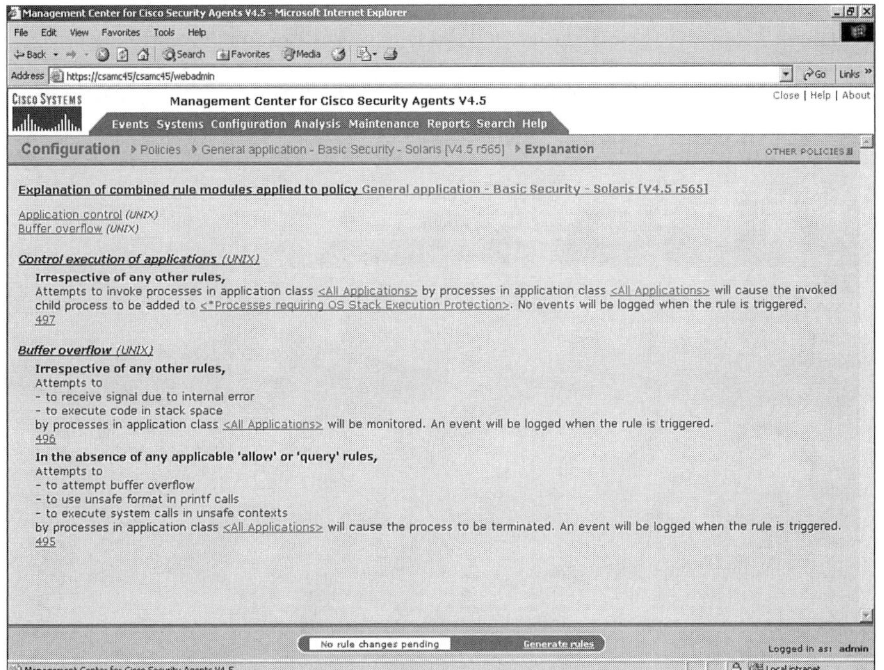

NOTE The **Explain Rules** link is available on the module, policy, group, and host screens. Clicking **Explain Rules** gives the rule explanations for the combination of policies at each level of configuration. The explanation generated from the link on the host detail screen is the result of the combination of all the rules in the combination of groups, policies, and modules associated with that host.

Builtin Desktop and Server Policies

CSA 4.5 contains builtin desktop groups for Windows and Linux operating systems. The following sections examine the policies assigned to each in detail.

Windows

Windows Desktop Groups are further divided into two types. There is the Desktops—All Types group that as the name suggests is applied to all desktops, and the Desktops—Remote or Mobile group that is used for roaming workstations or workstations used in a home office and not always connected to the corporate network. The Desktops—All Types group is associated with policies that are useful for all workstations in the organization, such as the E-mail Client—Basic Security—Windows policy. Figure 8-3 shows that the rule modules attached to that policy are the E-mail Client Module—all Security Levels, E-mail Client Module—Base Security, and the E-mail Worm Protection Module.

Figure 8-3 *E-mail Modules and Policy Applied to All Windows Desktops*

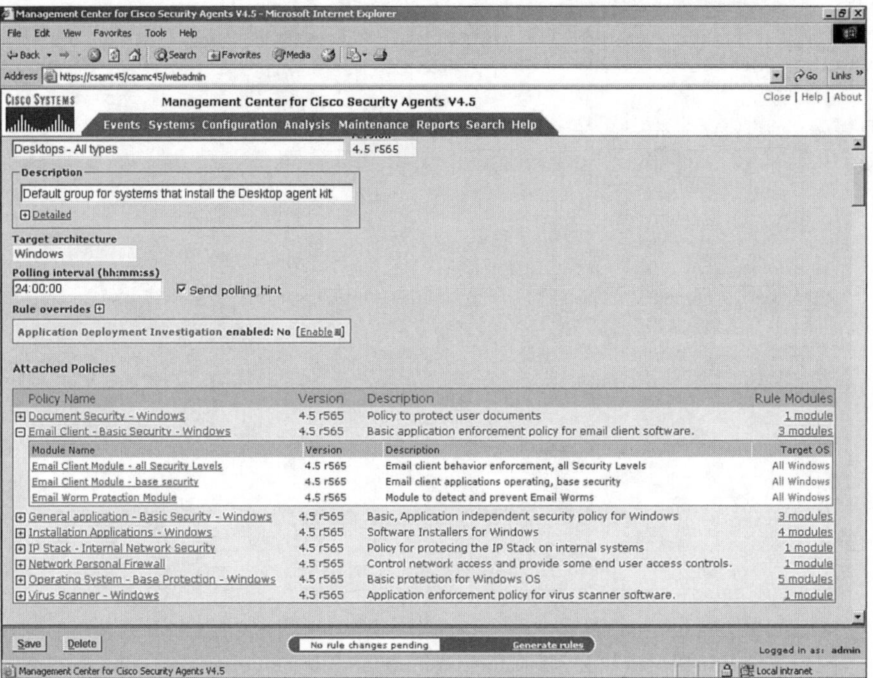

Notice the other policies associated to the Desktops—All Types group. Policies for document security, virus scanners, base system protection, and network filtering are also attached. When combined, these policies give the workstation a great deal of protection from common threats you face everyday.

NOTE Remember that some modules attached to a policy might not be active depending on the system state of the machine or the actual operating system of the machine. Therefore, some of the rules attached to groups with this policy association are not enabled even though those rules are present in the combined list of rules for that group. The next chapter explores this concept in greater detail.

The followings lists describe some of the highlights and more important protections provided by these policies. The points are grouped by the action taken whenever the given event occurs.

The following are actions always denied:

- E-mail applications are not allowed to launch user-invoked applications, NT virtual DOS machines, or command shells. An event is logged if this is attempted.
- E-mail applications might not write dynamically quarantined files, and any attempt to do so is logged.
- Any application processing that recently created untrusted content (such as a recently downloaded executable) is not allowed to access the Local User Account registry keys and attempts to do so log an event.

NOTE There is a rule in place to disable any attempt by the workstation to act as a server for any TCP or UDP services; however, the rule is not enabled by default.

The following are actions always allowed:

- Any application can invoke virus scanners, and virus scanners can invoke any application.
- Installers and applications invoked by installers can read and write all files.
- Document readers, e-mail applications, and Winzip applications can read and write document and user data files.

The following are actions that cause the user to be queried:

- Any application invoking a software installer causes the user to be queried, and an event is logged. If the user is not logged in or does not respond in a timely manner, the action will be denied.

- E-mail applications attempting to access wscript, vbscript, or file system objects prompt the user for a response and log an event.
- The user is queried when any application tries to write files in virus scanner directories. An event is logged.
- Any application attempting to trap keystrokes, monitor media devices (such as microphones or video cameras), or write memory owned by other applications cause a user query and logged event.
- An NT virtual DOS machine attempting to read files from removable media causes CSA to query the user and log an event.

The following reactions are denied unless allowed by some other policy and log an event unless otherwise noted:

- MS LSASS is not allowed to invoke any applications.
- Remote clients, network servers, and suspected virus applications cannot write startup files.
- Remote clients cannot access registry keys.
- No applications can access physical memory.

The following are events and actions that are simply detected and build dynamic application classes:

- All applications invoking MS sysocmgr are added to the Installation Applications application class.
- Processes executing untrusted content is added to the Suspected Virus Applications application class if they try to communicate using protocols normally used by e-mail applications.
- All applications invoking unusual system calls are monitored.
- Antivirus events and logon events are logged to the NT event log.
- Any detected nonstandard, non IP-based protocols attempting to load trigger an event.

There is also a group with two associated policies for remote or mobile desktops. The Desktops—Remote or Mobile group has the Cisco VPN Client Policy—Windows and the IP Stack—External Network Security policies attached to it. These policies contain rule modules that are useful for allowing remote access to the network and also have more strict controls on what network services are allowed to connect to the machine.

Some of the rule highlights from this group include:

- Although the attempt to modify CSA files by Cisco Secure Desktop (an optional component of the Cisco SSL VPN client) is denied, related events are not logged.
- The Cisco VPN client can invoke VPN helper applications.

- Port scans from all hosts fail.
- The machine does not respond to echo requests.

Notice that the policies that are valuable to both types of machines are applied to both the Desktops—All Types group and the Servers—All Types group. These policies could easily be associated with the **<All Windows>** auto-enrollment group, and the resulting policy set would remain the same. This illustrates that you can accomplish one goal several different ways in CSA and that you can creatively use groups and policy associations.

The Windows Servers—All Types group is associated with a subset of policies that are assigned to the Windows Desktops—All Types group. Referring back to Table 8-1, you see that the resultant set of server policies does not include rules for document security, e-mail client security, or network personal firewall, as the desktops do.

Linux

The Linux desktop policies are written to afford protections for Linux systems similar to the Windows protections detailed previously. In much the same way that Windows policies protect directories such as windows\system32 and the system registry, the /etc directory is protected on Linux systems and Solaris systems. Because Linux operates differently than Windows, other application classes and variables are used in policies, but the overall enforced policy is similar.

The following are some of the main differences in policy:

- The Red Hat Network Updater utility cannot act as a client or server for TCP services.
- During a change in run levels, setting up the network interface is allowed.
- All applications are prevented from loading any modules.
- Untrusted content, suspected viruses, web browsers, and e-mail clients cannot write Redhat Package Manager (RPM) database files.

Although these are some of the differences, there are key similarities to Windows and Linux policies. In fact many rules are exactly the same, particularly Network Access Control rules. Most applications cannot write or modify files in system directories, files recently downloaded from the web are untrusted, and in most cases applications cannot accept connections as servers.

Comparing Table 8-2 to Table 8-1 shows that Windows and Linux handle policy associations the same way with respect to desktops and servers' group policy mappings. The standard Linux desktop policy and server policy are identical except the desktop policy contains rules for IP stack security and network personal firewall.

Solaris

The manner that CSA addresses Solaris differs from the way that Windows and Linux are handled; all Solaris hosts are expected to be servers, and there are no builtin desktop policies. This does not mean that Solaris hosts cannot be used as desktops, but simply that CSA does not have default policies for Solaris workstations. Policies for Solaris workstations can be created and can use rule modules from Linux, and in most cases, they work fine without modification.

It should come as no surprise that the policies attached to the All Solaris group are Operating System—Base Permissions—Solaris and Application Classification. The Solaris Servers—All Types group is associated with General Application—Basic Security—Solaris, Installation Applications—Solaris, and Operating System—Base Protections—Solaris policies. Again, attaching all five policies to the **<All Solaris>** group would yield the same results as having a host that is a member of the Servers—All Types group. Table 8-3 outlines these relationships.

Table 8-3 *Relationship of Policies and Groups*

Host	Group	Policy
Sunserver1.csa.com	All Solaris	Operating System Base Permissions
		Application Classification
	Servers—All Types	General Applications—Basic Security—Solaris
		Installation Applicatins—Solaris
		Operating System—Base Protectins—Solaris

Another interesting point to note is that the Application Classification policy is associated with the auto-enrollment group for all three operating systems. This policy contains rule modules that target each of the operating systems.

Application Policies

There are several builtin application policies in CSA for popular applications commonly found on any enterprise network. These policies provide additional security for hosts that run these applications and make specific exceptions to base server, desktop, or operating system rules, so that the applications can function properly. Among others, policies for Microsoft IIS and SQL Server, Apache Web Server, DNS Services, DHCP Services, and Cisco IP SoftPhone are builtin. Of course, application policies for VMS are included and the Cisco Security Agent Management Console (CSA MC) host already has those policies applied by default.

NOTE Policies for Cisco CallManager and Unity Server are also available from Cisco. Check the CallManager and Unity sections of the Cisco website for software updates for the policy export files. These files can then be imported into the CSA MC using the import function found under the Maintenance heading in the MC.

The following section takes a look at a few of the application policies and what protections are included. Some of the policies examined are specific to a single operating system, whereas others are applicable to all CSA supported operating systems.

Web Server—Microsoft IIS—Windows

This module contains the Common Web Server Security Module and the Microsoft IIS Web Server module. The Common Web Server Security Module contains rules that apply to any web server running on a Windows host, whereas the Microsoft IIS Web Server Security module contains rules that are specific to IIS. The rules in this module are shown in Figure 8-4.

Figure 8-4 *Web Server—Microsoft IIS—Windows Rule Policy*

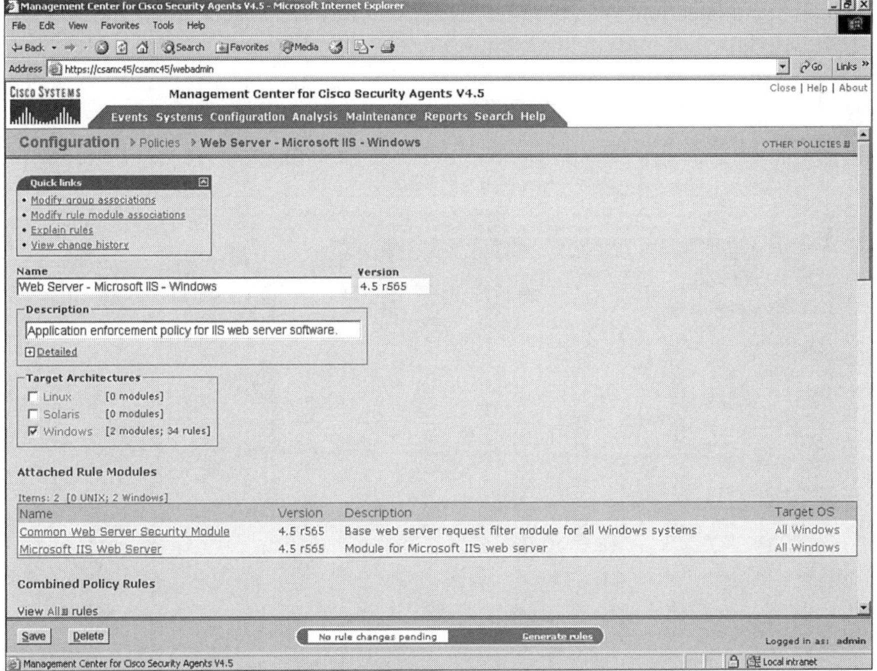

The overall effect of these policies is to secure the web server against common attacks and exploits encountered by IIS servers. Some of the policy highlights include:

- Common Windows file exploits are denied.
- IIS can act as a server for FTP and HTTP.
- Any application trying to write to IIS executable directories causes the local user to be queried. Because this rule is applied to a server and a local user is not commonly logged on, this rule usually results in a denial.
- CSA restarts IIS if the service does not respond to HTTP or FTP requests or if the service does not respond to the service control manager.
- IIS and Apache web services are protected from Cross-Site Scripting (XSS) attacks, SQL command injection attacks, common log file exploits, and common Windows command execution exploits among others.

Web Server—iPlanet—Solaris

The iPlanet Web Server policy is similar to the IIS module in that it is a combination of a generic Common Web Server Security module and the more specific iPlanet module. Many of the protections provided by this module are the same as the IIS module, except that they use Unix commands and objects instead of those found in Windows. Rules for XSS, SQL command injection, and common log file exploits are present in this module just as in the IIS module. The rules in this module are shown in Figure 8-5.

Figure 8-5 *Web Server—iPlanet —Solarisp Policy*

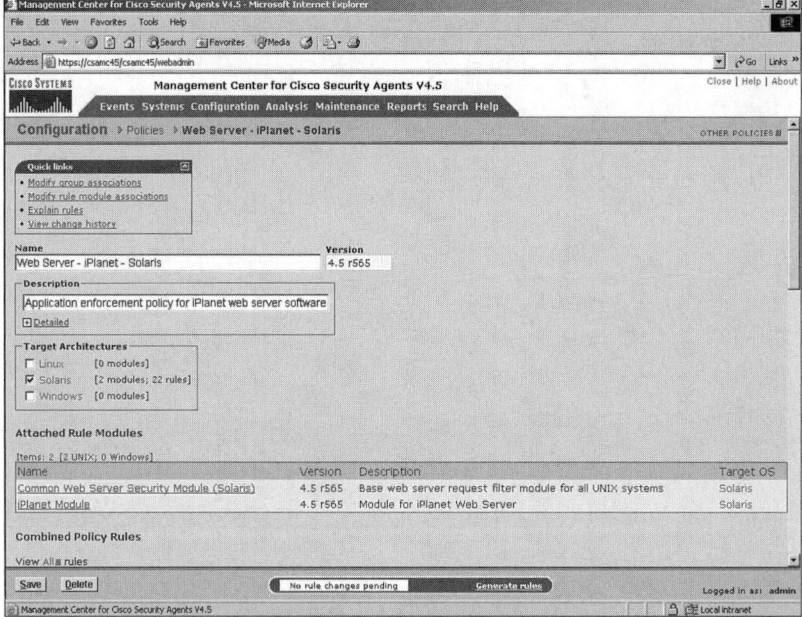

Web Server—Apache

The Web Server—Apache policy applies to all three supported operating systems. It contains six modules: the Common Web Server Security module for each of the operating systems and a specific Apache Web Server module for each operating system. The protections offered by this policy are similar to the protection in the preceding two policies. What makes this policy so convenient to use is that it is applicable to all three operating systems, so the same policy can be used for protecting hosts of all three types.

Notice that the Linux and Solaris rules in this policy are mixed together in the rule listing. This is because Linux and Solaris use the same conventions for objects, such as system directories and devices. This view allows you to compare the policy differences between the two operating systems on the same screen. The rules are also handled and processed essentially the same way on Unix and Linux systems. The Windows rules are in a separate list because of the wider differences in operating system type. This module is shown in Figure 8-6.

Figure 8-6 *Web Server—Apache Policy*

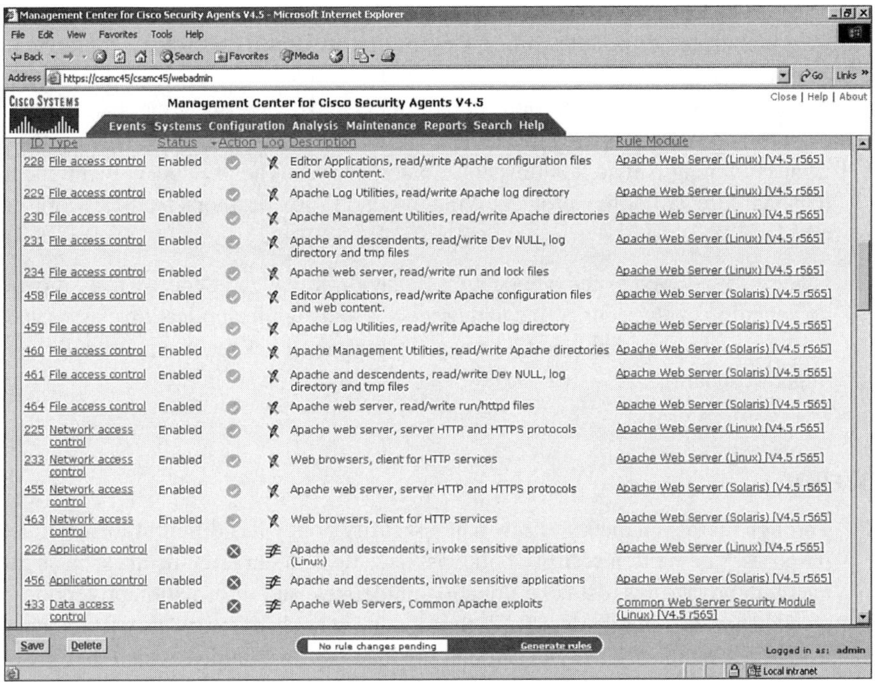

There are few differences between the Microsoft IIS policy and the Apache policy as applied to a Windows machine. The bulk of the rules from each policy come from the Common Web Server Security module. This module contains most of the data access control rules, although the IIS and Apache-specific modules address file access control and application execution control rules relevant to the web server application. The same is true of iPlanet and Apache on Solaris. No other Web Server packages have built-in policies for Linux because Apache has the largest market share by far for Linux web servers.

Microsoft SQL Server 2000—Windows

The Microsoft SQL Server 2000 policy simply contains the Microsoft SQL Server 2000 Rule module. The purpose of this policy is to protect the SQL Server system and data from harm and contains rules specific to SQL Server 2000. This policy allows SQL Server to write SQL data files, but no remote network applications can write those files. It also lets SQL Server write only SQL data files so that the xp_cmdshell stored procedure cannot be exploited to write to the file system. A service restart rule is also included to restart SQL Services in the event it is unresponsive.

Other Builtin Policies

CSA includes other policies out-of-the-box that are useful for protecting individual systems and the network as a whole. The Network Quarantine policy restricts *all* network traffic to or from a host and is useful for machines infected with a virus or malware. The Cisco Trust Agent (CTA) policy is used to enable CTA communications between the host and network devices running Network Admission Control (NAC). The previously mentioned Network Personal Firewall policy protects Windows and Linux desktops from network-based attacks.

Other policies such as the Application Behavior policy and Security Classification policy do not enforce any security, but add processes to dynamic application classes used by rules in other modules and policies. The next chapter discusses the Application Behavior policy in greater detail.

Summary

Throughout this chapter you saw that a security policy has different forms, functions, and purposes. The written security policy is made up of other documents, such as incident handling procedures, data classification guidelines, and information protection mechanisms and standards. CSA is the tool that actively enforces the written security policy using CSA policies. The CSA policies are made up of modules, which in turn are made up of rules, and applied to different system groups. Although Windows, Linux, and Solaris are fundamentally different operating systems, CSA provides each one a high level of protection. To safeguard hosts running different applications and services, application specific policies can be used to protect web servers, database servers, and other infrastructure servers.

CHAPTER 9

Advanced Custom Policy

The Cisco Security Agent (CSA) is an extremely flexible product that has granular policy enforcement capabilities. Included as part of the product installation on the management server is a suite of preconfigured policies that can be deployed to provide immediate protection and control. These policies are a great start and in many cases provide the security required by organizations. In addition, some minor tweaking might be required to allow for approved system use. If you are familiar with the flexibility and applications of the CSA product, you can extend the base capabilities to solve many host security issues in your deployment. In this chapter, you learn about:

- The importance and basics of tuning CSA
- Rule capabilities
- Importance and usage of state sets
- Using dynamic application classes
- Basic forensics

Why Write Custom Policies?

There are several reasons for adding to or changing the default policies that ship with the Cisco Security Agent Management Console (CSA MC). The most common and simplest reason for change occurs during the normal tuning process. The second most common reason for change involves writing custom application control policies to better secure your system. The final reason to change policy is to perform forensic data gathering across the deployment.

The Normal Tuning Process

The normal tuning process occurs during every CSA deployment and continues after deployment when software and patches are added to your systems. These custom policies are often called exception rules, which are rules the administrator creates to allow normal system and application interaction to occur. Often, this also includes changing rules that query the user into straight allow rules that require no interaction. This means you not only tune the policy to allow specific use but also streamline and simplify the user interaction with the agent, so it does not become a nuisance. If the product becomes too cumbersome for users, they tend to attempt to circumvent the security measure, which would completely go against your goals.

The following are a few reasons to create exception rules:

- **Installers**—You likely have a standard process for installing software in your environment, such as using login scripts and software deployment tools. It is important to allow these processes to maintain your systems unimpeded without user interaction and without weakening the security of your endpoint.
- **Application memory usage**—Many poorly coded applications (or cleverly coded, depending on your frame of reference) might attempt normal data or stack memory access or even attempt to access memory used by another process. You might need to allow these applications to perform this action for them to function correctly.
- **Code injection**—Some applications attempt to insert themselves or DLLs into other processes as part of normal usage.
- **Network access**—You often need to tune systems to allow inbound and outbound access to services on workstations and servers. This can include remote control applications and other network services, such as FTP, TFTP, TELNET, SSH, and HTTP.

Custom Application Control Policies

In addition to creating exception rules for your policy, you also need to craft additional policies that control how other applications are used in your network. Many of the policies written in CSA that control applications are a direct result of your written security policies and acceptable use documents that the users acknowledge. CSA allows you to take the verbiage in these documents and place actual enforcement controls on the systems rather than hoping that your users follow the rules.

Examples of reasons you might write custom application control policies include:

- **Preventing or controling certain application usage**—Your organization might want to prevent or control specific applications, such as P2P files sharing applications, instant messengers, e-mail applications, and remote control products.
- **Limiting system network exposure**—You can institute policies that control which services are available remotely when you connect to the corporate network rather than at a remote, untrusted location. Examples of such connections include a user's ISP connection, a wireless hotspot, or a hotel network.
- **Administrative policies**—You can create policies that limit which users and systems can access administrative tools and also provide higher levels of access to administrative users (or any other users or groups necessary).

- **Application installation policies**—You can create policies that allow CSA to permit mass deployment products to install software unimpeded (examples of mass deployment products include those available from BigFix, Microsoft, and Altiris). Other manual installs can either interactively prompt the user or be denied completely.

Forensic Data Gathering

Because CSA continually monitors system interaction on endpoints in your environment, you might want to leverage this product to report certain interactions you find interesting. By creating a specific set of rules that monitor interaction, you can create a "Honey Pot" policy that when deployed reports interaction of specific processes for you to acknowledge. Monitoring system interaction or at least specific interaction can provide an early warning system that can alert you to suspicious activity before it becomes a real security issue.

Preparing for the CSA Tuning Process

The CSA tuning process is more an art than a science, and you might need some practice before you become efficient. Understanding the points discussed in this section will make you more effective. These include understanding the components of CSA Policy, knowing what protection each rule type provides, and understanding how to use advanced components such as state sets and dynamic application classes. The following sections explain those components and provide a process to follow when you tune or create a custom policy.

NOTE This chapter reviews rather than thoroughly describes each component. For more detailed information, refer to the Cisco Systems website and the Cisco Press book *Cisco Security Agent*. Additionally, this chapter focuses on Windows components to illustrate our points.

Understanding Rule Capabilities

It is imperative that you know the protection provided by each rule type, so that you can quickly write rules without using the Tuning Wizard or researching endlessly. The following is a list of rules most commonly used when tuning. The list is ordered by frequency of use in tuning. You should memorize these components to save time when tuning an environment because memorization greatly simplifies your workload.

- **System API Control**—This rule provides many types of protection to hosts and is by far the most common rule tuned in any deployment. This rule applies to processes as defined by the associated application class and can provide the following common protections or exclusions:

- **Inject code into other applications**—To function, some applications need to insert themselves or DLL's into other applications. This type of injection can be malicious, however, because viruses often attempt to inject their DLL into a privileged process to gain administrative rights to the system. Be certain that this process is normal before you tune!
- **Write memory owned by other applications**—Occasionally applications attempt to use another application's memory space. This is somewhat uncommon but has been seen in off-the-shelf software.
- **Access systems functions from code executing in data or stack space**—Although this is a common buffer overflow action and should be treated with care, some applications do this to check their licensing. Verify that this is repeatable and normal through active testing or by confirming with the vendor, then tune appropriately. You can tune this rule granularly through the use of pattern matching, which the Tuning Wizard commonly performs.
- **Trap keystrokes**—Some software attempts to capture keystrokes as part of normal behavior. Verify this is not malicious before proceeding.
- **Monitor media devices**—You can control which devices in your system control or access media devices, such as video cameras and microphones.

- **Application Control**—This rule provides the ability to control whether an application is allowed to run. It also controls what applications can start other applications. It is an important rule type, especially when combined with dynamic application classes, which you see later in the chapter in examples of advanced custom policies.
- **File Access Control**—This rule controls which applications are allowed to read and write files and create directories.
- **Network Access Control**—This rule controls how a process is allowed to initiate, terminate, or listen for network connections.

Although you will become familiar with several other rule types through daily use of the product, you should completely understand the rule types in the previous list before beginning to tune and create customer policies in your own environment.

Discovering State Sets

State sets provide a level of granularity and control not provided by many other Host Intrusion Prevention System (HIPS) products. Become familiar with two types of state sets: user and system state sets. These sets provide mechanisms that enable a CSA administrator to deploy policy to endpoints that are enforced only when a specific environment is encountered, such as the administrator logging into the system or a specific IP address used by the computer.

User-State Sets Overview

User-state sets are matched on an endpoint when specific users or groups are in use on the system. You can both define as many of these sets as you want and use the state sets that are pre-installed with the CSA MC. These objects allow you to enforce policy that is not normally allowed. The following examples illustrate this, and a sample User-State Set configuration screen is shown in Figure 9-1:

- **Administrative access to manual installations**—Although your average user might not be able to install software locally, you could allow the administrator to log in and perform the installation. The state set would identify this user account and allow the installation by applying specific allow rules to the system temporarily while the administrator is logged into the system.
- **Remote access to the registry**—You might use management tools to set registry settings remotely that CSA would normally prevent. You could use a user-state set that matches a specific account or group used to authenticate to the local system and override the preventative policies.
- **Administrative CSA control**—You might define a rule module that allows the CSA to be viewed or stopped only when the matching state set is active.

Figure 9-1 *User-State Set Configuration*

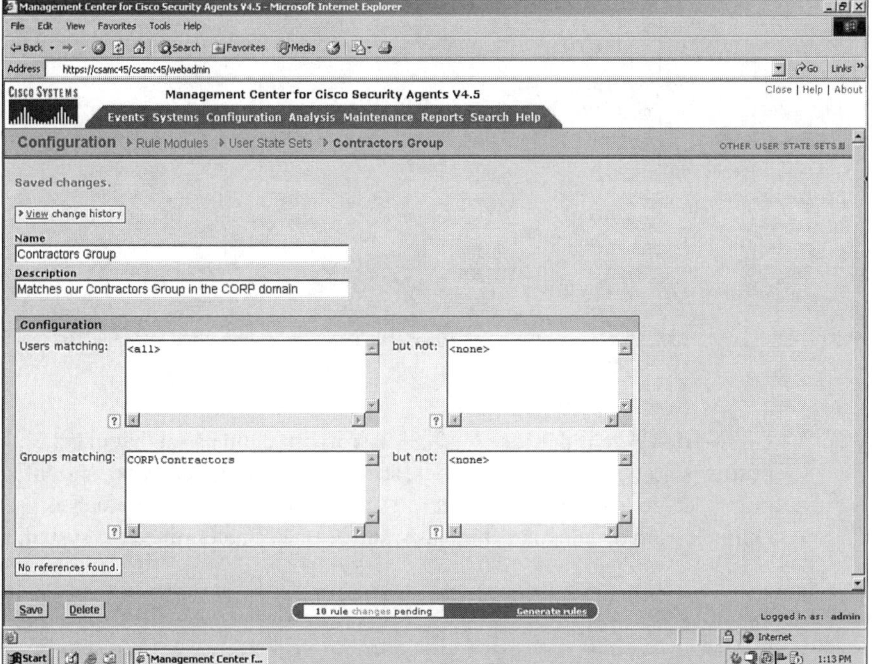

System State Sets Overview

System state sets are matched on an endpoint when various criteria are matched. There are several reasons to build a system state set, such as identifying when a system is on or off a specific subnet, when the CSA MC is reachable, when an installation is currently in progress, or when your Network Admission Control (NAC) posture token is changed or set among others. The following is a list of common settings that can be used alone or in conjunction to match a specific state and a sample image of what the System State Set configuration screen looks like in Figure 9-2.

Figure 9-2 *System State Set Configuration Options*

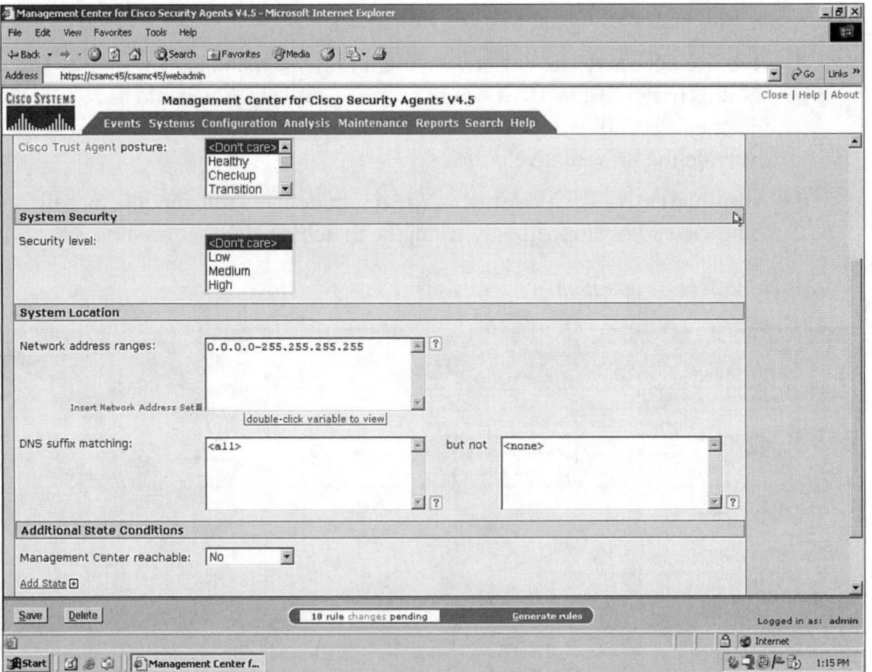

- **Cisco Trust Agent posture for NAC**—You can define a set that matches the various posture settings that NAC provides, such as Healthy, Quarantine, and Infected. You might decide to enforce different rules when the state matches, such as preventing Outlook from opening attachments when NAC has determined the system is infected.

- **Security level**—If you allow users to see the CSA in the system trays of their computers, you can also allow them to use the security-level selector that allows them to change the setting to Off, Low, Medium, or High. These settings can enforce different policies as defined by the CSA administrator.
- **Network address ranges**—This identifies the network to which the user is currently attached.
- **DNS suffix matching**—This identifies the users' DNS suffix, such as ServiceProvider.net, Company.com, and VPN.Company.com.
- **Management Center reachable**—This matches if the agent determines that the CSA MC can be contacted or not. This is a good way to know if the user is currently connected to your network or not connected. You might use this to enforce restricting inbound connectivity for the system if it is not connected to your network.
- **Installation process detected**—This matches when a process is placed into the **<*Installation Applications>** special dynamic application class. This state allows the alteration of the current running policy, so that the installation can continue without too many user-required query responses, if any at all.

Using the combinations of the variables that create system state sets is powerful when building custom policies for your environment. You should try to use these objects when creating policy to ensure granular security policy enforcement as an alternative to creating a policy that is too loose and allows negative actions to occur for all system states. An example of using multiple variables for a system state is determining if a user is VPN-connected. You could match on the system IP address, the DNS suffix, and the CSA MC reachable parameters to determine that a system is connected to authorized VPN concentrators. After this state matches, you can alter the system security policy to allow or deny system functions, such as file transfers or remote control functions if necessary.

Discovering Dynamic Application Classes

Just as state sets can provide great distinction in levels of policy enforced, dynamic application classes can also provide granular policy manipulation. If you use the dynamic application classes effectively and efficiently, you can simplify the amount of work you need to perform and the number of rules you need to create when tuning processes. In addition to simplifying the number of rules required to maintain your environment, dynamic application classes can provide much stronger security to the endpoint. The following examples describe some common uses of dynamic application classes and Figure 9-3 shows the configuration of a dynamic application class.

- **Telnet applications**—You can automatically add processes to this class when they attempt to access remote IP addresses over TCP/23.

- **Limit executable actions after accessing a protected file**—You could place processes in a special class after they read or write to a specific folder. You could then limit the capabilities of this process to ensure it cannot transmit files or perform other actions.

Figure 9-3 *Dynamic Application Class Configuration*

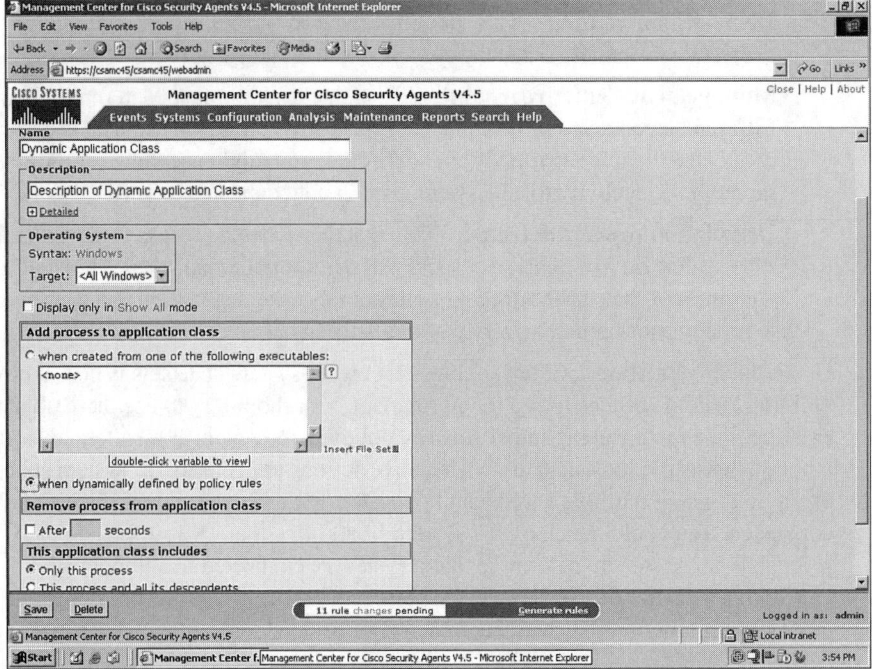

Best Practices for Tuning

There are many ways to tune a policy, and often there are multiple variations of policies that can accomplish the same tasks. It is often stated that there is no wrong way to tune, but there are definitely some advanced issues you should consider before choosing to tune any rule. Some of the issues to consider include: ease of migration of consistent policies among multiple environments (development and production), ease of transition during CSA MC software upgrades, and the flexibility and strength of the policy.

Understanding Importing and Upgrading

When you design your policy and make changes to the default policy included with the CSA MC, it is important to understand how any changes you make can impact the amount of effort it takes to exchange policies between your production and development environments and also when you upgrade minor or major revisions of the CSA product.

NOTE Many corporations use multiple environments to control their testing and implementation processes and change control impacts. It is not unusual to see this between two and four environments such as: testing, development, systems integration, and production.

When you import objects you have exported from another CSA MC (or a previous export from this CSA MC), you should understand which items are duplicated and renamed and also which items replace the original. Additionally, you should understand that part of every CSA software upgrade, such as moving from CSA v4.5.1.628 to CSA v4.5.1.639, also includes an import process as part of the upgrade.

During software upgrades on the CSA MC, the imports compare each individual imported objects against the current objects to see if there is a match by name. If there is a match, the system determines if the object is an exact match or not. If it is an exact match, the new object replaces the old object and the old one is removed. This means that any policy that uses this object now includes the new object version automatically. If the object is not an exact match and some of the parameters have changed with the upgrade, the new object is imported and displays the new version number, but it does not automatically replace the object in the current policy. You need to perform compares on the new and old object to see what changed in the newly upgraded object and determine if you would like to incorporate the changes.

During an import of an object that is not part of an upgrade procedure, the objects are also compared. If the object name already exists, the system creates the new object being imported but appends to the name to differentiate the newly imported object. The appended name contains an underscore character followed by a portion of the name of the import process you created to import this object, such as _import-name. You need to compare and apply these new objects as necessary using a manual process. Of course, if the new imported object does not match any existing objects, it simply adds the object to the system without changing the name of the object.

You can see that the previous two types of imports can cause you to perform manual tasks upon completion to apply the policy you want and to clean up the post upgrade and import environments. This can be a tedious task. Ensuring that you make as few changes as possible that cause the post-import tasks to grow in number greatly simplifies your job as an administrator. For this reason, it is important that you think about the objects you edit before you make the changes. At first, it might seem like a better idea to edit the settings in default objects, so that you do not have to create an additional rule to add the functionality you are attempting to add. However, if you do this you actually ensure that any imported or upgraded policy does not match and results in duplication that requires manual cleanup. You should always attempt to leave the default objects simple and unchanged if possible. This is not always the case because there are exceptions to the rule, but if you attempt to make this part of your decision-making process, you will have much simpler administrative tasks in the future.

Variable and Application Class Usage

When creating policy, many types of objects are available to you. Often, because many of the fields available to the administrator allow literal values to be entered along with variables, the administrator enters the value into the fields rather than creating a new variable (such as File Set, Network Set, and so on) or application class. It is recommended that you attempt to create variables and classes as often as possible to allow your future policy to deploy more rapidly. Any object that can be reused later in the software life-cycle simplifies your policy development and also ensures consistency among multiple administrators.

Sample Custom Policies

As with most events in life, seeing is believing. You need to be able to use all the CSA MC policy objects effectively. This section illustrates a few examples of how to build custom policies to assist in constructing your basic skills in this art.

NOTE The sample policies created in this section might need additional rules and components to be completely effective in your own environment. The following examples help illustrate the processes involved.

State-Based Policies

As discussed earlier, state-based policies can be powerful. Using states can be an effective way to lighten policy enforcement on a single machine temporarily without completely degrading the entire deployments security permanently.

Install Technician Agent Control

Often, you encounter the need to allow a local technician of a system to perform actions that would not normally be allowed to the system user. This could be a technician's manual installation of a software package or hardware driver. To accomplish this, you can either use a state-based set or place the system in a special group or test mode so that the installation can be performed. The problem with the last two options is that the CSA administrator would need to be involved in every daily task. In addition, it's possible that the security is completely removed in test mode rather than just slightly degraded and controlled. In this example, we use the following procedure to start to configure the objects.

Step 1 Create a user-based state set named **INSTALL-TECH** that matches a local group with the same name. This is effective only if you have a group called INSTALL-TECH on your system and have a user in that group perform the installation. This state set is displayed in Figure 9-4.

Figure 9-4 *INSTALL-TECH State Set*

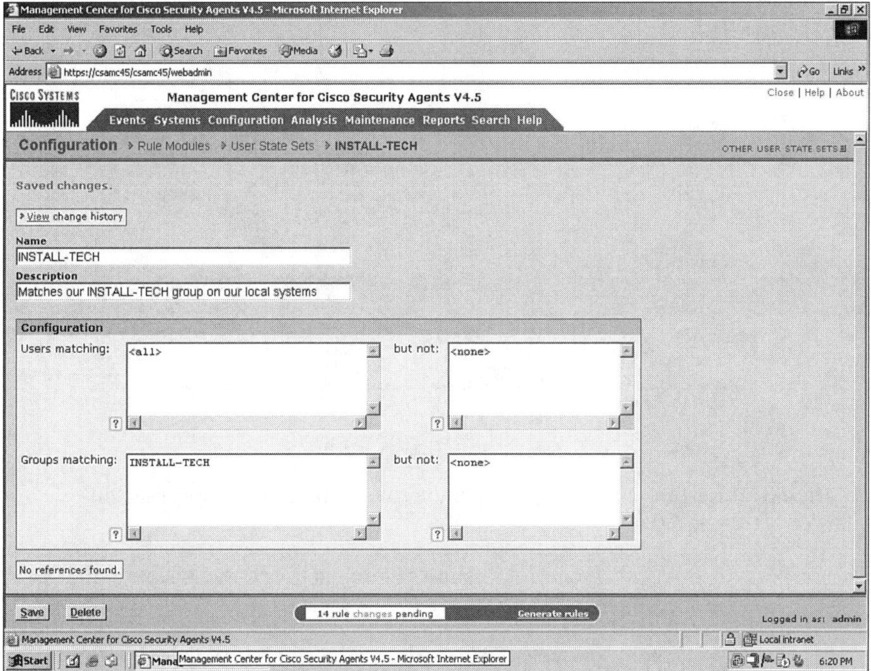

Step 2 Create a policy named **Install Allowed Policy** and also a rule module named **Install Allowed Rule Module**. The rule module should be enforced only when the INSTALL-TECH state set matches. The configuration for the rule module can be seen in Figure 9-5. The rule module should be associated with the policy.

Figure 9-5 *Install Allowed Rule Module with State Set*

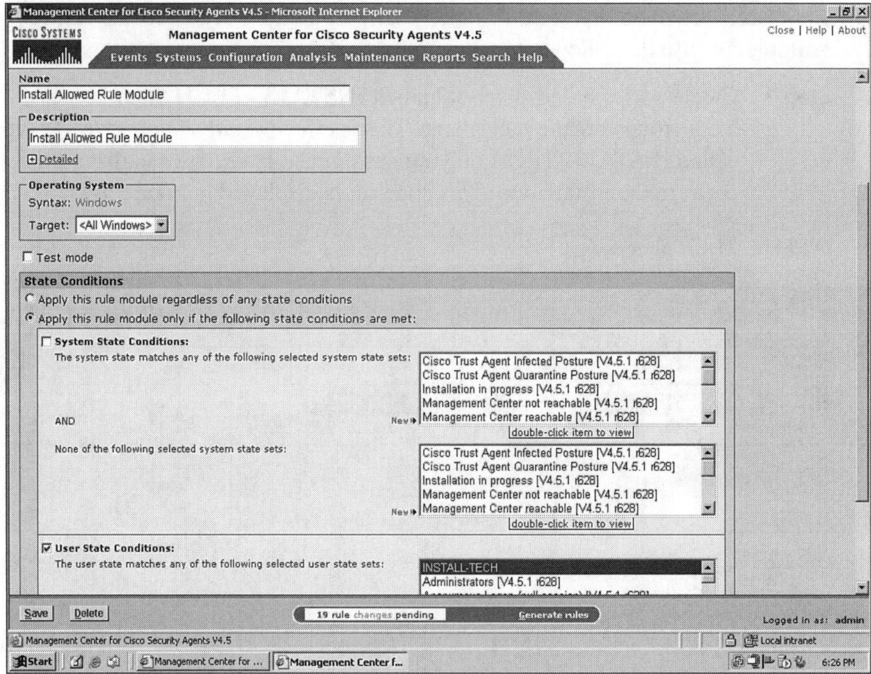

Step 3 Insert the following rules in the rule module. See these rules in Figure 9-6.

— Agent UI control—Allows the agent to become visible to the install technician.

— Agent service control—Allows the agent service to be stopped by the install technician.

Step 4 Attach the policy to groups as necessary.

Figure 9-6 *Add Necessary Rules to the Rule Module*

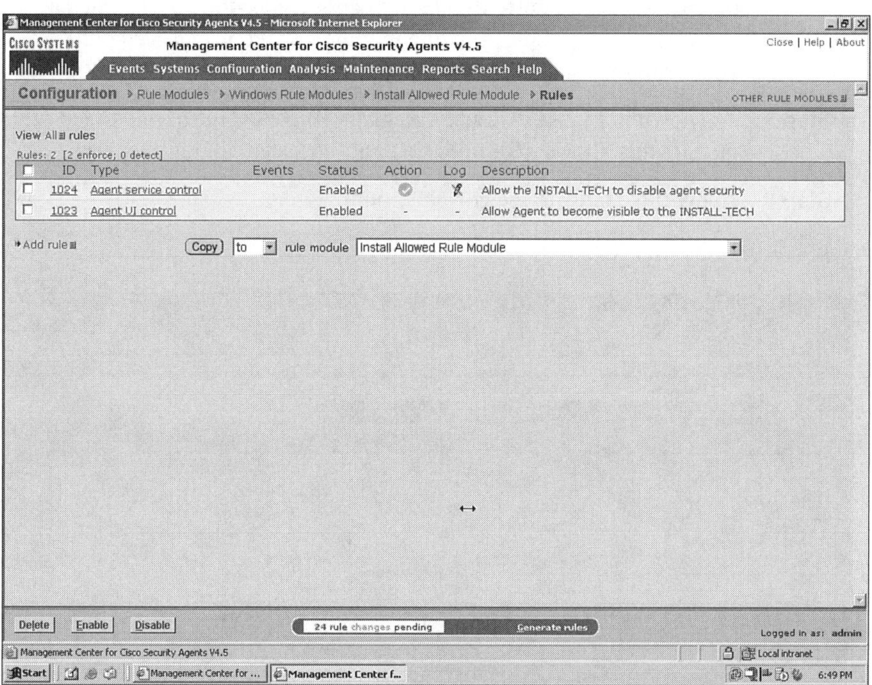

At this point, an install technician should be able to log in on any system that carries the policy and install software. They can receive query messages and stop the agent service when necessary.

Remote Registry Access

It is not unusual for certain systems in your environment to attempt registry access to workstations for various purposes. To allow this access, yet not open up remote registry access to all systems, you need to use a user-state set. Follow these steps to create the policy required to accomplish this task.

Step 5 Create a user-based state set named **MGMT** that ties to a group that the user who will attempt the remote access is a member. When a user who is a member of this group authenticates to the remote system, the state set will match and your rules will temporarily apply to the system.

Step 6 Create a policy named **Remote Registry Access Policy** and a rule module named **Remote Registry Access Rule Module** that you can associate to the policy. This rule module should be enforced only when your state set matches on the system.

Step 7 As shown in Figure 9-7, add a Registry Access Control rule to the rule module that allows **<Remote Clients>** to access all registry keys.

Step 8 Apply this policy to the correct groups.

Figure 9-7 *Remote Registry Access Rule*

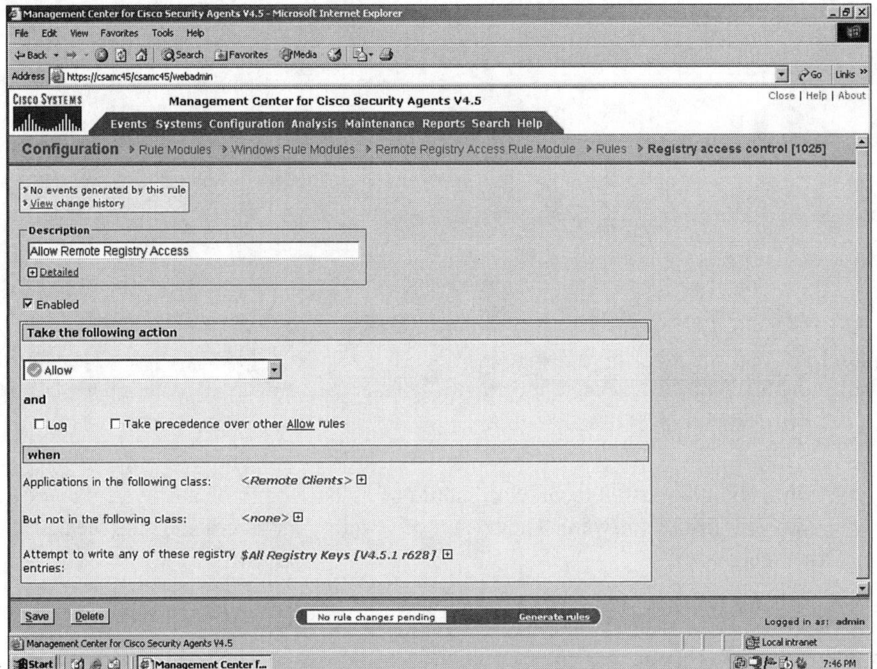

Remember, if you apply this correctly, you allow access to the registry remotely only after a successful authentication of a specific user or group member. This is much more secure than allowing all access to the registry at all times.

Securing the System When Away from Home

When systems connect to your network, corporate firewalls, intrusion detection systems (IDS), intrusion prevention systems (IPS), and other security devices protect them. When they disconnect and travel to remote networks at coffee shops, hotels, or even their home, they lose all that protection. Therefore, it might be desirable to raise the level of network security enforced on these systems when they travel abroad. In many cases, endpoints run many services that listen on the network, such as mass deployment and system management software, remote control packages, file sharing, and web servers. The following example creates a system state set and a policy to help you lock down your systems when they leave your premises.

Step 1 Create a system-based state set named **OFF-NET** that matches IP addresses that are not part of your address space. Also, be certain that the CSA MC is not reachable as shown in Figure 9-8. When a system does not have an IP address you own and also cannot reach the CSA MC server, you can assume that the system is not local.

Figure 9-8 *OFF-NET Systems Set*

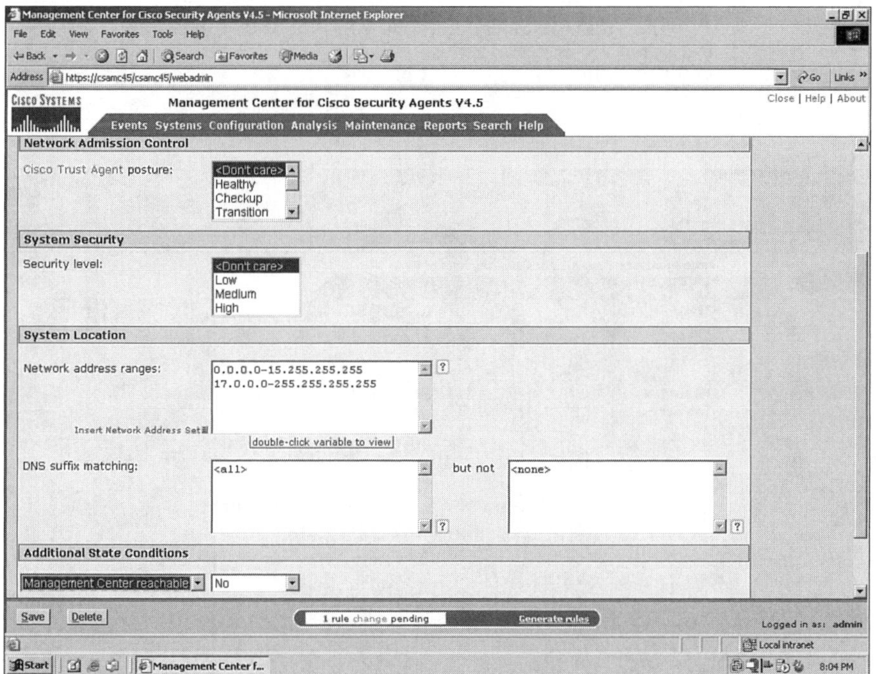

Step 2 Create a policy named **OFF-NET Protection Policy** and a rule module named **OFF-NET Protection Rule Module** that you can associate to the policy. Enforce this rule module only when your OFF-NET state set has matched on the system.

Step 3 Add the following rules as displayed in Figure 9-9:

— Add an NAC rule to the rule module that denies all applications from acting as a server on all TCP and UDP ports. This should be enforced only when you are not connected to the corporate network.

— Add a Network shield rule that prevents all malicious packets and various scanning mechanism but does not log the messages. Your systems are guaranteed to be scanned and see some of the worst the Internet can throw at them when they are off your network. It is therefore advised that you do not log these attempts as you have little recourse when the host is miles away from any protection you can provide. Additionally, you are not likely to receive these messages until the host next connects via remote access or locally, which most likely guarantees you would be too late to react.

Step 4 Apply this policy to the correct groups.

Figure 9-9 *OFF-NET Rules*

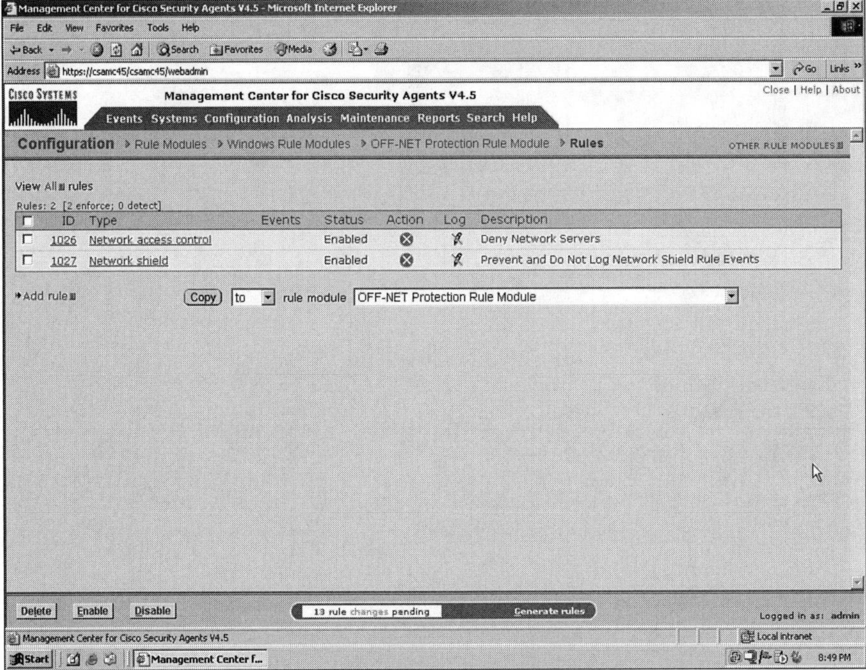

You can add any other rules that would control the system when it is not attached to your network. You might decide that no client connections should be made out of the system except virtual private network (VPN) initiation back to the corporate facility for example.

NAC Policy

If your company decides to implement Cisco NAC, you will find it advantageous to use the CSA to complement the solution. You can use the NAC posture token returned by the Cisco Access Control Server (ACS) Policy Server to match a policy and therefore cause an additional policy to become effective. This example uses the pre-defined Cisco Trust Agent Infected Posture system state set to determine when the NAC server deems your system infected. After you have matched that set, you initiate a rule that does not allow e-mail applications to start other applications, such as viewers.

Step 1 Create a policy named **NAC Infected Policy** and a rule module named **NAC Infected Rule Module** that you can associate to the policy. This rule module should be enforced only when the Cisco Trust Agent Infected Posture system state set has matched on the system. View the system state in Figure 9-10.

Figure 9-10 *Cisco Trust Agent Infected Posture State Set*

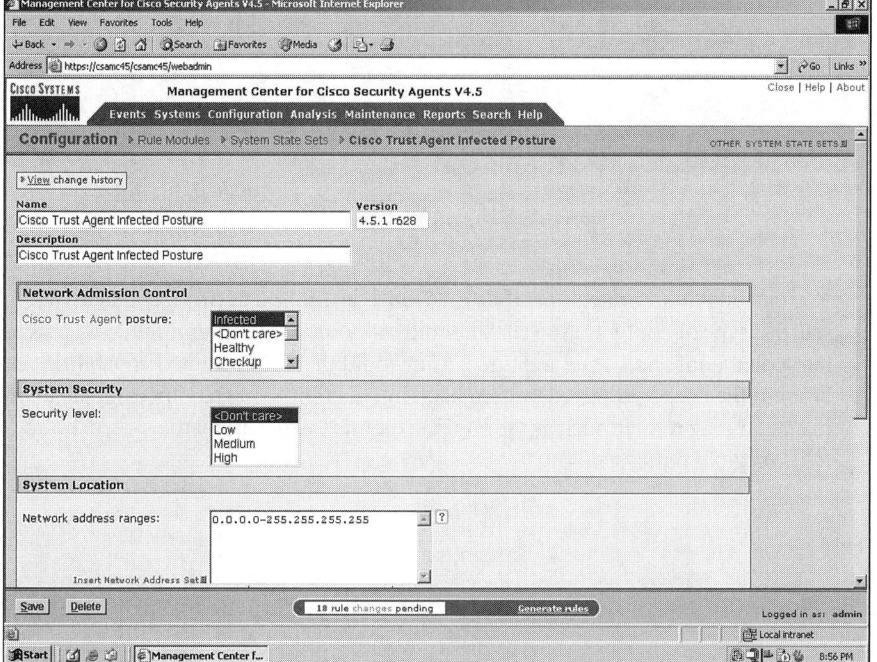

Step 2 Add an application control rule to the rule module that prevents e-mail applications from starting any other application as displayed in Figure 9-11.

Step 3 Apply this policy to the correct groups.

Figure 9-11 *Application Control Rule*

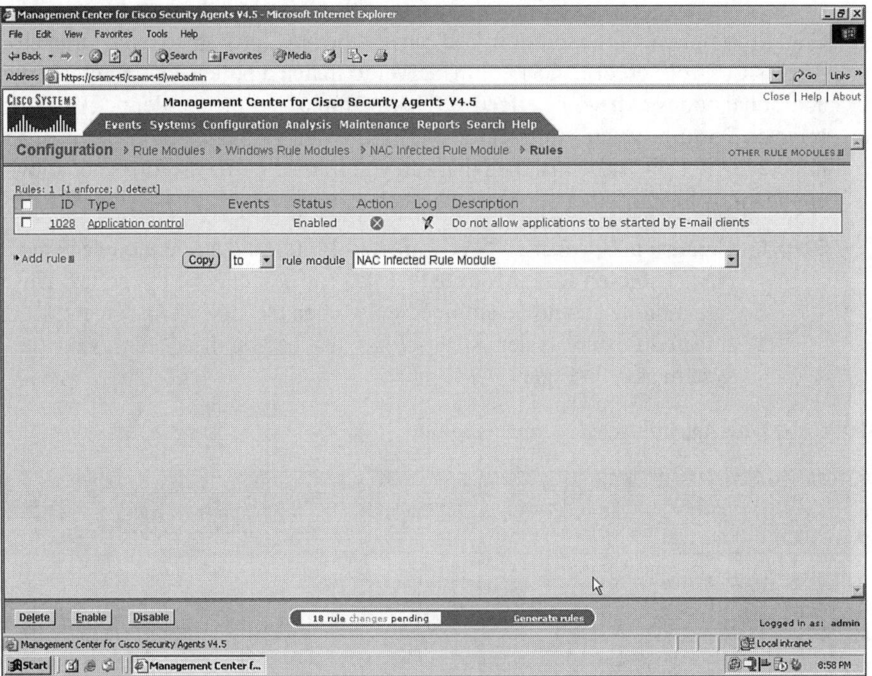

You can add other protections if desired, such as limited network connectivity. As you can see, this type of configuration can alter the endpoint capabilities if the NAC process deemed that you are infected or quarantined. You would then have limited capabilities until you brought the agent-protected system back into a compliant state by using an endpoint management product, such as the BigFix Agent, at which point the system policy can revert to its original policy.

Using Dynamic Application Classes

Dynamic application classes are a key component in the CSA architecture. Learning to use these effectively allows you to complete complex tasks using a limited number of rules rather than a great number of static rules. After you understand how to use this type of control, you will use it often and continue to become a more effective and efficient CSA administrator.

An example of dynamic application classes follows. The example tunes an item many corporations use to simplify their environments. Many companies use mass deployment software distribution products to install software, software updates, and patches to their systems automatically. Because the software deployment mechanism is trusted, no CSA administrator wants to tune the policy for every software installation and update. Instead, you can build a rule module that makes use of a dynamic application class to provide the capabilities needed to all the installers that are started by the trusted deployment mechanism.

For this example, assume the software distribution mechanism is named **AUTO-INSTALLER.EXE** and is pre-installed on every system. The following steps walk you through a high-level approach that enables you to create your own policy that allows your enterprise software distribution system to function.

Step 1 Create an application class named **AUTO-INSTALLER.EXE** that includes your application as shown in Figure 9-12.

Figure 9-12 *AUTO-INSTALLER.EXE Application Class*

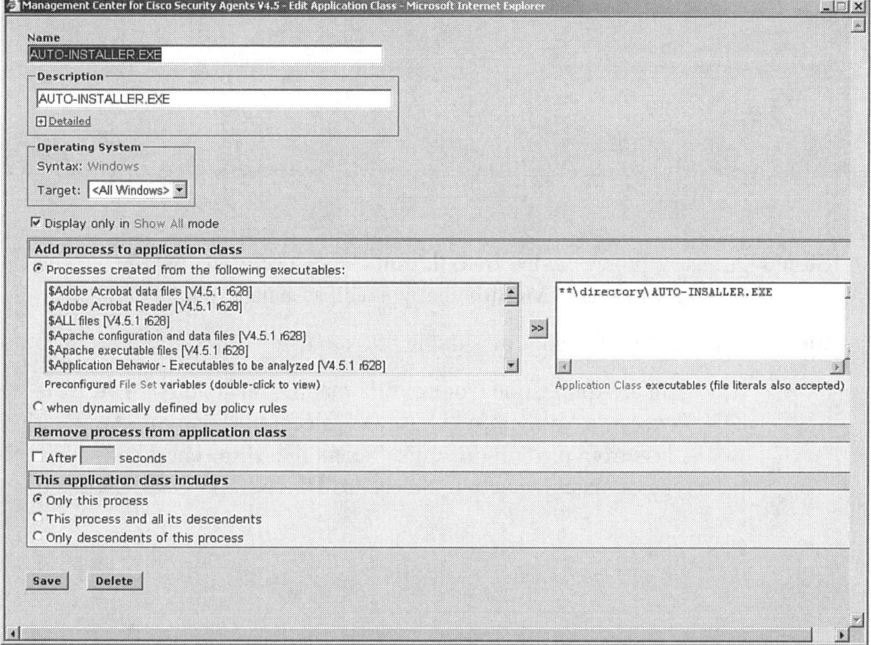

Step 2 Create another application class named **Processes Started by AUTO-INSTALLER.EXE and Children**.

This is a dynamic application class that includes processes started by AUTO-INSTALLER.EXE and their child processes as well. You select only **When Dynamically Defined by Policy Rules** to make this a dynamic application class. Do not select **This process and all its descendants**. You can see the configuration of this in Figure 9-13.

Figure 9-13 *Dynamic Application Class*

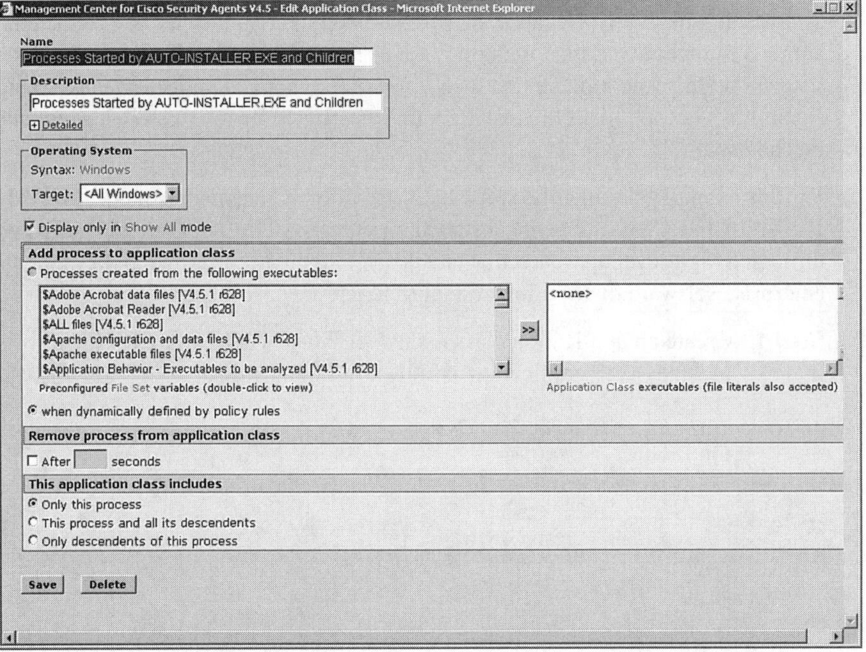

Step 3 Create a policy named **Installation Policy** and a rule module named **Installation Rule Module** that you can associate to the policy.

Step 4 Create the following rules in the rule module.

(a) Add an Application Control rule that has an action of **Add New Process to Application Class** and select **Our Dynamic Application Class** from the dropdown list. Select the **Allow** checkbox to list the type of matching action. Select **AUTO-INSTALLER.EXE** and

Processes Started by AUTO-INSTALLER.EXE and Children as the application classes to monitor. Finally, select **All applications** under **attempt to run**. This is shown in Figure 9-14.

This rule can be interpreted as, "When AUTO-INSTALLER.EXE, processes started by AUTO-INSTALLER.EXE, and all subsequent processes start any allowed application, add the new process (as a child) to the dynamic application class."

If you turn on logging for this rule, you can see the process tree of who starts whom. You might not want to do this in a production environment due to the load it can create on the CSA MC, but it can be useful at times.

Figure 9-14 *Tagging Child Processes*

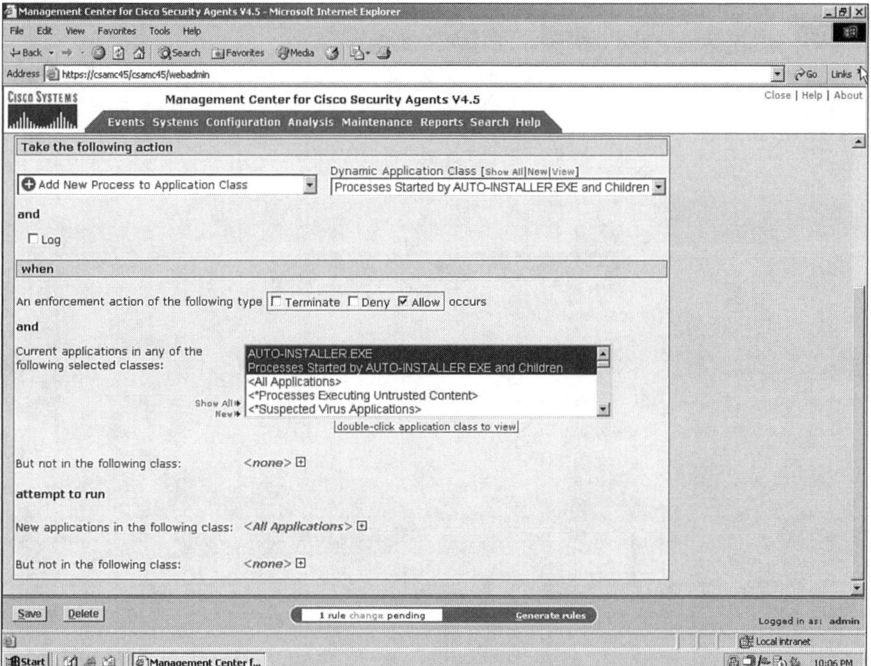

(b) Clone the Application Control Rule described previously by selecting the rule from the rule module and pressing the **Copy** button to copy a clone to the same rule module. Edit the new rule and change the action associated to the new rule to **Allow** and also the description as shown in Figure 9-15.

This rule allows the installation program and any software package, patch, or update to start any programs required to complete the installation. This also allows the installer to start the patches and other installers in the first place.

Figure 9-15 *Allow the Installers to Execute Applications*

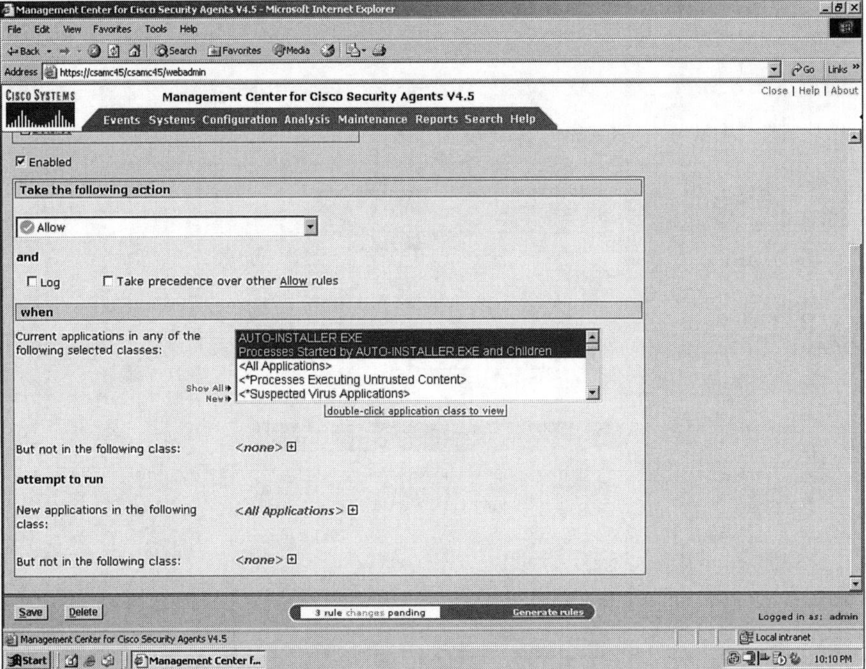

(c) Add a File Access Control rule to allow AUTO-INSTALLER.EXE and the contents of the dynamic application class to **Read File**, **Write File**, and **Write Directory** on all files. This allows the installer to write to all locations required, which includes writing DLLs and services. It is important to test your installers before allowing your mass distribution system to install the software.

Remember, you assume that anything installed by your installation and distribution program is trusted 100 percent. This rule is displayed in Figure 9-16.

Figure 9-16 *Allow the Installers to Write Files*

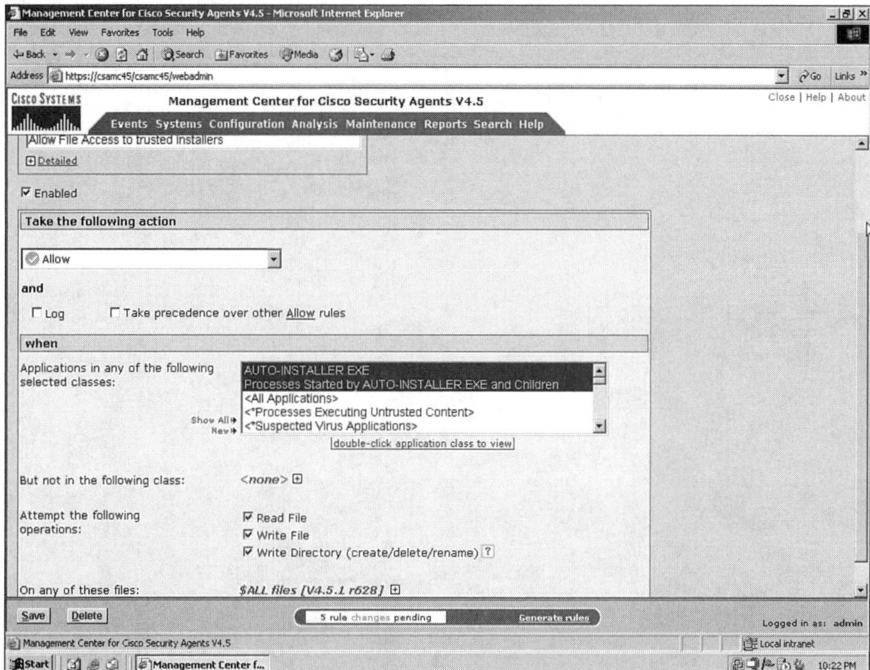

(d) Add a Registry Access Control rule to allow the same two application classes to write to all registry locations.

(e) Add a System API Control rule that allows whatever temporary security controls you want to provide to the installers. Common installer System API rule violations could include: trapping keystrokes, accessing memory of other applications, injecting code into other applications, and accessing functions in data or stack.

Remember, this policy does not weaken the entire system, but just provides these specific installation applications the temporary rights they need to complete an installation without causing the CSA administrator the headache of providing updated policy every time a new installation occurs. The key to everything in the previous example is the dynamic application class and the amount of intelligence and control it provides you. Mastering this concept ensures a successful deployment. The list of rules we added, as seen in Figure

9-17, might not be a complete configuration for every installation application on the market, but should provide you a start in creating your own policy.

Figure 9-17 *List of Rules from the Installation Policy*

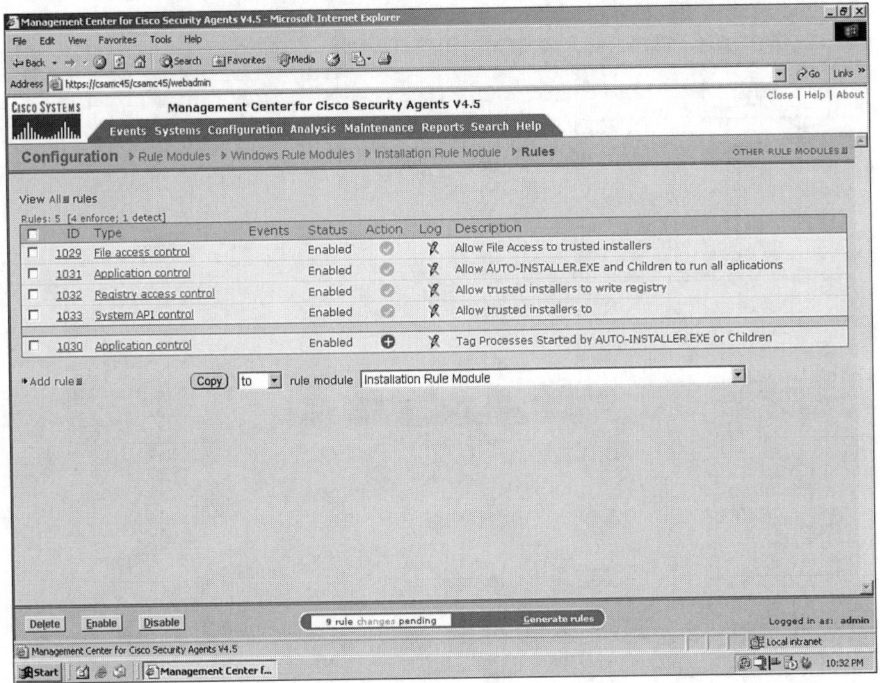

Forensics

You can use the CSA and various rules and features of the product to report behavior you want to monitor on certain systems. The two methods used are: Monitor Rules and Application Behavior Investigation. The remaining portion of the chapter discusses these two methods.

Monitor Rules

You can create rules that do not enforce any security Allow or Deny actions but rather log an event only when the matching rule is triggered. These rules use an action of Monitor. You can create any type of rule with this type of action. The following are examples of rules that might be useful:

- Monitor execution of a specific application, such as a known P2P, Instant Messenger, or other unapproved application.

- Monitor FTP, TFTP, IRC, and other connections that should not leave your corporate network.
- Monitor file access of certain directories and file types.

You can use these rules when needed or create a Rule Module that includes several different types of rules with the Monitor action, each tied to a specific empty application class. Using this approach, you can add an executable to this application class when you locate a process you want to monitor, and you instantly begin to receive forensic data about the process after the next rule generation. This can provide you a Honey-Pot approach to monitoring that is available to you anywhere in the deployment at any time.

Application Behavior Investigation

The CSA product also provides a mechanism for monitoring a process natively named Application Behavior Investigation. This is configured by selecting **Analysis>Application Behavior Investigation>Windows Behavior Analyses**. Select **New** to create an investigation. You define the matching application class and the host the investigation should target. After completion and after a specified period or number of executions, you receive a report that displays all the network interaction, file interaction, COM object interaction, and registry interaction of that process. This can be a useful way to collect data about what a process does as part of research and also prior to creating and application control policy for this software.

Summary

Creating your own policies is a major part of operating a successful CSA deployment. To accomplish this, you must thoroughly understand the components available to you and the methods of research available. Understanding the rule types and the events caused by those rules helps you move forward in your deployment and perform day-to-day support. A solid grasp of the fundamentals and advanced components not only makes you an effective administrator but also an efficient one.

PART V

Monitoring and Troubleshooting

CHAPTER 10

Local Event Database and Event Correlation

The Cisco Security Agent Management Console (CSA MC) provides the security administrator access to logged data collected from agents throughout the CSA deployment. A database stores this data, and you access it through the Event Log and Event Monitor screens. This chapter provides the information necessary to best locate and sort the data required to complete various tasks, such as tuning the deployment and investigating possible security breaches in the environment.

In this chapter, you explore the following topics:

- Event database
- Event Log and Event Monitor views of the database
- The filtering of logs

CSA MC Event Database

The CSA MC stores all events collected from the CSA in a database format. By default, if you install the CSA MC software on a single server, the CSA MC installation software installs a Microsoft Desktop Engine (MSDE) database. The MSDE database holds CSA events as they are sent to the server. As an alternative to a MSDE database, you can optionally install a copy of Microsoft SQL Server to fulfill this functionality. If you choose to install MS SQL instead of MSDE, you can opt to install the database locally on the CSA MC or on an additional server that could be dedicated to providing this functionality. Regardless of the database option selected, you must use a database to store all event and configuration information.

NOTE If you choose to store the data in an MS SQL database rather than MSDE, you are capable of querying the data and reporting natively from that source. Experienced SQL administrators should access the data in its native format because an incorrect command can corrupt the implementation and is not supported by Cisco. In addition, you should be aware that an MSDE database is supported only by Cisco in deployments of up to 500 agents and can store only 2GB worth of data.

The CSA MC provides two options for natively viewing the events in the event database. The first option is the Event Log, which provides access to all events in the database. The second option is the Event Monitor. The Event Monitor provides a view into the database that differs only from the Event Log view in that it automatically refreshes the data on the screen at regular intervals.

The Event Log

The Event Log is the most common viewer used in the CSA MC. It provides the administrator a record of events in the order they occurred. As displayed in Figure 10-1, each record displayed includes the following:

- **Event Number**—The number listed here corresponds to this specific event in relation to the number of events displayed for the current display criteria. The display criteria and total event count related to the criteria are shown at the top of the Event Log page.
- **Date**—This field shows the date and time that this specific event was triggered on the host that logged the event. The date and time is taken from the host itself, so an incorrect date on the host would not be altered when the CSA MC server receives it. This is because the systems that lose contact with the CSA MC, such as laptops, locally store the events triggered until communication is reestablished. These events are sent in bulk to the CSA MC and inserted into the database with the appropriate timestamps. If the host is from another time zone than the CSA MC, there is an adjustment made to account for the time difference and it is stamped in the database with the time associated with the CSA MC.
- **Host**—This displays the host that recorded this particular event. Clicking on the host name directs you to the Host Information page that includes all the information in the configuration database specific to this host.
- **Severity**—This field lists the severity of the event as mapped in the database. The entry here ranges from Information to Emergency.
- **Event**—This is the largest field in the record. It includes the specific information about the event, such as what occurred and who performed the task. It also includes options to see more complete details, a link to the specific rule that triggered the event, a link to launch the wizard that is used to tune this event, and Find Similar that allows you to sort the event log searching for similar events to the one in question.

Figure 10-1 *The Event Log View*

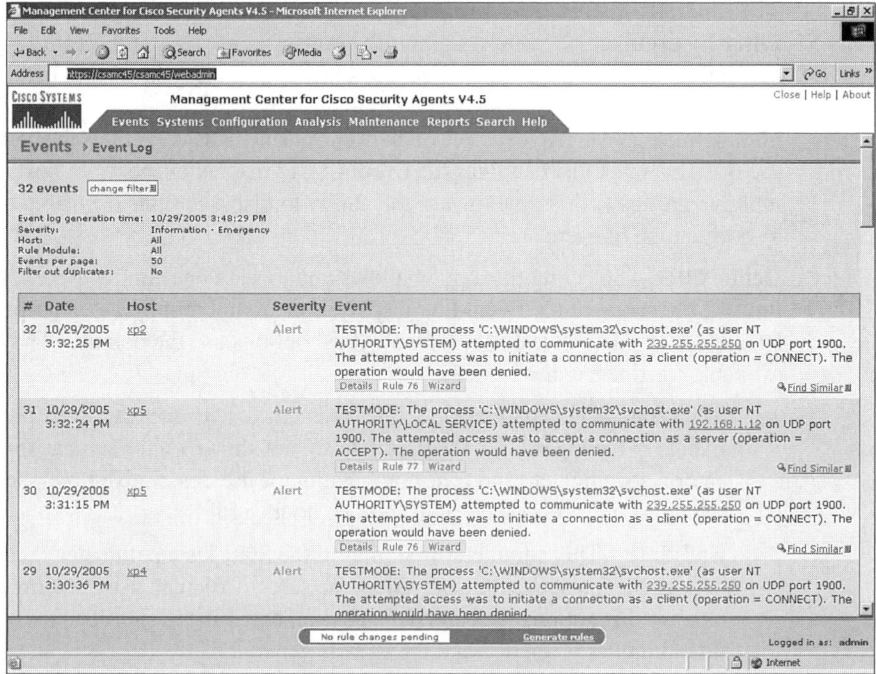

When you attempt to locate specific data, you can configure the Event Log in different ways. Some of the filter capabilities are results of clicking on links on other pages within the CSA MC, but there are also basic ways to filter the data directly from the Event Log screen itself.

Filtering the Event Log Using Change Filter

When you attempt to specify events to complete a management task, such as tuning or security investigation, it is advantageous to limit the data presented on the screen, so that the administrators can quickly and easily see patterns emerge that allow them to accomplish their goal. The Event Log Change Filter option allows the administrator to filter the Event Log using specified criteria.

To view the current filter criteria, look to the top, left corner of the Event Log screen. The screen displays the current filter in place. Above the current criteria is the total number of events that match the current criteria and the option to Change Filter. Selecting the Change Filter link presents a pop-up option that presents the Change Filter options, as displayed in

Figure 10-2. There are two major options that must be selected before applying the Change Filter criteria to the displayed Event Log. These options follow:

- **Filter by eventset**—To apply a granular eventset as a filter to the Event Log, select this option and then proceed to select the specific eventset you wish to use. Eventsets include some filtering options that are not available through any othr CSA MC filtering mechanism. An example of an eventset-only filter criteria is the creation and use of an eventset that can filter the Event Log to display events from hosts across multiple groups at the same time or the ability to display events occurring only from a specific type of event.
- **Define filter**—Selecting this option allows you to set a one-time filter capable of limiting the scope of the Event Log display. You are not required to enter parameters for each of the definable options. Nondefined options use the defaults. The criteria available for filtering the log are:
  - **Start date**—This parameter defines the start date of the displayed events. Events in the log prior to the start date are not shown on the screen. You can enter a specific date and time combination or use descriptive time phrases such as—now, three days ago, and two hours ago.
  - **End date**—This parameter is similar to the Start Date parameter except it defines the latest event displayed on the screen. You can use the term now or leave this option blank and it displays all matching events up to the actual time the filter is applied and the view is generated.
  - **Minimum Severity**—This parameter allows you to select the lowest severity level on any event to be displayed ranging from Information to Critical.
  - **Maximum Severity**—This parameter allows you to select the highest possible severity level to be displayed ranging from Information to Critical.
  - **Host**—You can enter the name of a host directly into this field to display only events from this host. If desired, you can click the change link to open a dialog window complete with drop-down boxes that enable you to select the host from a list or select a group. Leaving this field blank or unconfigured defines all hosts as the matching criteria for this parameter.
  - **Rule Module**—This parameter allows you to select a specific rule module that causes events to be triggered. Rules contained only in the selected rule module cause events to display.
  - **Rule ID**—You can enter a specific rule ID in this field to display only events resulting from this specific rule. Although you can enter this here, it is more commonly populated through links derived from other pages, such as the Most Active Rules link available on the Status Summary page and the Find Similar filtering option.

- **Events per page**—This parameter defines the number of events to display per page because of this newly defined filter. The default is 50 per page and the maximum is 500 per page.
- **Filter text**—By entering a word or phrase into this field and selecting either include or exclude, you ensure that any event either including or excluding this text is required or excluded from the search results. This is helpful when searching for events related to a specific user or file.
- **Filter out duplicates**—This option allows you to filter any identical events that occur in your search criteria results. The first result is displayed and duplicates are removed. By default, duplicate events are not removed.

Figure 10-2 *Change Filter*

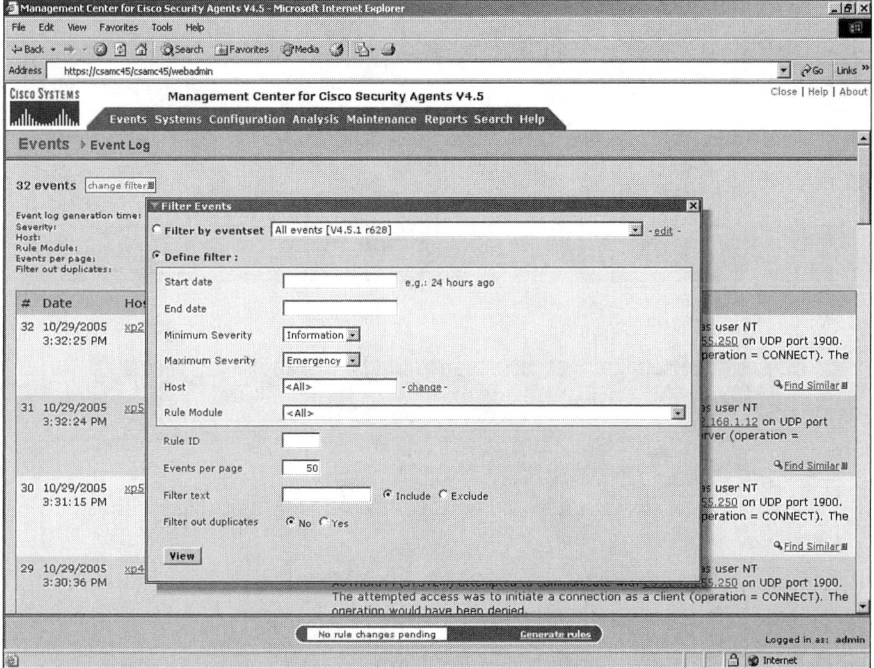

To test the Change Filter option, create a simple filter and verify the results. For this example, filter the Event Log so that it displays only events that include dns.exe. To accomplish this, the only parameter you need to set is Filter text. Set the Filter text field to dns.exe and also ensure the selection of the included radio button to the right of the text entry field. View the parameters in Figure 10-3. Figure 10-4 displays the outcome of the filter that now shows three events. Also note that after applying the filter, the filter criteria displayed at the top of the page reflects the changes made in the filter.

Figure 10-3 *Sample Filter Criteria*

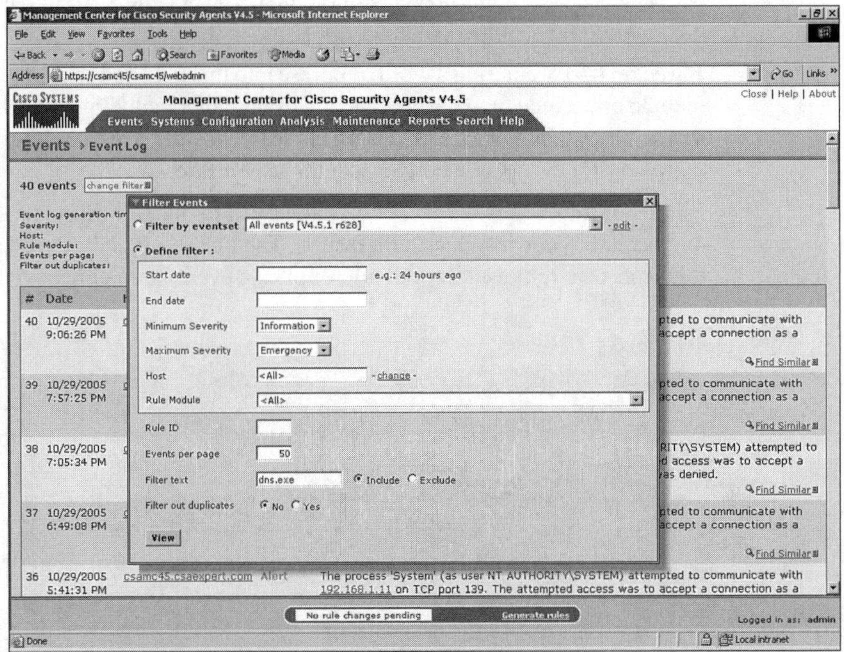

Figure 10-4 *Resulting Event Log*

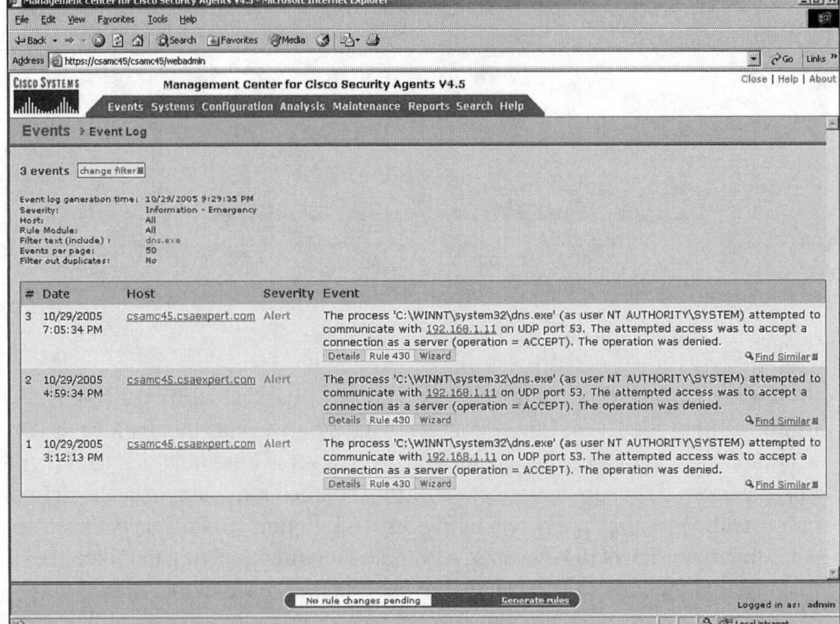

Filtering by Eventset

The Eventset filtering option is an excellent way to filter the various logs using consistent, reusable criteria. To filter the data, it is recommended that you use the Eventset method for a filter that you continue to use often. Eventsets are made up of various settings that apply as a filter granularly. These settings include:

- **Name**—You must enter a name for this eventset to identify it among the others in the list.
- **Description**—You can add a description for this eventset.
- **Event Types**—You can include All Events by type or specify various Rule Type and Action combinations.
- **Severity Levels**—You can specify a single, various, or all event severities.
- **Groups**—You can include all hosts or specific groups.
- **Rule Modules**—You can include all rule modules or specific rule modules. Use CTRL+Click or SHFT+Click to select multiple entries.
- **Timestamps**—You can include all timestamps or specific timing via the following options: Custom Start and End, Today, Last 24 Hours, Last 7 Days, Last 30 Days, or Older than a specified number of days.

Using an eventset allows certain types of filtering options and multiple-selection criteria that is not possible any other way. In addition, filtering using this method produces consistent results and is used effectively during normal daily filtering of the Event Log by administrators, desktop support personnel, and helpdesk personnel. Figure 10-5 shows a common eventset filter created for reusable purposes.

Figure 10-5 *Using Eventsets as Filtering Criteria*

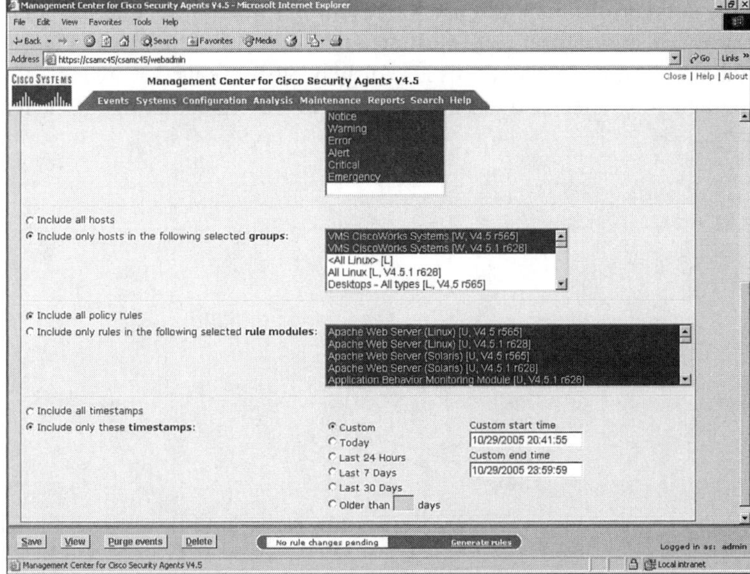

Filtering the Event Log Using Find Similar

Another method that you can use to filter the Event Log is to select Find Similar from any of the specific Event Log entries that you would like to isolate. You are somewhat limited in the type of parameters that can be set from this filter mechanism; however, in certain circumstances, it is efficient. The criteria used to filter the Event Log from Find Similar follows:

- **Same host**—The host that triggered this event is listed in this field by default. If you do not want to limit the resulting filtered view to events triggered by this specific rule, you must deselect this option.
- **Same policy rule**—The rule ID that triggered this event is set by default. If you do not want to include only the events specifically sent by the triggering of this rule, you must deselect this option.
- **Same severity level**—The severity level of the event you use to Find Similar is set by default. If you do not wish to filter events to display only events of this severity level, deselect this option.
- **Same type**—This criteria specifies the identification of similar events that were triggered by the same rule type and action combination.
- **Same time frame**—This option allows the administrator to specify a timeframe to which the similar events should be limited. You can specify a timeframe in minutes, hours, or days and an interval that will include the time before and after the event you use to create the Find Similar filter.

To illustrate this type of filter, look for events that include dns.exe. This time, you need to manually locate an event of that type. After locating the event, select **Find Similar** from that event and specify the following criteria: Same policy rule and Same time frame (+/- 15 minutes). The criteria selections can be seen in Figure 10-6 and the resulting Event Log is shown in Figure 10-7. Notice that the results of Find Similar filter do not provide exactly what we had hoped to receive (illustrated in the previous example in Figure 10-5). Because of the limited criteria, the results also display other events that are similar in nature. It is important you understand when best to use the different filtering mechanisms.

Figure 10-6 *Find Similar Filter Criteria*

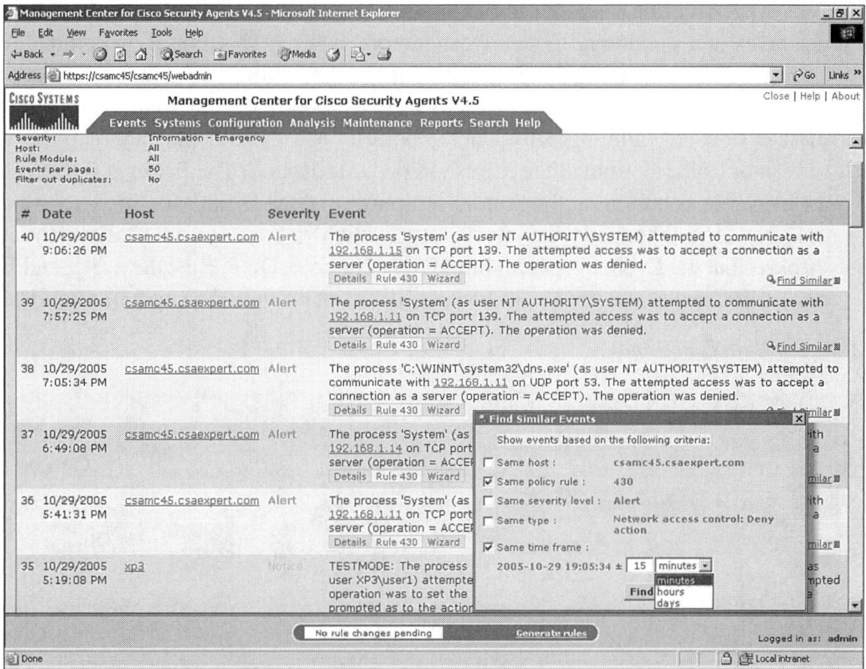

Figure 10-7 *Resulting Event Log*

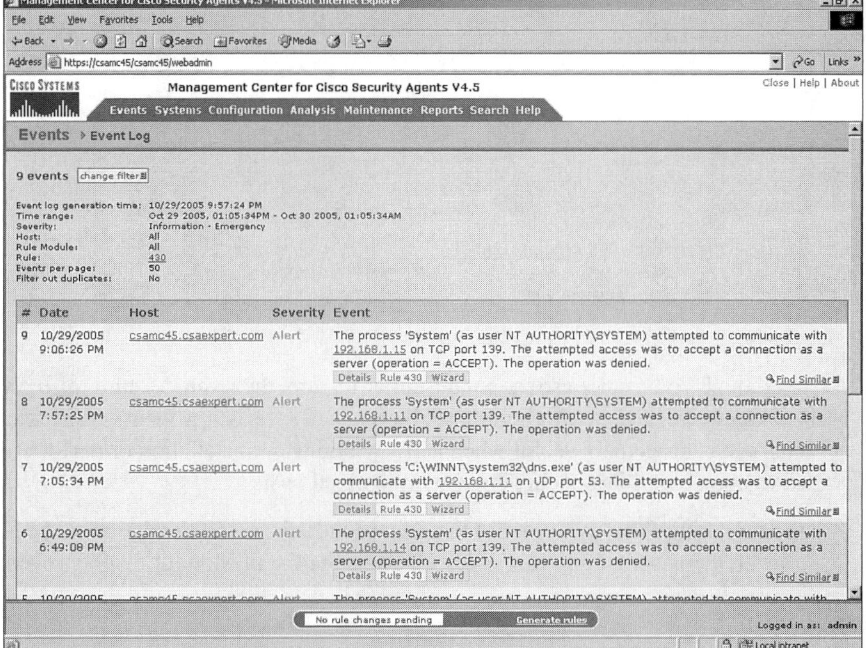

The Event Monitor

The Event Monitor is similar to the Event Log except that it auto-refreshes the view displayed at a set interval. The refresh interval is set to 15 seconds by default. You can increase this by changing the time setting in the drop-down box at the top of the screen next to Refresh Interval. The options are 15 seconds, 1 minute, and 5 minutes. In addition to these options, the administrator can temporarily pause the display and halt the automatic refresh or cause an immediate refresh to occur if desired. The Pause and Refresh options are available as buttons at the bottom-left portion of the Event Monitor screen as displayed in Figure 10-8. The fields displayed in the Event Monitor View are nearly identical to those displayed in the Event Log including: Event Number, Date, Host, Severity, and Event. The only difference is that the Event Monitor does not provide the capability to Find Similar.

Figure 10-8 *The Event Monitor View*

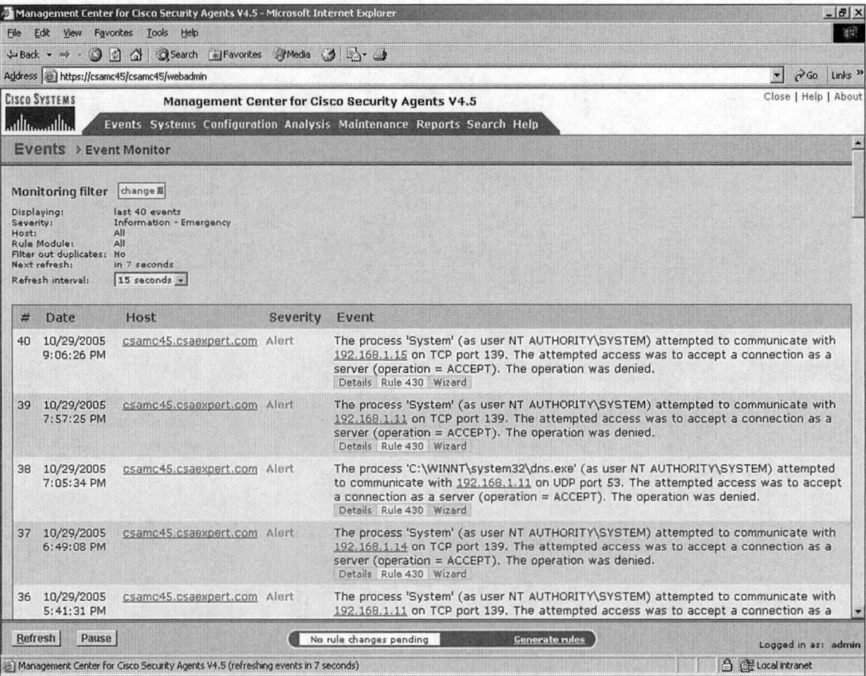

Even though you cannot use the Find Similar feature, the Event Monitor also provides the capability to create a monitoring filter. Filtering a near real-time view for specific incoming events can be extremely useful when actively tuning an installation or performing an investigation based on specific criteria or involved hosts.

The Monitoring Filter is similar to the Event Filter discussed in relation to the Event Log. However, there are subtle differences. Because the Event Monitor displays events as they occur and it is not used in reference to historical events in the database, the options differ. The options available, as displayed in Figure 10-9, follow:

- **Filter by eventset**—Similar to the Event Log filter, you can apply a granular eventset as a filter to the Event Monitor to limit the real-time incoming events.
- **Define filter**—Selecting this option allows you to set a one-time filter capable of limiting the scope of the Event Monitor display. The criteria available for filtering the log are:
  - **Minimum Severity**—This parameter allows you to select the lowest severity level on any event to display in a range from Information to Critical.
  - **Maximum Severity**—This parameter allows you to select the highest possible severity level to display in a range from Information to Critical.
  - **Host**—You can enter the name of a host directly into this field to display only events from this host, or if desired, you can click the change link to open a dialog window complete with drop-down boxes that enable you to select the host from a list or select a group if desired. Leaving this field blank or unconfigured defines all hosts as the matching criteria for this parameter. This option is helpful when attempting to troubleshoot a specific host issue in near real-time without having to view all events from all other hosts rolling in to the database.
  - **Rule Module**—This parameter allows you to select a specific rule module that caused the triggered events. Only rules contained in the selected rule module cause the display of events. This option allows administrators to limit their view only to events added to the database that are tied to a rule module they are actively tuning at that time.
  - **Rule ID**—You can enter a specific rule ID in this field to display only events resulting from this particular rule. This is also another field that is used to assist during the tuning process.
  - **Display last**—This parameter defines the number of events displayed per page because of this newly defined filter. The default is 50 per page and the maximum is 100.
  - **Filter text**—By entering a word or phrase into this field and selecting either include or exclude, you ensure that any event either including or excluding this text is required or excluded from the search results. This is yet another useful parameter when either performing an investigation or undergoing active tuning.
  - **Filter out duplicates**—This option allows you to filter any events that occur in identical search criteria results.

Figure 10-9 *Change Filter*

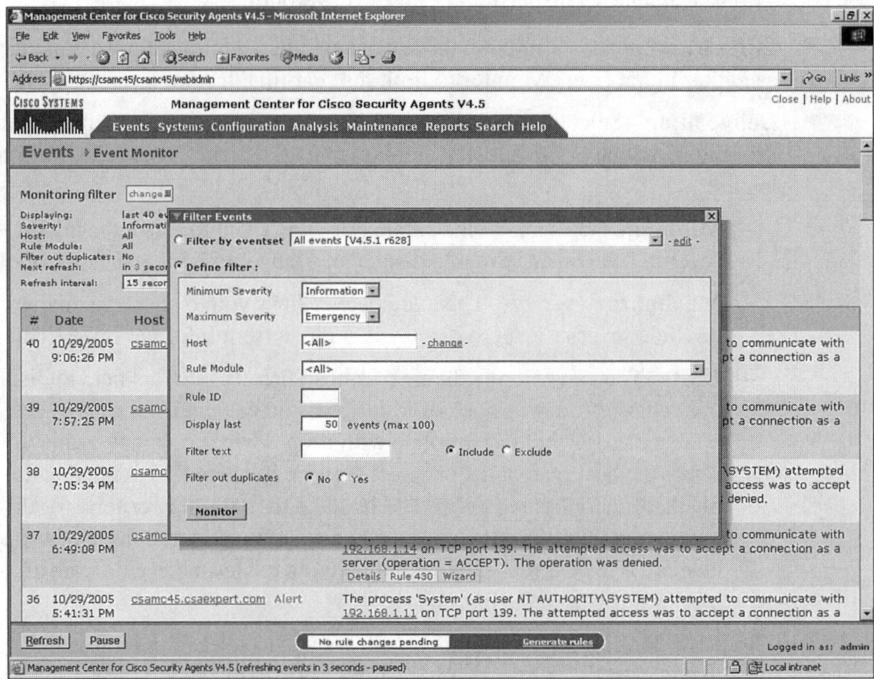

Filtering the Event Monitor is a common practice. Becoming adept at the different parameters available ensures your ability to quickly isolate and fix issues in your environment.

Automated Filtering from Directed Links

You can click on links that direct you to an automatically filtered view of the data to filter the Event Log available throughout the CSA MC. The following list outlines a few samples of directed links that provide filtered Event Log views:

- **Most Active Hosts—# Events**—When viewing the most active hosts' pop-up window that is available from the Status Summary page, you can use a directed filtered link by selecting the # Events (such as 11 events) next to the specific most active hosts, as displayed in Figure 10-10. You can produce a filtered view of events from the host that occurred in the last day. You can also change the Sort By field to Rules Triggered and filter the display to add an additional filter in addition to the host and also include the events derived from this host and a specific rule, as seen in Figure 10-11.

Figure 10-10 *Most Active Host Events Directed Link*

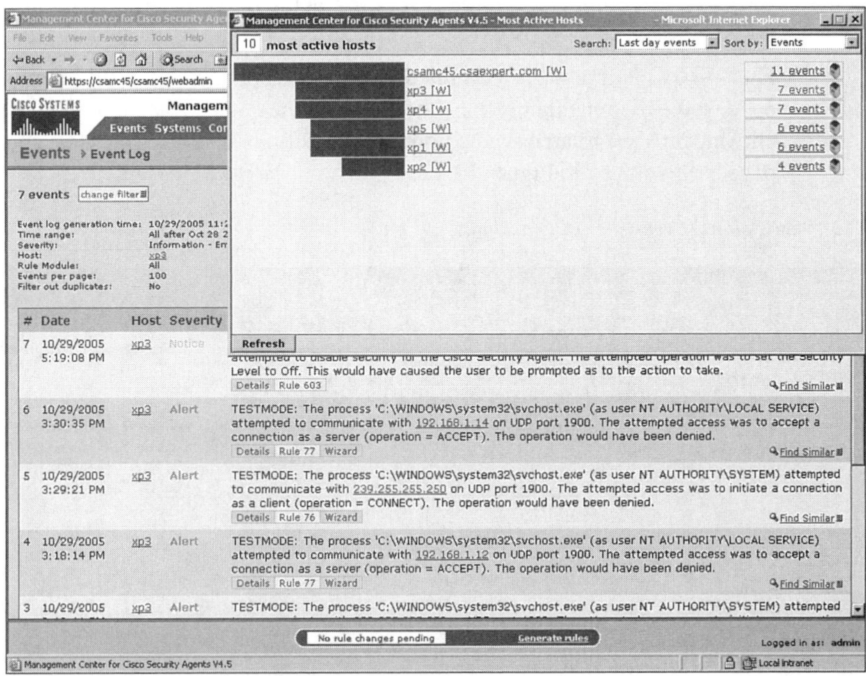

Figure 10-11 *Most Active Host Events Secondary Criteria*

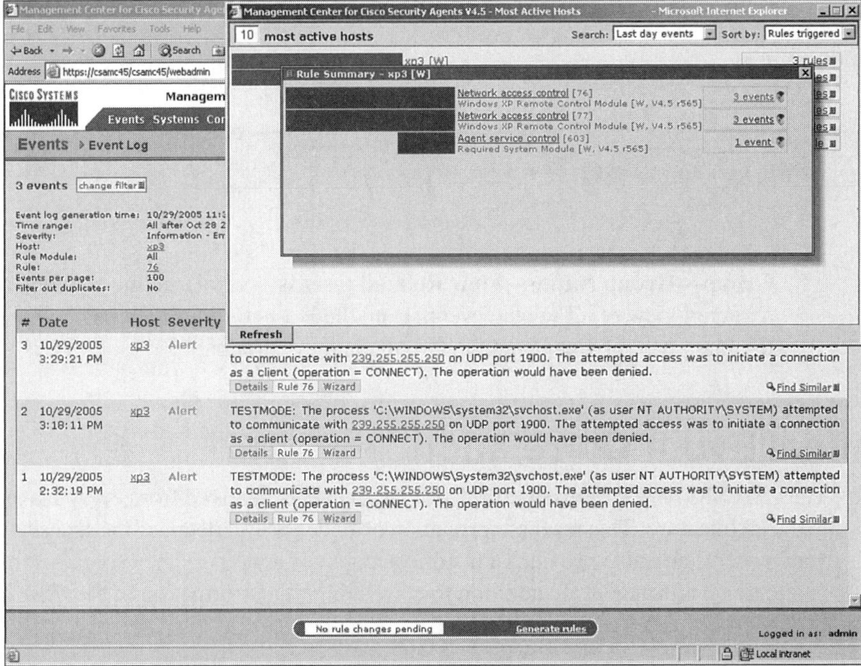

- **Most Active Rules—# Events**—This directed link provides a similar output as most active hosts, except that it initially focuses on the rule most triggered rather than the hosts.
- **Host—Host Name—View Related Events**—When viewing a Host configuration page, you can immediately view the events in the database from this specific host by clicking on View related events from the Quick links section of the Host configuration page, as displayed in Figure 10-12.

Figure 10-12 *View Related Events—Host Quicklinks*

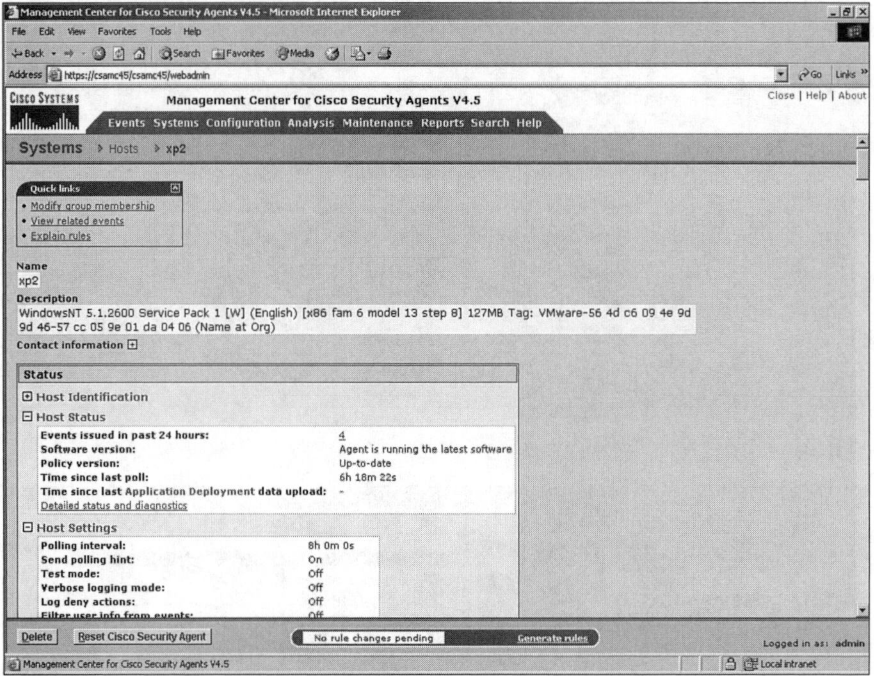

- **Group—Group Name—View Related Events**—Similar to the way you can create a filtered view of all related events from the Host configuration page, you can create the same type of view from the Group configuration page.

Additional Event Correlation

The CSA MC performs event correlation of all events received from every managed agent in the architecture. This level of correlation provides useful detail of the security posture of your systems and also provides a historic account of actions as they spread across the computing environment. In addition to correlating this information in the CSA MC, you might wish to send the data to another collector for further correlation with additional non-CSA messages, such as network IPS, firewall, and other security-based data sources. Examples of collection tools available from Cisco Systems include Cisco MARS Appliance, CiscoWorks SIMS, and the Security Monitor included in the CiscoWorks VMS Suite.

Summary

One of the most important features of the CSA MC product is the event database. To run an efficient operational deployment of the CSA product both during and post implementation, you must be able to effectively isolate events in the Event Monitor and Event Log. The data available in a properly filtered view can ensure rapid policy tuning and data interpretation during a security investigation. If necessary, continue to practice the skills and tools covered in this chapter until you are confident you know which options are best used in specific circumstances and how to quickly gain access to the data you require.

CHAPTER 11

Troubleshooting Methodology

As with any technology, problems will arise during a Cisco Security Agent (CSA) deployment. Knowing what tools are available and how to use them to troubleshoot problems with CSA helps immensely. At the end of this chapter, you will also understand common problems with the systems and services that CSA relies on, such as Domain Name System (DNS) and SQL Server. This chapter examines:

- Troubleshooting common issues
- Troubleshooting tools available to NOC personnel
- Tools installed with the agent
- Troubleshooting Cisco Security Agent Management Console (CSA MC) SQL Server 2000 issues
- Contacting Cisco for support

Common Issues

Most CSA problems you encounter are caused by a short list of problems that repeatedly occur. Some of these problems show up on the server, whereas some are on the agent machines in the field. The top three sources of CSA problems are licensing, name resolution, and the network shim installed on the agents.

Licensing

Often the most basic problems with CSA result from licensing issues, mainly the shortage of available licenses. Fortunately, these are easy to diagnose and fix. Make sure that there are unused licenses available for the machine type that tries to register with CSA by going to the License Information option under the Maintenance heading in the CSA MC. This screen shows the license files installed on the MC and how many agents have registered. You can confirm this information by checking the csalog.txt file on the MC in the

CSAMC45 directory in the CiscoWorks VMS installation path> as shown in Examples 11-1 and 11-2 that follow.

Example 11-1 ***License Errors in csalog.txt on the CSA MC***

```
[2005-08-20 00:03:40.046] [PID=4816] [webagent]: Agent Req 'Registration'
Failure(2035),
ip=192.168.100.114, huid={A5EFBC01-4588-4744-8835-F9DD5D884A71}
[2005-08-20 00:03:50.453] [PID=4816] [webagent]: No such feature exists
Feature:       desktopagent
Feature:       desktopagent
License path:  C:\PROGRA~1\CSCOpx\CSAMC45\cfg\CSAMC.lic
```

Example 11-2 ***Corresponding Error in the Remote Agent Log***

```
[2005-08-20 00:03:40.390] [PID=396] [Csamanager]: Registration failed without
message Error code=2035
[2005-08-20 00:03:40.390] [PID=396] [Csamanager]: Registering with server csamc45,
Failure (2035)
[2005-08-20 00:03:40.390] [PID=396] [Csamanager]: Will retry to register in 10 sec
```

Examples 11-1 and 11-2 show that a desktop agent tried to register with the server and no desktop agent licenses were available. A few keywords give some clues about what is happening. The third line of Example 11-1 shows that feature—Desktop is trying to be enabled—but the second line shows that no such feature (or license for that feature) exists on the MC. Line one of Example 11-1 and each line in Example 11-2 show that there was a problem with agent registration. Agent registration problems showing up in both errors simultaneously almost always points to license issues.

To resolve this problem, you must either add additional licenses for systems of the correct type or delete hosts from the CSA MC to put those licenses back into the license pool. CSA has no licensing grace period; a license is either available for an agent or it is not. It is a good idea to have a few extra licenses available in dynamic environments where machines are added, replaced, or reimaged regularly. Figure 11-1 shows the licensing screen on the CSA MC.

NOTE Remember that the CSA MC automatically deletes hosts that have not polled for 30 days from the database. This should keep the count of used and available licenses from becoming too stale. Recall that when a host is deleted from the database, the license is available again for the next registering host. Also, all events from the deleted host are deleted along with any other record of that host.

Figure 11-1 *License Screen Under the Maintenance Menu on the CSA MC*

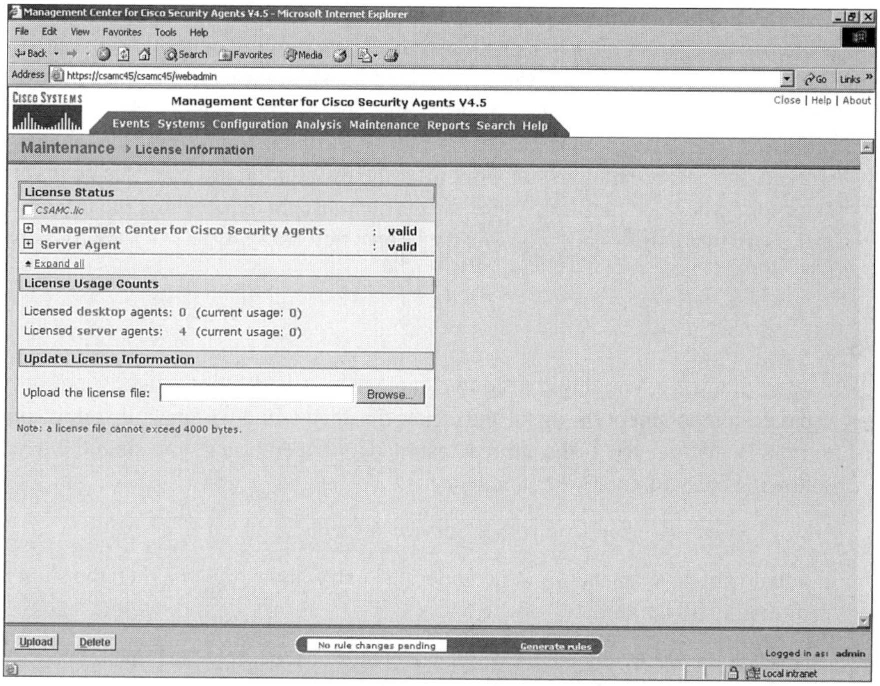

NOTE In rare cases, a corrupted license file can prevent the CSA MC from launching correctly from VMS. In these cases, call Cisco Technical Assistance Center (TAC), as discussed later in this chapter, and confirm that you have access to the console and all log files in the CSA MC directory and CSA license files.

Name Resolution

CSA depends on name resolution for communications from the remote agents to the MC. CSA does not care if the name is resolved by DNS, WINS, or even host files. First, open the agent panel to verify that the CSA MC is listed. Then try using the NSLOOKUP utility to determine if the DNS Server that the host is using is able to successfully look up the IP address or get the address through recursive lookups. If that does not work, switch to a different DNS server in NSLOOKUP and try again. Then check the system's host file. A cached entry from a host file can override lookup attempts to a DNS server. Make sure to flush the DNS cache of Windows machines.

Network Shim

The CSA network shim provides additional host protection, but can also cause problems on some machines, particularly laptops and machines running network tools and diagnostic software, such as packet analyzers. Although the shim protects machines from network attacks, it is also a likely source of problems when you have network communication problems with network interface cards and VPN connections. If a VPN connection profile worked fine before but does not work after the installation of CSA, it is not too difficult to determine where to start looking for the problem. Begin by checking the CSA event logs to make sure that a rule is not blocking the connection attempt. Then check for network shim.

Windows

As part of testing, you might need to disable the network shim. Luckily, the shim is a separate component of the agent and can be disabled without uninstalling, but you will need to modify the registry. If the shim is installed and operational, you should have the following entry in your system registry:

HKLM/System/CurrentControlSet/Services/csanet/Enable=1

If you do not have an enable value under that entry in the registry, then the shim is enabled and running by default.

To disable the shim, change the value for enable to 0 or create an enable value with a dword value of 0. To enable the shim, simply set the dword value back to 1 as shown in Figure 11-2.

Figure 11-2 *CSA Network Shim Registry Key and Value*

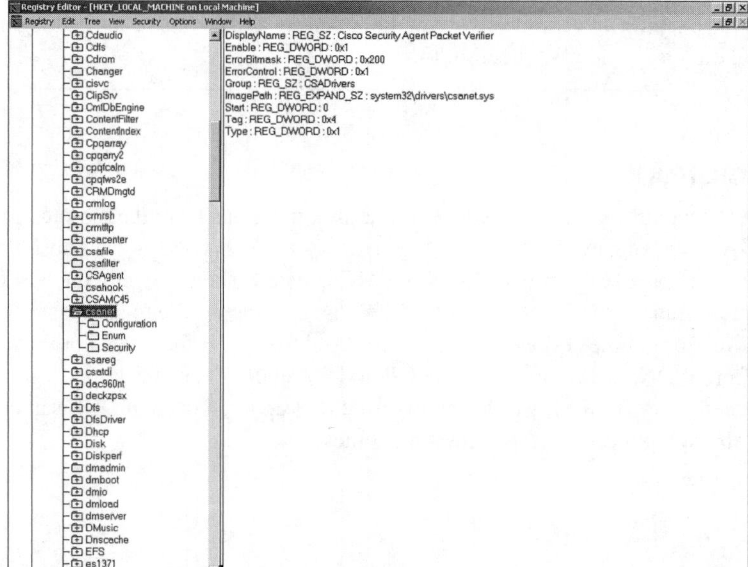

UNIX / Linux

The network shim runs as a separate process on UNIX systems and can be stopped without stopping the entire agent. The csaadapt script can stop, start, disable, or remove the network shim from a UNIX or Linux system. Be aware that csaadapt must be executed as a privileged account, such as root. As shown in Figure 11-3, running csaadapt without any parameters returns a list of valid parameters.

Figure 11-3 *csaadapt Parameters*

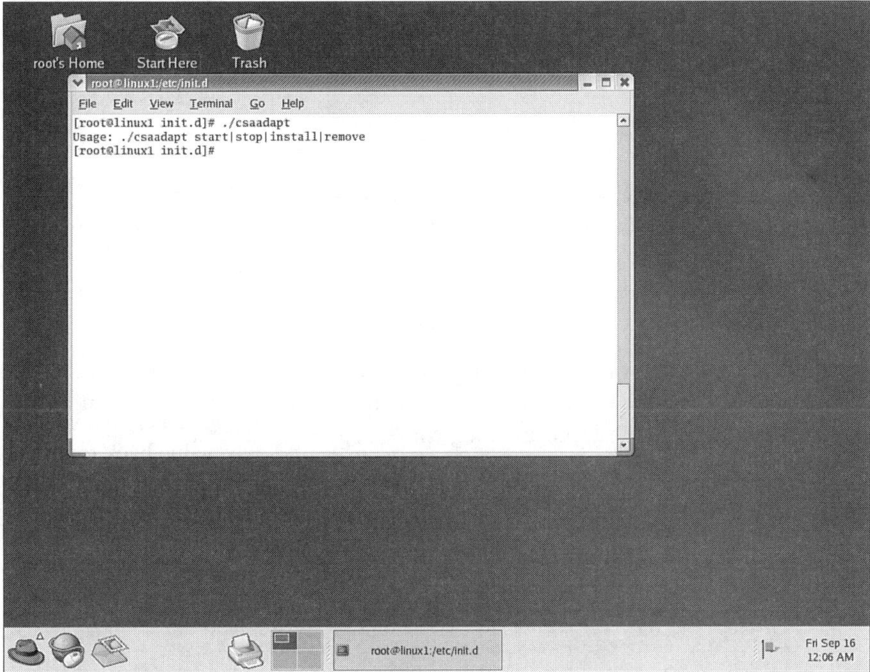

All the tools mentioned at this point in the chapter run either from the CSA MC or the agent host. Some of the tools used to troubleshoot CSA problems are the same tools that are used for resolving issues with any other network application.

NOC Troubleshooting Tools

Troubleshooting CSA is not any different from troubleshooting other applications on your network. Follow the same troubleshooting best practices that you would for other client/server applications, such as e-mail and database applications. Look at system event logs before making any configuration changes to see if a simple explanation of the problem is presented. Next, look at the application log files. Run system diagnostics to check the operations of the application and find out where things might have gone wrong. Examine the affected systems to see what is happening because end-user reports might not be accurate. Test the network connectivity between the endpoints to make sure that communications aren't broken at a lower layer.

Whatever you do, document the steps you take and change only one thing at a time when troubleshooting. That way you know exactly which steps were taken to fix the problem and which step actually fixed it.

Event Logs

Event logs provide a wealth of information about what has happened on a machine, and in some cases, event logs provide information on current activities as well.

NT System and Application Logs

Windows event logs hold information about whether an application or service started or stopped and specific information that the application deems important or interesting. Check the system log to make sure that the CSagent service started correctly by filtering the Windows system log with a source of Service Control Manager. It might also be wise to check that the service is set to start automatically.

Look at the Windows application log to see what events CSA might have logged. Most events logged to the CSA MC are also sent to the local system's application log. These events show up in the application log with CSagent as the source. Denied actions typically are stored in the log as error-level events in the application log. Keep in mind that the severity level of the event in the application log, such as that shown in Figure 11-4, does not necessarily match up to the severity level of the event in the CSA MC event log.

Figure 11-4 *Windows 2000 Application Event Log*

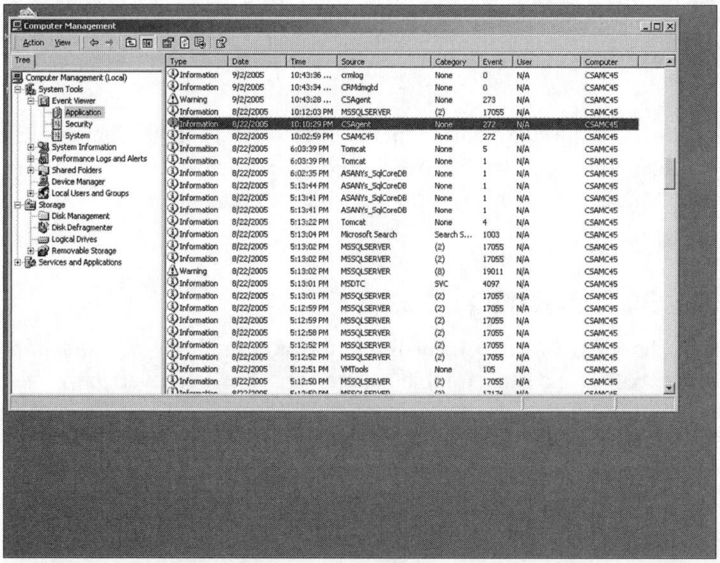

UNIX and Linux Messages File

The messages file, often in the /var/adm directory on Solaris machines, and /var/log serve the same purpose as the system log in Windows. Check this file to see if the agent did not start correctly and why.

SQL Server Logs

Sometimes you encounter problems that have nothing to do with the agent on the endpoint, but instead are caused by errors on the local MC or database. SQL server logs are a good place to check. Another benefit of these logs is that the information is often understandable to people who are not database experts.

CSAMC45-install.log

The CSAMC45-install.log file stores information about the steps taken to install the CSA MC on a system and the results of those steps. This file is useful for letting you know which prerequisites, services, and files were checked and when the checks occurred. Often, if a system does not perform properly from the time of installation, careful inspection of this file will show the reason. The default location of this file is C:\Program Files\CSCOpx\CSAMC45\log.

CSAgent-install.log

This file lists all the steps taken during the agent installation on a host. All modifications to the system and checks performed and the results are shown in this file. Most of the time, any errors are readily apparent in this file and are useful to get to the root cause of the problem. The default path to this logfile is C:\Program Files\Cisco Systems\CSAgent\log.

Remote Control

When all else fails, you can connect to the remote machine to see what is happening. Terminal Services, Telnet/SSH, and virtual circuit number (VNC) among others give you several options for remote control of machines. Of course, make sure that CSA policies allow remote control of the machine you are trying to connect to.

Terminal Services

Starting with Windows 2000 Server editions, Microsoft Terminal Services is an optional component that can be installed to give a user a remote desktop session on a machine. This feature is now installed by default on Windows XP workstations and Windows 2003 servers, although it requires manually enabling the machine to accept connections. What makes this feature so powerful is that remote users have access to the machine with the same privileges they would possess if logged in locally. After you connect using Terminal Services, you can use the full range of builtin utilities to troubleshoot problems, including event log and the local agent GUI, assuming CSA allows user interaction.

Terminal Services uses the Remote Desktop Protocol over TCP port 3389. Windows XP and Windows 2000 and Windows 2003 Server editions include clients. A free client for UNIX called rdesktop is available and most Linux distributions include an RDP client.

Telnet/SSH

Mainly used on UNIX and Linux hosts (although included but disabled by default on Windows machines starting with Windows 2000); Telnet and Secure Shell (SSH) allow remote command-line access. You are probably familiar with Telnet because almost all Cisco network equipment is configurable through the Telnet protocol.

Telnet works over TCP port 23 and all data is transmitted in clear-text (unencrypted). SSH uses TCP port 22 and encrypts all traffic. Each of these utilities gives you remote command-line access on the destination host as if you were local. After establishing a Telnet/SSH connection to a host you can then use tools, such as vi to look at logs, and csactl to modify the agent status.

NOTE Do not use Telnet on the Internet because the username/password pair is sent over cleartext making this protocol particularly susceptible to eavesdropping and man-in-the-middle attacks. (A man-in-the middle attack occurs when a host is inserted into the middle of the data transfer and tries to impersonate one or both of the endpoints in the conversation.) Most security professionals do not like to use Telnet internally even on large corporate networks. SSH should be used on any device that supports it.

VNC

VNC is a powerful network control utility that is free and is available for most operating systems. A powerful feature of VNC is the ability to remotely control the console of a machine without installing any software on the client/viewer machine. Unlike Terminal Services on Windows machines, which usually creates a session dedicated to the remote user, VNC redirects the local console video display to the remote client so that every action performed by the remote user is visible to anyone monitoring the local console.

VNC uses TCP port 5900 when used with VNC Viewer software and TCP port 5800 when used over HTTP. An interesting and powerful feature of VNC is that it can be used with or without additional client software. Most workstations with a web browser and Java

Runtime Engine installed can connect to a VNC server simply by connecting to port 5800 over HTTP in a web browser. Similar to other remote control services, VNC allows you to use any troubleshooting tools available on the machine.

NOTE VNC is available for download at http://www.realvnc.com among other sites.

CAUTION Install and use VNC with caution on your network! VNC can be configured to encrypt traffic over SSH tunnels, but by default, all traffic is sent in the clear. Also, the free version of VNC requires only a password to connect, and after connecting the remote user has all the privileges of the locally logged-in user, in effect becoming that user. This tool is susceptible to brute-force password attacks because only one piece of information, the password, must be supplied. (Hackers use brute-force password attacks to try to guess a password by using every possible combination of acceptable characters.) And remember that the best feature of VNC—that almost any workstation can connect to a VNC server without installing software—is also the scariest feature to security professionals.

Remote Access, Reachability, and Network Tools

A logical place to focus troubleshooting efforts is basic network connectivity. The tools discussed in this section are powerful and used by network administrators and hackers alike.

Before you spend too much time troubleshooting agent configuration, make sure that basic network communications are taking place. Again, follow the same basic troubleshooting procedures for CSA as for any other network application. These tools are available for almost every operating system and run on even the oldest hosts, making them quite popular. Simply search for the applications with your favorite search engine to obtain these tools.

Ping

What IT professional has not used the trusty ping utility when troubleshooting a network problem? Tried and true, ping is still one of the best and most basic utilities in the tool bag to test connectivity to remote machines and networks. If you are having trouble with a remote agent, make sure that it can ping the CSA MC before making any policy changes. Also ping the remote agent from the MC if possible to make sure that bidirectional traffic is flowing. CSA policies applied to workstations and desktops by default do not block ping (echo) requests.

If ping succeeds, at least you are sure that basic IP connectivity is in place. However, a ping failure does not mean that IP connectivity does not work. Instead, some Internet Control Message Protocol (ICMP) filter might be in line between the nodes. In short, ping tells you that you have connectivity if it succeeds, but only that you *might* not have connectivity if it fails.

Traceroute

Use traceroute (tracert on Windows operating systems) to check connectivity to the MC if ping fails to see how far the request goes before it is dropped. Again, this utility uses the ICMP and can be filtered, but it is still useful to let you know what route traffic takes to the destination. Traceroute tells you the address of each interface the packet enters on the way to the destination. Use it from both endpoints, the remote agent and the MC, to get a good idea of the paths used because the traffic can take different paths depending on the flow direction.

Pathping (Windows 2000 and Later Only)

Pathping combines attributes of ping and traceroute and not only tells you if the destination is reachable and which interfaces are traversed, but it also computes statistics on the latency at each hop along the way. This utility is useful for finding slowness along the path that a packet travels and can be used when policy updates and agent upgrades take longer than expected to download.

Ethereal

All network administrators have had to use a protocol analyzer (also called packet sniffers) to look inside the datagrams traveling across a network. Network interface's running in normal mode accept only packets that are bound for that interface's MAC address. Sniffers run in promiscuous mode, which means that they accept all packets regardless of the address of the destination. This lets them capture all data "on the wire," not just the packets sent to the sniffer host. To determine if two hosts communicate properly, a sniffer is a good tool to use because it can discover a great deal of information about the packets and communications between hosts.

Ethereal is a free packet sniffer that is popular and available for most platforms. By placing a machine running Ethereal on the same network segment as the MC, you can analyze all communications between the remote agents and the CSA MC. This is useful if you suspect that poll hints are not being sent to remote agents or if you think that agent poll messages are not reaching the server.

NetCat

NetCat (nc) is a simple listener and client for remote connections. NetCat can listen for connections on a given port and send those commands to a program or application on the host, which is most often a command shell. This is useful to determine if communications reach the endpoint without being filtered or translated to another port or address.

NMAP

The venerable NMAP utility has been around for a long time and is still one of the most useful and powerful network utilities. The ease of use and breadth of features make NMAP the most popular port scanner available. NMAP scans ranges or addresses and ports for listening applications. The data returned from NMAP tells you if a system has an application listening on a given port and whether that port is open to accepting new connections. Figure 11-5 shows the options and parameters to use with NMAP.

CAUTION Be careful when you determine where to install and use NetCat and NMAP. Not only are they powerful network utilities, they are also powerful hacker utilities. The unauthorized presence of either application on a system on your network almost certainly means that you have a problem. It is wise to build CSA application control rules to prevent the execution of either of these utilities by unauthorized personnel or systems.

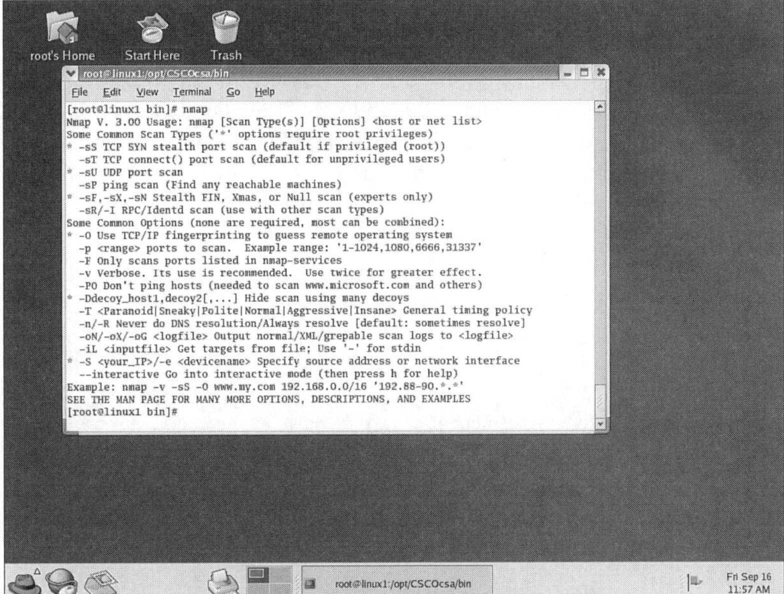

Figure 11-5 *NMAP Options and Parameters*

Agent Troubleshooting Tools

There are several tools, utilities, and log files that are useful for troubleshooting problems with CSA. CSA installs several utilities and creates log file recording information useful for determining what took place. The following sections describe other useful tools included with the operating system and Microsoft SQL Server.

CSA Installed Troubleshooting Tools

CSA installs several diagnostic utilities for troubleshooting problems with agents. The tools vary between Windows and UNIX/Linux but basically give you the same functionality across the platforms.

NOTE The agent installation program does not add the CSA install directory to the path system environment variable. The default installation path on Windows is c:\program files\Cisco Systems\CSAgent and /opt/CSCOcsa on UNIX/Linux. The utilities discussed in the sections that follow are in the bin subdirectory of the agent installation path.

ICCPING.EXE (Windows Only)

ICCPING checks that the CSA MC is reachable from the remote agent machine and confirms that all the proper network ports are open and that the MC is responsive to the agent. ICCPING also tells you the delay or latency between each request and response.

The default path for ICCPING.exe is c:\Program Files\Cisco Systems\CSagent\bin. There is no UNIX or LINUX equivalent to ICCPING because that functionality is present in the CSACTL utility.

When using ICCPING, you can optionally specify the number of ping requests to send and whether or not the traffic should be sent over SSL or not. This is useful to determine if certain ports are filtered across the network or if the MC is not responding to the agent on one port versus another.

The syntax for ICCPING is:

```
iccping webadmin [number of pings] [SSL]
```

If the MC is reachable, you receive success messages similar to the following:

```
C:\Program Files\Cisco Systems\CSAgent\bin>iccping webadmin 4 ssl
Ping[  0] ssl=yes, dst=WWWcgi45, size=4, status=success, time= 1352 ms
Ping[  1] ssl=yes, dst=WWWcgi45, size=4, status=success, time=  320 ms
Ping[  2] ssl=yes, dst=WWWcgi45, size=4, status=success, time=  351 ms
Ping[  3] ssl=yes, dst=WWWcgi45, size=4, status=success, time=  330 ms

Num of failures/4 pings = 0 !!!
```

If ICCPING returns a high ratio of failures to requests (for example, more than three out of ten), you should focus your troubleshooting efforts on network connectivity between the agent and the MC. Also, if ICCPING is able to get responses from the MC over SSL and not over the standard communications port, look at the routers between the hosts for packet filters or access lists that might be the cause of the problems.

RTRFORMAT.EXE

RTRFORMAT reformats trace file into ASCII formatted text that can then be sent to Cisco for analysis. RTRFORMAT requires a trace request (.rtr) file as an input parameter and can also pipe the output of the translation to a file. Otherwise, the output prints to the console.

The syntax for RTRFORMAT.EXE is:

```
rtrformat rtr_file [> output_file]
```

If the agent is active and you choose to pipe the output of RTRFORMAT to a file, make sure to specify a path outside the CSA directory, because CSA itself prevents the creation of the file. Simply stopping the agent service would also suffice.

NOTE The CSA default installation path contains spaces that are not handled by RTRFORMAT correctly. Be sure to put the entire path and filename in quotes. Also, you can stop the agent, copy the RTR file to the CSAgent/bin directory, and output the file locally and then restart the agent service.

Now that you understand how to use RTRFORMAT, you should note that there is not much information in the file that is usable outside the Cisco TAC. There are some keywords and references that can be picked out of the trace output, but for the most part, leave the analysis of trace files to Cisco.

CSACTL for Solaris/Linux

Solaris and Linux use a command-line interface (CLI) to manage the local agent. Although Linux has a GUI, more options are available from the CLI and it gives you access to just as much information. In fact, CSACTL provides a way to poll from the command line, a feature absent in Windows. The default path to CSACTL is /opt/CSCOcsa/bin.

NOTE Remember that when running CSACTL, you might need to prepend "./" if you do not use the absolute path to the program.

An important feature of CSACTL is the ability to generate an event to send to the CSA MC log. You can select the severity level of the event and specify text to store in the event as details.

CSA Diagnostics

CSA installs a diagnostics information-gathering utility in a program group on the Start menu on Windows machines, as shown in Figure 11-6. The agent gathers useful diagnostic information and bundles it into a csa-diagnostics.zip file, which is placed in the Cisco Systems\CSAgent\log directory. There is a great deal of useful information bundled in this file:

- Agent.bundle—This text file includes the original agent version installed on the host, registration ID, CSA MC name, and the IP address of the MC at the time of MC installation, HTTP, HTTPS, and alternate communications ports
- Agent.rul—Rule file (not plain-text readable)
- Agent.state—CSA system state and oser state information with other information from Agent.bundle
- Agent.var—Local CSA variables and query information
- Arp.txt—ARP table entries
- CSAgent-Install.txt—Log of steps taken during agent installation
- Csalog.txt—The csalog log file
- Driver_install.txt—Log file of driver installation events
- Env_vars.txt—System environment variables
- Ipconfig.txt—ipconfig from local agent
- Nbtstat.txt—nbtstat command output
- Netstat.txt—netstat command output
- RTR files—RTR (request trace) files
- Routes.txt—Route print command output
- RuleEngine.state—Diagnostic file (not plain-text readable)
- Sslca—SSL certificate file
- Sysvars.cf—Some CSA-specific control variables

Figure 11-6 *Location of CSA Diagnostics Utility*

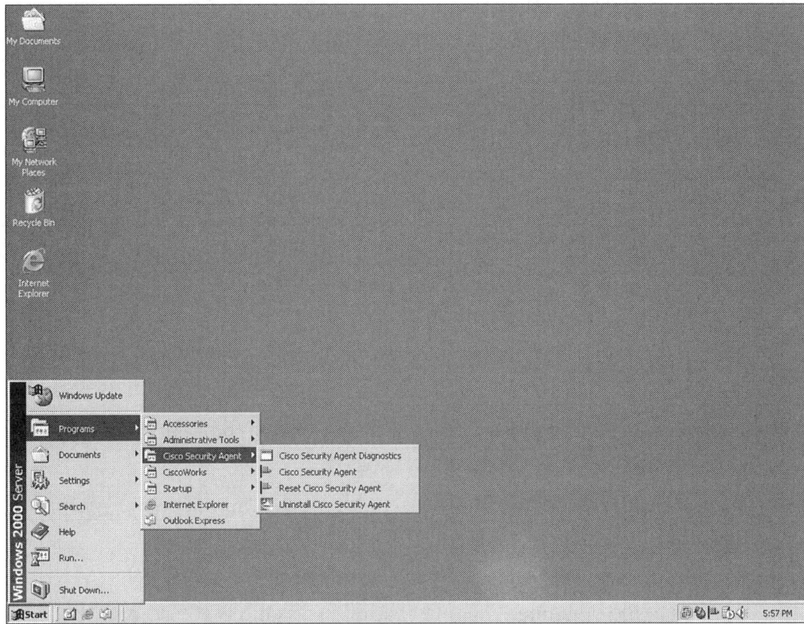

You are prompted when diagnostics are complete, as shown in Figure 11-7. After the diagnostics are complete, send the file to Cisco TAC with your support case notes.

Figure 11-7 *CSA Diagnostics Complete*

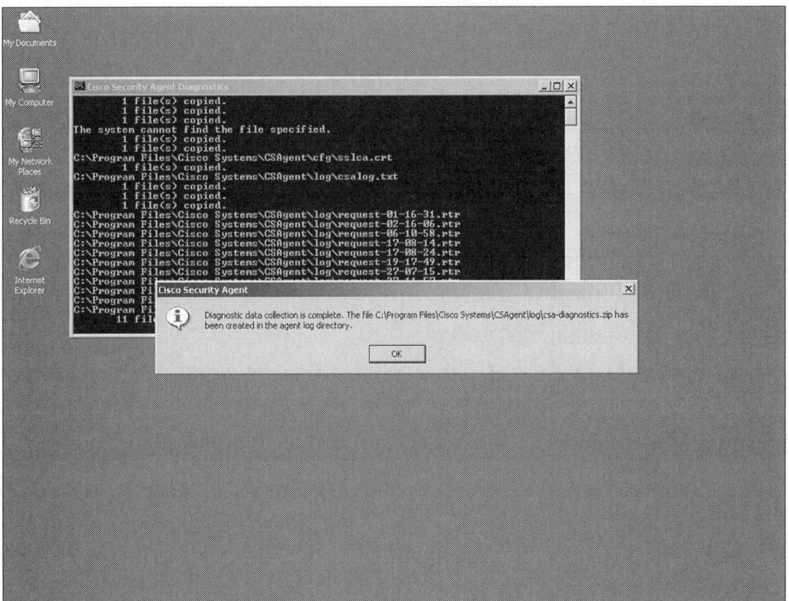

Log Files

CSA creates several log files during installation and later through the course of normal operations. These files include information on installation details and errors, driver installation and registration, events related to the operation of CSA itself, and finally security-related events that are recorded according to the policy applied to the host. These files are located in the agent log subdirectory. The files described are:

- CSAgent-Install.log—This log records the steps taken during agent installation and the results of those actions. This log also records any problems encountered during agent installation. This file is not overwritten during updates or upgrades, but it is appended with information from the newer versions, so that a complete record from the first time installation of the agent is retained.
- csalog.txt—This file contains information about the operation of the agent itself. It does not contain security event-related information. This file is periodically archived.
- csalog???.txt—These files are simply archives of the csalog.txt, where ??? is a version number increasing incrementally from 001.
- driver-install.log—This file lists the steps taken and the information gathered during installation of the network shim.
- securitylog.txt—This is a record of security events as defined by the CSA policies applied to the machine. The information in this file is the same as that logged to the MC.
- request-??-??-??.rtr—Request trace files are machine language files that list events related to agent polling and rules updates.
- *.dmp files—These are dump files written by CSA when a process tries to execute a buffer overflow. The files list the contents of the memory owned by the process and can be analyzed to determine which system call triggered the System API Control rule.

Service Control

If for some reason the machine cannot be rebooted during your troubleshooting efforts, you might need to stop and restart the relevant CSA services. There are many ways of doing this, from both the GUI and command line.

On Windows, the simplest way to stop and start services is via the Services applet found in Administrative Tools. For command-line aficionados, there are no less than three ways to stop CSA from a command prompt.

To stop or start just the agent, either of the following work:

```
net {start ¦ stop} csagent
sc {start ¦ stop} csagent
```

Another method to stop the agent uses the csacontrol executable in the csagent\bin directory.

To stop the agent:

```
csacontrol -c e -t c
```

To start the agent:

```
csacontrol -c s -t c
```

NOTE Simply run csacontrol.exe without any parameters and a popup window displays all the parameters and their functions.

UNIX and Linux systems use the **ciscosec** command to stop and start the agent service. **Ciscosec** has a single parameter with two possible values: start and stop.

SQL Troubleshooting

SQL Server 2000 with Service Pack 3a stores all the event data and configuration for all groups, policies, and other objects used by CSA. Most security analysts and administrators are not database administrators and are not familiar with the concepts and tasks required to maintain a database of any size. Although CSA administration and maintenance does not require high-level DBA skills, it helps to be familiar with some of the basic tasks and troubleshooting concepts of SQL Server.

NOTE SQL Server is used mainly for large-scale CSA deployments. MSDE is used as the database for small (under 500 hosts) deployments and does not have the suite of SQL Server utilities.

SQL Server Basics

An effective CSA administrator does not need advanced skills to manage SQL Server, but a basic understanding helps. Performing basic queries and tuning server settings are about the most complicated database tasks you have to complete. Knowing how to check that SQL Server is accessible by other applications is also valuable.

Basic Queries

Basic queries performed against SQL Server provide important information. First, they demonstrate that SQL Server runs and responsive. Second, they list the data in the selected table or tables. Finally, they display the time the query took, so that you can judge the performance of the SQL Server.

SQL Server has two primary interfaces for performing basic queries:

- The SQL Enterprise Manager—The SQL Enterprise Manager shows administrators all databases and allows administrators to make changes to databases and the settings of the server itself. The GUI is friendly (by database standards) and easy to use. Running a query from Enterprise Manager is as simple as right-clicking on a table and returning either all rows or a selected number of rows from the beginning of the table.
- The SQL Query Analyzer Tool—The SQL Query Analyzer tool is basically an enhanced CLI for the inner workings of SQL Server. The Query Analyzer is more powerful than the Enterprise Manager, but not nearly as easy to use.

  To run a simple query from the Query Analyzer, select the CSA database (the default database name is CSAMC45), and then enter the query in the query window. The statement used to perform the query is the SQL SELECT statement.

  The syntax for SELECT is:

  ```
  select * from "tablename"
  ```

Figure 11-8 shows the Query Analyzer and output from a select query.

Figure 11-8 *SQL Query Analyzer*

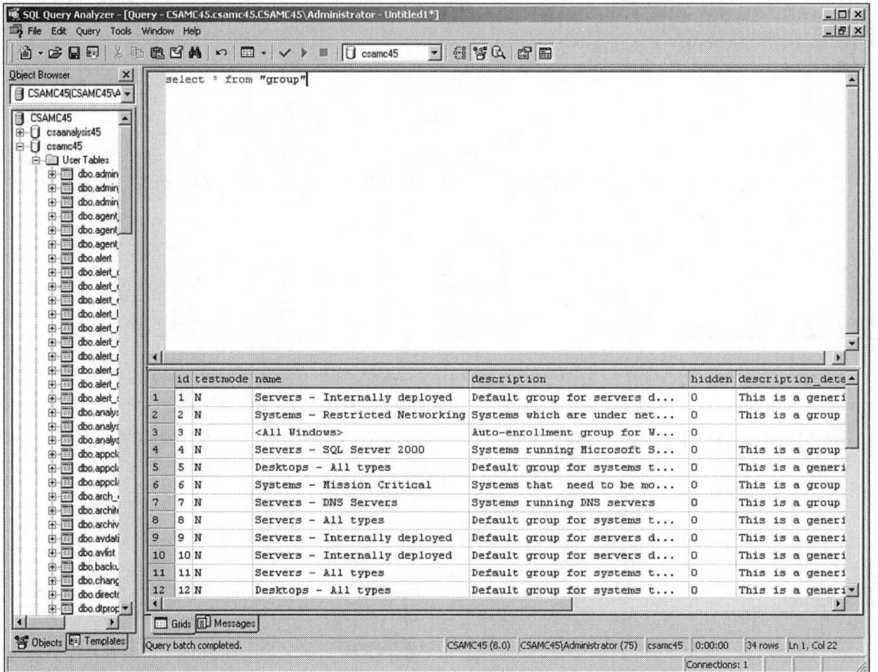

You need to put the table name in quotes. The results of the query are displayed in the lower window in Query Analyzer.

Processor Utilization

SQL Server is a resource-intensive application and can consume all the available resources on a host by itself. Performance problems on single-server CSA MC implementations are not uncommon. High-processor utilization is often realized in the form of performance problems and generally sluggish response of the server. Windows Task Manager is useful to determine what process uses most of the processing capacity of the machine and the total-processor utilization of all processes.

You can configure SQL Server to use single or multiple processors. If CSA is installed on a single server with four or more processors, you can enhance performance by allowing SQL Server to use only two of the processors and reserving the other processors for CSA application processes and tasks. Figure 11-9 shows the processor tab of the SQL Server properties.

Figure 11-9 *SQL Server Processor Settings*

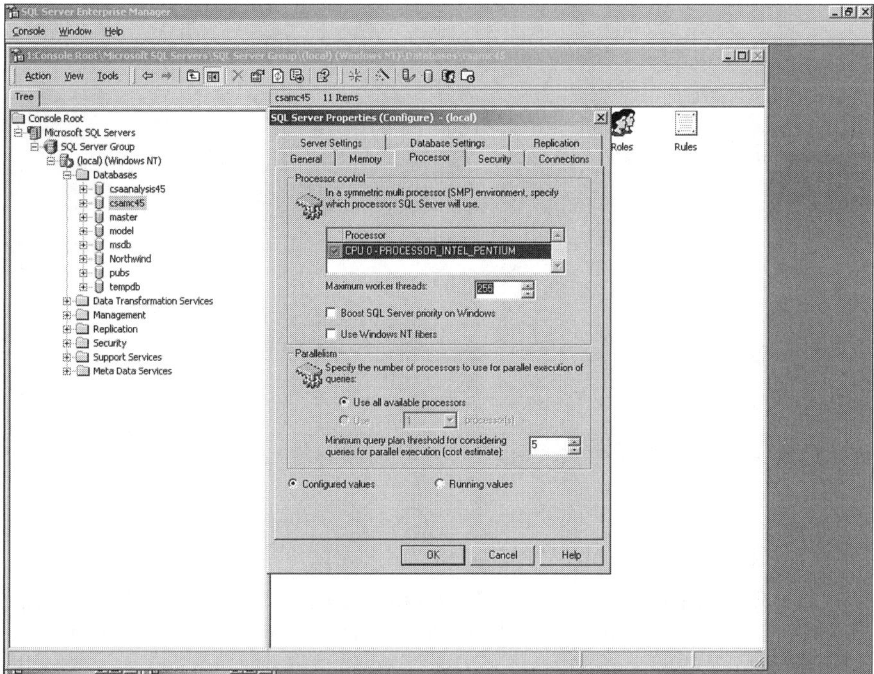

Memory

Early versions of SQL Server required administrators to set the amount of memory reserved for SQL Server and any changes required reboot to take effect. SQL Server 2000 can dynamically tune memory usage and reservation and generally does a good job of it, but tweaking the settings can still yield performance increases. On large servers running CSA and SQL Server, be sure to reserve at least 1 Gigabyte of memory for Windows and CSA applications, and let SQL Server use the rest. In most cases, SQL Server uses only what it needs, but it is wise to set a limit so that any large or complex queries or database operations do not use all the machine's memory. Figure 11-10 is the Memory tab of the SQL Server properties.

Figure 11-10 *SQL Server Memory Settings*

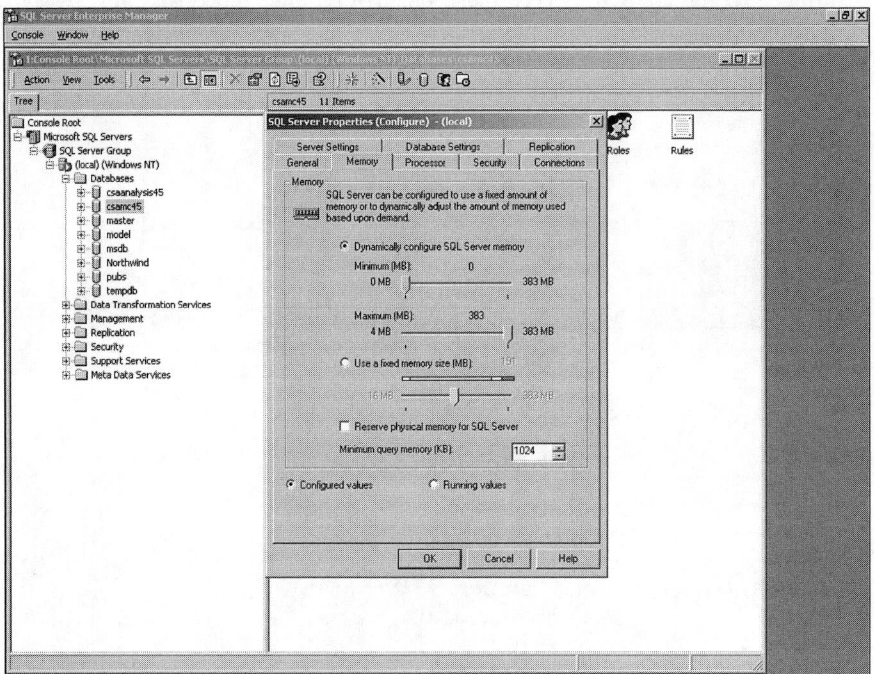

ODBC Connection to Remote Database Server

Open Database Connectivity (ODBC) is the interface CSA uses to access SQL Server. ODBC connections are accessed through the Administrative Tools menu on the server. The CSA setup routine configures the ODBC connection to the SQL Server automatically using the information you provide.

The CSA MC does not work at all if the database connection is broken. Use the ODBC applet to test database connectivity and change configuration settings if needed. The ODBC configuration applet is wizard-based and clicking **Next** and accepting the defaults should take you to the final step where the database connection can be tested. Figure 11-11 shows the System DSN tab of the Data Sources Administrative Tools applet.

Figure 11-11 *System DSN List*

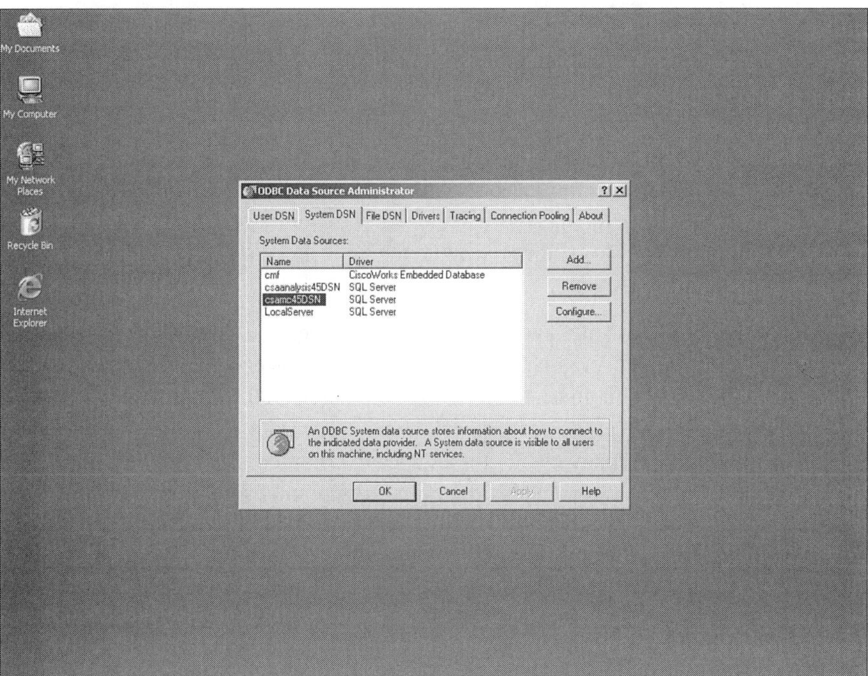

Deleting Events and Shrinking Database Size

One of the advantages of storing all CSA information in a single database is the simplicity of having all configuration and event information in one place. However, a drawback is that the database can become large and fragmented because of the way that information is written to and deleted from the files. New events are typically written to the end of the database. Old events are stored closer to the beginning of the file. Configuration changes also mix up the order of the data pages in the database. As old or unimportant events are deleted from the database, holes form in the file. These holes, or unallocated pages, sit in the middle of the file and the file does not shrink. The database file stays the same size because SQL Server does not automatically return this space to the file system. Performance becomes sluggish as the system has to search for data in a file that is unnecessarily large and fragmented.

Large, fragmented databases perform poorly, so to keep your CSA MC in top shape, the database needs to be defragmented just like a hard drive. Pruning and deleting events from the database fragment the file more than any other activity. The SQL Server tool DBCC (Database Consistency Checker) defragments the database file and also shrinks the file to the smallest size possible to store all the data.

Pruning Events from the Database

Events are written to the database as they occur in a continuous stream. The database stores these events in the order they reach the MC. Events are written chronologically and are not sorted or grouped by host, group, policy, and so on. As you perform queries on hosts or rules, SQL Server searches through all the events looking for a match. Sometimes the events are grouped together in the database coincidentally because they occurred at about the same time. However, it is more likely that the events are distributed throughout the table, and the database has to read each row in the table and either include that row in the results or ignore it and move on.

Although this sounds like a lot of work, SQL Server was designed specifically for these types of tasks. However, a large amount of data can overwhelm SQL Server, making the performance very sluggish. As the file grows larger, SQL Server has that much more data to sift through. Queries and reports take longer accordingly. In some extreme cases, the database stores too many events for a query to complete before the timeout. The Status Summary page might not display the event graphs and event filters, and event sets can also stop working. This occurs because SQL Server spends too much time trying to search through the data, build the result set, and present the result set to the CSA MC application.

To speed up the searches and to keep the database tidy, older and unimportant events should be regularly deleted. By creating and scheduling event log management tasks, events are purged from the database. This helps keep SQL Server from searching through too many events when a query is run.

NOTE Be sure to follow the regulations and guidelines for your specific industry when you delete data and events from the database. Some industry regulations, such as those governing security at financial institutions, might have a minimum amount of time that security event data must be retained before it is purged. If so, you can use data warehousing techniques to move old events out of the active CSA database to keep the file size down while retaining these events for future inspection in an offline or archival system.

DBCC Shrinkfile

Simply deleting old events fixes only part of the problem with database size and performance. Although they do not cause the SQL Server application to sort as much data, the holes in the database mentioned earlier, force SQL Server to search through and skip over unallocated or empty portions of the database during queries.

Another problem is availability of space on the volume storing the database. If the file grows to fill the volume so that there is no space left, the database crashes, and so does the CSA application. At that point, you either have to delete data from the database manually, or move the database to a larger volume. Neither option is much fun.

After deleting data from the database, the free space needs to be returned to the file system. Sometimes this free space at the end and the database is truncated, lopping off the end and giving those blocks back to the file system. More likely, the free space is sprinkled throughout the entire database.

DBCC SHRINKFILE rearranges the data in the database, filling the holes left by deleted rows in the tables and truncates the database file. DBCC is run from the SQL Query Analyzer and has several parameters. SHRINKFILE itself is an option of the DBCC command and requires several parameters. The simplest method to use DBCC SHRINKFILE is to use the filename and target size parameters.

DBCC SHRINKFILE syntax is as follows:

```
dbcc shrinkfile (filename,target_size)
```

The database filename is the logical name of the file in the database, not the physical database filename on the disk. This has nothing to do with the name of the mdf file stored on the system. Look at the database properties to determine the logical filename; however, the filename is almost always csamc45.

The target size parameter specifies the desired size of the database at the completion of the operation. The file size is always large enough to store all the data, so do not worry about using too low a number. For example, the current file size is 10 Gigabytes, but only 8 Gigabytes of data are in the file because of unallocated space left over from data deletion. Running a shrinkfile with a target size of six shrinks the file to 8 Gigabytes. This safety mechanism prevents unintended data deletion and corruption. Figure 11-12 shows the DBCC SHRINKFILE syntax and output from a successful execution.

Figure 11-12 *DBCC Shrinkfile Syntax and Output*

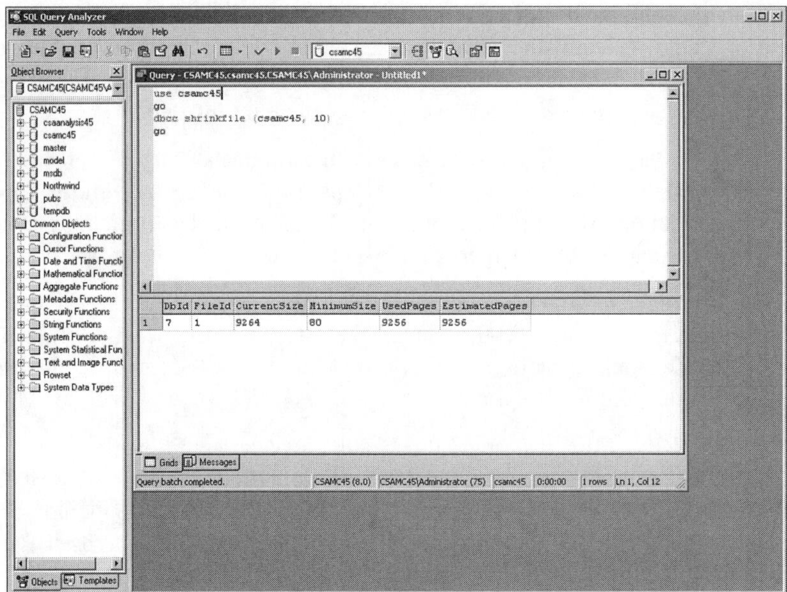

NOTE More information on DBCC and other Transact-SQL statements can be found at http://msdn.microsoft.com.

Cisco TAC

If all else fails, call for reinforcements. The Cisco TAC handles support calls for all Cisco products and services. When you call TAC, a case is opened and a priority is assigned to the case. Priority 1 cases (system down or unusable) are handled first and most often are opened via phone. Priority 2 cases (system barely usable) are also usually opened via phone. Priority 3 and 4 cases (severe inconvenience or inconvenience or question) are opened and resolved most easily at the Cisco website.

When opening a case, make sure that you have several key pieces of information. Keeping this information handy in case of problems is wise because the TAC is able to help you resolve your problem faster and will not have to look the information up in the support database. The following is a list of vital information to have available:

- CCO ID—This is the Cisco Connection Online ID that you use to log in to the Cisco website to download updates.
- Smartnet account or contract number—Smartnet is the Cisco support and maintenance mechanism and is purchased as a separate item from any other services or products. Smartnet is a support subscription service that is renewed annually.
- Phone number—In case you are on the phone with a TAC engineer and the call is disconnected unintentionally, the TAC engineer needs a way to reconnect with you immediately to continue working to resolve the issue.
- Any information that is relevant to the problem—You would be amazed at how many users call for support without doing any research into the problem. Gather all information about the problem that you can before the call so that you do not waste time during the call and can be more effective at solving the problem.

When in doubt (and you have Smartnet), call TAC if there is a problem that you cannot solve. The engineers work with you until the problem is resolved, and you almost always learn something new about the product. When you encounter a problem, be aware that you are probably not the first to encounter this particular issue and TAC engineers have access to internal documents and other support cases and resolutions. Even if you are the first to encounter an issue, TAC can help because they have access to the CSA developers and are able to troubleshoot much deeper than an end user typically can.

Open Priority 1 and 2 cases by calling 1-800-553-2447. These cases can also be opened online at http://www.cisco.com/go/support. Priority 3 and 4 cases are often handled most easily online as well.

licensing@cisco.com

The licensing desk at Cisco handles all licensing issues for CSA (and any other Cisco product). From personnel experience, the license desk is responsive and helpful, provided you have all the proper information, such as support contract number, order number, and so on. A simple e-mail to licensing@cisco.com takes care of replacing a missing or corrupt license file and other problems associated with licensing. The only licensing problem that they cannot easily solve occurs when you run out of host licenses, and then deleting hosts or buying more licenses is the only solution.

Summary

CSA is a complex application with a lot of pieces, but solid troubleshooting practices can be applied to solve most issues. Follow a logical approach, make one change at a time, and make notes about your troubleshooting steps as you go. Use all the network tools and logs that are available to you. Often, a text file or log contains all you need to know about the issue and how to resolve it. Remember that CSA relies on your network infrastructure. As with other applications, the faults or failures of your network infrastructure can affect the operation of CSA.

Do not forget the fundamentals of troubleshooting just because CSA is new and complex. Tech support first asks everyone, "Is it plugged in?" for a reason. Check the basics.

Finally, call for help if you need it. The Cisco TAC is capable and usually quick to respond. After all, you did pay extra for support, right?

APPENDIX **A**

Best Practices Deployment Guidelines

The main portion of this text discusses the technical management of Cisco Security Agent (CSA). Successful deployment of CSA requires a solid technical understanding of CSA, and support from management, server administrators, and users are as important. Management has to support the CSA implementation team, and the users and server administrators must understand the goals of the CSA implementation, or users will encounter considerable friction during the deployment.

Although most technical professionals hate to see this, in a large organization the political aspects of a CSA deployment can sometimes be more important than the technical details. CSA is inherently limiting to your users and administrators, and your general user base is probably not pleased with anything that limits them, even if it does increase system stability and operating efficiency. Good communication throughout the deployment is key to success with your users and management and getting everyone on your side. You will have a smooth deployment if you keep these issues in mind throughout the project. This appendix covers the following functions:

- Gathering the information needed for a successful CSA deployment
- Conducting an orderly pilot or trial of CSA
- Deploying the agent in Test mode to the general deployment scope
- Switching the general population from Test mode to protect mode
- Maintaining and supporting CSA as an ongoing process

Overview

What does a CSA implementation entail? The short answer is—it depends. It depends on the size of the organization, the security posture that the organization has adopted, the value of the assets to be protected, and the diversity of those assets. A small organization can deploy CSA to a few servers and desktops in a few weeks. The authors of this book have worked on large deployments that have taken close to a year.

In a perfect world, CSA simply enforces the procedures already in place within an organization. The users are security conscious and can be counted on to choose wisely when prompted. In addition, all applications follow best practices with respect to security of the host system. Buffer overflows never happen. Tuning CSA is easy because the default policies correctly handle every application behavior.

In a perfect world, CSA would not be necessary. However, a new virus is released every day, users manage to install new spyware and applications that monopolize resources faster than you can identify them, and, thanks to the connected nature of the modern world, bad guys are trying to get access to your network and systems 24 hours a day.

Having read Chapters 1–11, you already understand how CSA works and the protections it provides. This appendix describes a sample deployment plan. This deployment plan covers each of the steps and concerns that need to be addressed with a CSA deployment of any size. Most CSA deployments take time and are broken into six well-defined phases. The authors would be hard-pressed to name a rushed CSA deployment that was successful when phases were skipped.

Remember that security is a process not a product. CSA does not change that. It enforces the process and greatly enhances operational security, but security is not a destination. Bearing that in mind, CSA tuning does not end when the deployment phase is over. As applications are upgraded and new applications are installed, CSA must be adjusted because CSA shifts from deployment to operational maintenance mode.

As previously mentioned, a successful CSA deployment goes through six phases. This scenario discusses five. Phase 0—determining the need for CSA—is assumed to be complete.

NOTE Several good documents on the Cisco website help make the business case for CSA. These non-technical white papers explain the value of CSA, and another paper explains the Return on Investment (ROI) for CSA and effectively justifies the costs of CSA to management. You can find these documents at http://www.cisco.com/go/csa.

Gathering Information

Throughout this entire phase, CSA does not need to be touched. Because CSA can potentially control almost every action of every host on your network, a good deal of information needs to be discovered and gathered before any agents are deployed.

However, you do need a good working knowledge of the capabilities of CSA and what it does. As you gather this information, think about how you can use it to plan the deployment. Determine which parts of the written Security Policy CSA will enforce. Make a list of past security incidents that CSA could help you avoid. Create an inventory of systems CSA will protect. Most importantly, state your goals using well-defined criteria.

Security Policy

First, dust off your organization's Security Policy. The Security Policy is most likely a framework document that references specific child policies and procedures, such as an Acceptable Use Policy and incident handling procedures. All security policies are different, but they can be summarized to specify several lists of:

- Actions that are always forbidden
- Consequences of forbidden actions
- Actions that are permitted, but require approval and the approval process
- Actions that are always permitted

The preceding list is compiled from all the documents that make up the Security Policy. The following section discusses the most important of these documents

NOTE If you do not have written security policies, there are many standard or generic policies that serve as a great starting point. Go to http://www.sans.org/resources/policies for a comprehensive selection of sample policies that can be modified to fit almost any organization's needs.

Acceptable Use Policy

The Acceptable Use Policy specifies what end user initiated actions are allowed or prohibited on any of the systems under the jurisdiction of the Security Policy. Usually, this policy simply states something like, "All systems should be used only for approved business purposes." That statement can be a guiding principle for the policy, but it is useless on its own. This policy should list specific actions or behaviors that are explicitly prohibited and might also list specific allowable actions.

A good example of a specific action is listening to music on a workstation. Most modern workstations are equipped with sound cards, speakers, and media player applications. Some organizations do not allow users to play music on their PCs. Others might allow the user to listen to music on a CD, but do not allow the user to copy the music to the hard drive or connect to any streaming music sources.

Whatever your organization's position on listening to music and other actions taken by end users, the Acceptable Use Policy should be specific about what is allowed and denied. Most policies have a clause stating that the security administrator must approve anything questionable.

Security Problems

Every organization has security problems that worry the information security staff. Some organizations have strict controls on every device but still feel vulnerable to day-zero attacks. Others are not in such a good position and have to worry about these types of situations: critical data transferred using cleartext protocols, unused and vulnerable services running on most servers, and every user being a local administrator of every PC. All organizations have security needs that CSA can address. List problems that you have had that CSA could prevent. Also make a list of ways in which CSA can help you with actions your organization has been unable to address in the past, such as copying data to USB storage devices.

Past Incidents

A good place to start assessing your current security needs and requirements is to look at previous problems. CSA is often deployed because of a specific incident. Lots of organizations have security incidents, such as denial of service (DoS) attacks against web servers and virus outbreaks.

Calculate Single Loss Occurrence Costs

Determine how much revenue is lost because the network is down or degraded. It is prudent to classify different levels of disruption to help gauge the costs. For example, a total network outage can cost your organization $150,000 per hour, whereas a degraded network might cost only $15,000 per hour.

Calculate ALE Costs

The Annual Loss Expectancy (ALE) is how much revenue an organization can expect to lose over the course of a year. It is computed by simply multiplying the Single Loss Occurrence (SLO) by the number of events expected to happen during the year.

To get a truly comprehensive understanding of the ALE, calculate the value for each level of SLO. This is important because each level of disruption has a different likelihood. Then add each of the individual ALEs together to get the overall ALE for the organization.

This information is useful to show the value of CSA to the organization.

Ongoing Issues

Make a list of other problems that CSA can fix. These can be intentional actions by users that are not malicious, but are simply counterproductive.

For example, support costs are reduced because users no longer fill their hard drives with music or videos or install weather monitor applications that tax slow wide-area network (WAN) links.

Inventory

You have a much better chance of successfully protecting your assets if you know what they are. When taking inventory, gather lists of hosts you want to protect, the applications those hosts run, and how critical those hosts and applications are to your business.

Classify Critical Assets

Identify the organization's high-value assets. These can be computers supporting a critical business process or even data in the form of files or databases. This information should already exist in your organization's Disaster Recovery Plan and Business Continuity Plan. (If you do not have either of these plans, developing them should be your organization's next project.)

Applications Used

Look at the applications that support your critical business process. Examine the function of the applications and how they should normally operate. Make a list of normal operating procedures and how the application works. Start with the following list:

- What are the primary executables used by the application?
- Where does the application write files to the system?
- Does the application access the registry?
- What remote systems does the application communicate with and on what ports?

Number and Type of Agents

This step is critical to determine costs for CSA support, Cisco Security Agent Management Console (CSA MC) server sizing, and licensing costs. The CSA documentation contains guidelines for the type and number of CSA MC servers that are appropriate for the number of agents deployed. It is a good idea to exceed the server requirements listed in the specifications. Hardware is inexpensive compared to numerous things, including the cost of CSA licensing, the frustration of a poorly performing CSA MC, and the time it takes for rule generation.

Knowing the number of agents to be deployed is also critical for licensing purposes. When the installed license limit is reached, no more agents can register with the server and those hosts are unprotected. Although it is expensive, it is a good idea to purchase some amount of extra licensing. As machines are reimaged and retired, some agents are inactive, and those inactive agents can prevent hosts that are in use from registering with the MC.

Determine Goals

If you do not know your objectives, you do not know if you reach them. Define goals that are meaningful and measurable. A meaningful goal is: to protect the network from day-zero attacks, prohibit unauthorized processes and data transmission, and increase system stability. This clearly states an easily understood and important objective of CSA deployment, but the stated objective is not readily measured.

An example of an objective statement that is both a meaningful and measurable goal is: to reduce downtime and lost revenue through the implementation of CSA. Management loves simple and clear statements like this—non-technical and promising tangible benefits.

Of course, a statement such as the previous example is vague and does a technical implementation team absolutely no good, but it does get your team political support from management. Your technical objectives are discussed in further detail in the following sections; they should be specific and technical.

Applications/Systems/Processes Protected

There are two main criteria to keep in mind when selecting which applications and systems CSA should protect: the value of those applications and systems to your business and how easily exploited applications and systems can cause interruptions on your network and truly critical systems and processes to fail. Some applications or systems in your organization might not be worth the time and expense to secure them with CSA. Determine what level or importance is the threshold for CSA protection. However, other noncritical processes, such as a brochure-ware website running on an unprotected server, can be compromised in such a way that they can take down all other business operations on the network.

It might be that your goal is threefold: to install CSA on every host in the environment, to protect all applications to a basic degree, and to ensure that critical applications have special protections from specially crafted policies. You might not have the time or money to install CSA on all your hosts and tune policies. If that is the case, carefully choose which hosts and applications are protected by CSA with regard to value and vulnerability.

Organizational Impact

The organizational impact felt by a CSA implementation is different for every organization. Organizations that follow rigid processes and do everything according to written policies should not experience much impact, but most organizations experience some pains caused by CSA. Unless your organization is in need of radical change, your goal should be to minimize the negative impact experienced throughout and after a CSA deployment. Of course, the positive impact of fewer security incidents should be maximized.

Many of the problems that users and server administrators complain about occur when the written Security Policy is not followed. CSA forbids prohibited activities from taking place, such as a server administrator running an rsh daemon on a server for easy administration or a user installing application upgrades from the Internet before the proper support mechanisms for the new application are in place at the helpdesk.

This is a good place to note that management needs to be aware that problems caused by CSA, although sometimes real, are often greatly exaggerated. Explain that CSA is powerful and monitors and regulates all processes on a host, and CSA sometimes blocks legitimate actions because that activity looks suspicious. Because CSA is powerful and flexible and few people within an organization understand what CSA does, it is a convenient explanation of anything out of the ordinary.

In the early stages of one deployment, one of the authors was informed that CSA caused approximately 1500 users located across 20 branch offices throughout four states to be totally down and unable to access any network applications or data. Management was upset that this new software, which had been installed to prevent such problems, was actually the cause of a large outage. After a brief investigation, the actual problem was identified as name resolution configuration on two workstations and the other 1500 users and workstation were unaffected and operating as normal. Be prepared to defend CSA from the blame of every glitch on the network. Sometimes CSA does cause problems, but careful planning helps prevent them.

Patch Cycle Extension

CSA gives IT organizations more time to test patches for compatibility issues with applications. The manufacturer often rushes the latest security patches out the door with little testing for real-world application interaction. Sometimes the cure is worse than the disease.

Lengthening the patch cycle has many intangible benefits; the time to perform thorough testing is probably the most important. Another benefit to your organization is the ability to schedule a time when patches are applied on your terms, rather than as they are released. Setting a schedule also makes the lives of the server administrators who have to apply the patches easier, because they will not be expected to apply patches for vulnerabilities during maintenance windows with little notice.

System Stability

Organizations using CSA properly enjoy increased system stability and worry less about day-zero attacks and incidents. Increased system stability leads to greater revenue and profitability for your organization, and it also helps you at performance review time.

As described in Chapter 8, "Basic Policy," the goals of information security are confidentiality, integrity, and availability (CIA). The objective of all security measures is the CIA Triad. Stability is assured by making sure that the three pillars of information security are upheld.

Specific Vulnerabilities

Another technical goal might be to protect against a specific vulnerability present in your systems. If you want CSA to protect against something like buffer overflow vulnerabilities in a specific application, make sure you state that in your project goals and that you test it. Again, look to problems that you had in the past to create a list of specific vulnerabilities that you want CSA to cover.

Pilot Phase

The pilot phase of a CSA deployment provides you the chance to gather information on how CSA performs in your environment and starts to give you some insight into what the full deployment requires. Another benefit of the pilot phase often overlooked is the political aspect of a CSA deployment. If you can show management that systems in the CSA pilot deployment were protected from attacks and had greater uptime than systems outside of the pilot, you are likely to receive positive support from management as the project progresses.

Determine Scope

Determining the scope of systems to be protected and what those systems are protected from is the single most important task of the pilot phase. A poorly planned and defined scope is the most likely weakness that can doom the rest of the project because this phase will probably not be successful. *This cannot be overstated.*

Poor results from the project pilot cause the CSA general deployment to lose support from management and from those who will manage and use the systems protected by CSA.

Define the scope and get the project team and all stakeholders to agree to it. After that is finished, nothing outside of the scope exists for the CSA pilot deployment. Certainly, extreme circumstances such as a virus outbreak or some other catastrophic network event can cause the reevaluation of the scope, but when changing the project scope, make sure that everyone involved understands the risks.

Pilot Applications

If the scope of the *general* deployment includes all systems and applications, simply choose a representative sample of all workstations and servers for the pilot scope. If only certain applications or processes are protected, several workstations and servers should be chosen that are integral to the function of those applications.

Pilot Systems

If available, Development, QA, or Disaster Recovery environments can run CSA to give you an idea of how systems behave with and react to CSA in your production environment. If an enterprise-wide deployment of CSA is planned, choose a representative sample of servers and workstations on which to install CSA for the pilot phase of the project. It is often a good idea to choose the workstations used by department managers, so that they can explain to you the tasks that the department carries out and any issues that arise from CSA deployment.

Determine Conditions

To get an honest evaluation of CSA in your environment, do not choose conditions that influence the results either way. Choosing to test only static workstations and servers used by expert users makes CSA seem like a breeze to implement. On the other hand, choosing to test CSA on a poorly written application that rarely works correctly on the best of days can create an unfair impression. At best, CSA might appear ineffective and at worst detrimental to your environment.

User Agent Interaction

Most organizations disable agent-user interaction because they simply do not trust the general user population to make wise or correct choices when prompted by the agent. This prevents your users from making bad choices, but requires you to spend more time tuning the policies to allow suspicious but benign activities. If you cannot decide what to do with this, you can probably determine whether to allow or disallow Agent UI interaction early in the pilot because of the number of helpdesk calls generated, user complaints, or other information that you gather from reviewing the logs.

NOTE Create a policy that allows user interaction to administrators or members of a specific group and does not allow interaction to other users through the use of user-state sets.

Allow User to Stop Agent

During the pilot, it is useful to allow the user to stop the agent on servers or workstations. There might be situations where critical business processes are interrupted, and at this point, allowing users to stop CSA and determine whether CSA is the cause of the issues is valuable. Because CSA is so powerful and controlling, stopping CSA is a good troubleshooting step. At the least, you know if the issue persists—whether CSA is active or inactive—and that is important.

Remember that an event is logged at the CSA MC whenever an agent is stopped. This also gives you, as the CSA administrator, a feel for how likely it is that users try to stop the agent and how often. In many cases, lack of control and fear of the unknown make CSA a convenient scapegoat for any issues on a system, and because of that, administrators will probably stop CSA as a basic troubleshooting step.

Determine if allowing users to stop CSA will be an issue for your organization and create a process and procedure that specifies when this is and is not allowed. Most administrators do not remember (or desire) to restart CSA after the issue has been resolved or when CSA is no longer suspected of causing the original issues. Therefore, remember to add a statement in the procedure that relates to restarting CSA after troubleshooting is complete.

NOTE It is a good practice to use user-state sets to enable only administrators, power users, or other select user groups the ability to interact with and stop the agent.

Interval and Polling Hints

For the pilot phase, it is advantageous to use poll hints on all groups and shorten the polling interval. Because the number of machines in this phase is small, the network is not adversely affected and policy changes are rolled out rapidly.

Lengthen the polling interval and be more selective about poll hints as the project proceeds to general deployment. Large distributed networks with slow WAN links can experience network contention issues with too many agents polling too often. Also, sending poll hints to all agents can, in effect, cause a DoS attack against your internal WAN if all distributed machines use all bandwidth as they try to poll and download new agent policies. Business-critical traffic can potentially be excluded from the network by CSA administrative traffic.

Create the CSA Base Policy

Decide which policies you want to use for the initial pilot deployment. The default policies are a great place to start. Of course, you will use policies such as the Virus Scanner policy and Operating System-Base Protection policies. You should, however, look at other policies as well—the Instant Messenger policy and Document Security policy. These policies might not be appropriate for all machines, but look at the rules and determine if there is any benefit to applying these rules to some group or groups of hosts.

The default policies attached to the default groups that you are likely to use provide an excellent starting point for policy creation and customization. However, some of the rules in these policies might be too restrictive for your environment, especially if Agent User Interaction is disabled. For example, web browsers saving PDF files to the desktop query the user for approval, and this action is denied if user interaction is not allowed.

It is worth the time to start building some exception policies and modules to allow these suspicious but legitimate actions. Other exception policies that you might want to build are policies for applications, such as Microsoft Systems Management Server (SMS) or any other systems management or operations software.

NOTE At this point, it is good to develop a naming convention to be used on all groups, policies, modules, application classes, and variables that you create. This saves time later. Appending or prepending your organization's name or initials is useful to help distinguish your policies from Cisco policies.

Deploy Agents in Test Mode

The safest way to begin deploying CSA is in Test mode. As you recall, Test mode logs actions that would have been denied, but takes no protective measures. Build an agent kit that attaches the host to all the appropriate default and any custom groups you might have created, and also the Systems-Test Mode group.

Create a Communication Plan

Your users and server administrators need to know what kind of information you need for the rule tuning and how to reach you to address urgent issues that they might think have been caused by CSA. This communication plan not only tells them how to reach you, but what kind of information to have on hand when they call. Helpful information includes who was logged in at the time, the time the event occurred, what application was running, and what the user tried to do. Armed with this information, you can decipher the logs more easily. Any issues that you run into make more sense if you have this background information.

Build Groups

CSA groups can be based on geographic or physical location, department, host function, or any combination of that and other factors. Try to create and use as few groups as possible because maintenance and finding hosts within the system is easier and rule generation completes faster. Use the default groups, such as Desktops-All Types and Servers-All Types, and create your own groups, such as Servers-ABC Corp. Attach all exception policies to the groups, that you create and leave the default groups and policies alone.

Build Agent Kits

For the pilot, the agent kits you build might not be quiet installations or force reboots. Because you are dealing with a slightly different and more informed user population who have agreed to take part in the pilot, if the kits are installed manually you may want to allow your "test subjects" to see what happens on their systems to make them feel included and to gain more support. If an automated process installs the kits, a quiet install is best. Whether or not to force a reboot at the completion of installation or install the agent shim is best left to your discretion and the knowledge you have of your organization.

Install Agents

After the groups are created, the agent kits built, and the rules generated, all that is left for this step is to install the agents. Login scripts are a popular way to install the agent. If you use login scripts, it is best to force a reboot at the completion of the installation because the user has just logged in and cannot be too involved in any application or other work.

NOTE Most security-conscious organizations have trained their users not to go to websites and click on links received via email. Some users actually follow this advice. In this case, a manual installation is not likely to cover all your users.

The only way to be certain of the deployment of all the machines in your pilot scope is to use an automated installation process. Allow your pilot users a reasonable period of time to manually install the agent, and if the agent is not installed at the end of that period, discuss with the user whether that host will remain in scope or schedule an automated installation. You might have to amend the scope accordingly, but it is best to try to keep that host included in the pilot if a full general deployment is your goal.

Test Applications and Review Logs

Now that the agent is running in Test mode on the hosts, perform a full battery of tests against the applications running on that host. Try every function and option that is reasonable. Look at the logs on the CSA MC to see what actions ran against an applied policy. Build exceptions for legitimate actions that the applied policies would block.

Create Basic Exception Policies, Modules, and Rules

You need to create exceptions that are evident from the first boot of host systems after the installation of the agent. For example, processes such as mouse and multimedia or special function keyboard drivers appear to be trapping keystrokes, when they are simply monitoring for a combination of hotkeys to be pressed. Build exceptions for these things, so that events that require your attention are not covered up by all these benign events.

The first time you build an exception for a group use the Exception Wizard because it automatically builds the policy, module, and rule, and attaches each one correctly. When using the wizard, build the exception policy based on a custom group that you create for your organization. Doing this makes the rules more easily identifiable. In addition, the rules are retained with the custom group when the CSA MC is updated with newer versions. This issue is discussed in greater detail later in this appendix.

After that, it pays to be able to build exceptions manually, so that the rules can have wildcards where appropriate, and you understand exactly what the exception does. Even though the wizard allows you to modify the rule before it is saved, in most cases, it is easier to create the rule manually from the beginning. With practice, you will find it is actually faster than using the wizard.

Test Applications

Now that the basic system and driver exceptions are built and out of the way, put your applications through their paces with a full battery of system tests. Make an application test plan that details all the commonly used and critical functions of your applications. Test the application according to your plan and make exceptions when needed.

Most office or productivity applications require little tuning. You might need to build some system API control rules to allow buffer overflows in some applications, but these applications generally do not do anything that CSA would find suspicious. Systems management and operations applications are different. These applications require indepth tuning and testing because many of the functions of these applications are in direct violation of some of the default rules. Automated software distribution applications, such as Patchlink or WinInstall, exhibit virus-like behavior to CSA and many of the actions that they take, such as writing to the registry or system directories, are flagged by CSA while in Test mode.

Review Logs

In addition to looking at the logs during application testing, take time to inspect in detail the logs captured over several days or a week. Other applications that you did not test might have caused a warning or alert event, or system backups might cause log events when trying to back up CSA itself on some of your servers. When reviewing the logs, take advantage of the filter options. Filter out duplicates, so that you do not see the same event repeatedly and can see different events that might require exceptions.

Another log review technique is to view the top 10 active hosts and rules from the Status Summary screen. Seeing the top 10 hosts lets you know where to focus your tuning efforts, and knowing the top 10 rules shows you what type of events cause the most alerts. Keep building exceptions based on the top 10 hosts and rules until the log records activities that are out-of-the-ordinary and therefore, either do not take place often, or are actually malicious.

NOTE Repeat the process described in this section several times to make sure that the conversion from Test mode to Protect mode is smooth.

Convert Agents to Protect Mode

At this stage, you start to see how CSA works in your environment. Careful planning in the previous stages prevents issues from arising in this stage.

Your actions at this stage of the pilot are similar to those in the previous stage. Use your communication plan for information gathering, test the applications as you did previously, review logs, and build exceptions.

There is an extra step in this stage that you will want to try. Test the protection capabilities of CSA by intentionally trying to break the policy rules that are in effect. This is a good way to test that you have not loosened the rules too much and to confirm that CSA is providing the kind of value you expected.

Test Applications

Take the test plan that you developed in the previous stage and run through it again now that the agent protects the system. This will make you aware of any rule violations that were not logged. Carefully inspect the logs and make sure that the applications behave as they did during your previous tests.

Review Logs and Build Exceptions as Required

You should not build too many exceptions in this stage. If you were thorough in your Test mode testing, there should be few exceptions to build.

Test Agent Protection Capabilities

You see the first real rewards of a CSA deployment when you first test the agent protection capabilities. Try to perform activities that are always denied by policy, such as trying to delete system files using FTP, erasing the CSA files, or installing software from a CD. Document the test results and see if the policy needs to be refined.

This is also a good time to schedule a demonstration of CSA for management and the whole implementation team. The project will continue to have support once the benefits of CSA are shown to work in your environment.

NOTE Repeat the process described in this section several times to make sure that all the policies and configurations are correct before moving on to documentation and general deployment.

Documentation

Thoroughly document everything that has been done so far in CSA. Document the policies, exceptions, application classes, network address sets, host configuration (including OS, service pack, patch levels, and so on), and application versions and patches that were tested. Make a list of the application tests performed, the result, and any CSA logs resulting from those tests.

Your goal is to have a list of all tests and test conditions in effect during your trials. This information is useful for troubleshooting during general deployment when issues arise.

Document CSA Configuration

Make a list of all policies applied to the hosts tested. Take advantage of the reporting features of the CSA MC and export Policy Detail, Group Detail, and Host Detail reports. Record whether the network shim was installed and what groups the hosts are members of. Document polling intervals and use the audit trail to gauge how long rule generation takes as more hosts were added and exceptions and groups built.

Document Host Configurations

Gather all the host configuration information that you can. A good way to do this on Windows is to use the System Information application that is under **Accessories > System Tools**. This application can export all services that are installed and their states, service pack, driver versions, patch levels, and other information.

You need this information because you will probably have many issues to deal with during general deployment. Most organizations are not able to keep all the hosts on the network at the same patch level and configuration, and sometimes these small differences can cause big problems during the deployment. Having complete documentation on your test conditions helps in later project troubleshooting.

Document Test Procedures

Document all the tests that were performed, how the tests were performed, the expected results, and the actual results. CSA requires considerable testing, and few people can remember the tests they performed and the results of the tests. Document all your test results and conditions to show not only what happened, but that the tests were actually performed.

As you deploy CSA to the general host population, there is more potential for it to be blamed for problems on the network, whether it is in Test mode or not. Another reason to document these results is to use hard facts to prove that CSA is not causing problems on your network.

NOTE It is worth repeating that CSA involves mainly process and procedure enforcement. When deploying CSA, make sure that everyone follows and documents all processes and procedures.

General Deployment Phase: Test Mode

Install the agents on the hosts in the general deployment scope in Test mode slowly. The only way to successfully accomplish the general deployment is through an automated installation method. Relying on the users to manually install the agent kit simply does not work in most organizations.

For large organizations with many hosts in each group, it might be easier to put the target groups into Test mode rather than making each host a member of the Systems-Test Mode group. Later when the selected hosts are taken out of Test mode, it is easier to turn Test mode off for the group rather than moving the individual members of that group out of the Systems-Test Mode group.

Create a Deployment Schedule and Phased Installation Plan

Develop a deployment schedule and install the agent in phases throughout the enterprise. Group the agent installations by department, location, or any other administrative unit that your organization uses. Schedule the agent installation to happen during off-hours, preferably when users are not even logged in. To enable the network shim, if you chose to install it, be sure to make the agent kit force the machine to reboot.

Deploy Agents and Monitor Progress Against System Inventory

Now that the agents are scheduled and starting to be deployed, monitor your progress. Run Group Detail reports to see what hosts are registered with the CSA MC and compare that to lists that you get out of your directory services infrastructure or the general deployment scope. A "mop-up" plan is often required because even automated installations might not take care of every host. After the deployment schedule finishes, manually install the agent on any host that has not registered with the MC.

Create Application Investigation Jobs and Run Application Deployment Reports

There is a good chance that you do not have complete information about what applications run on all the hosts. Use CSA to gather this information by creating application investigation jobs. This is important information because the basic default policies can prevent applications from operating properly without application-specific policies applied. This step is more important for the servers than workstations because server applications typically run nonstop and accept rather than initiate network connections. In addition, server applications are more likely to write files to the host.

Run Application Deployment reports to see which hosts have the applications installed and also which versions are running. Using product and verbose network data collection can also help you fine tune network address sets. The Network Data Flows reports often reveal a good deal about the network that nobody knew.

NOTE These reports can actually help document the host configurations for Disaster Recovery and Business Continuity Planning.

Place Machines in Proper Application Groups

Now that all the information is known about the hosts, place the hosts in application- or function-specific groups. Use the builtin groups, such as Servers-SQL Server 2000 and Servers-DHCP Servers. This helps ensure that these applications run correctly because of the application-specific policies applied to these groups. This also helps keep the hosts in the MC organized by function.

Test CSA MC Functionality and Response

As more hosts register with the CSA MC, more groups are created and more policies and exceptions are applied, the CSA MC has more calculations to perform when generating rules. Review the audit trail to make sure that the timings of rule generation are acceptable. Review disk usage to make sure that there is enough drive space to retain the log data that you want. Also investigate network traffic and bandwidth use to remote sites. If anything on the CSA MC is unacceptable, it is best to fix those problems while the agents are still in Test mode.

General Deployment Phase: Protect Mode

Working through the process methodically take hosts in the general deployment population out of Test mode. Do this one group at a time. Publish a conversion schedule and be sure to make your organization's helpdesk aware of the changes that will take place.

Convert Selected Hosts to Protect Mode

Following your schedule, take each group out of Test mode. Pay special attention to the first few groups that come out of Test mode. Stay in constant contact with the helpdesk to make sure that there are no reports of problems or anything out of the ordinary. An abnormal rise in call volume to the helpdesk is probably a sign that CSA is causing some issues.

Monitor Logs and System Activity

Monitor CSA MC logs and the activity on the CSA MC. Verify that all machines that should be taken out of Test mode are polling and are communicating with the MC properly. Pay special attention to network shield rules and proper network operation machines that have the network shim installed.

Review Security Policy and Acceptable Use Policies and Build Appropriate Exceptions

No matter how thorough you test in the pilot phase, some application exceptions will probably have to be built. However, just because there are logged events showing that some benign actions have been denied, do not create exceptions without reviewing your organization's written Security Policy and Acceptable Use Policy.

There will probably be complaints and calls to the helpdesk concerning actions that users are used to performing that CSA now blocks. The helpdesk should be prepared for these calls by being able to cite the Acceptable Use Policy that the user agreed to. There are also legitimate business functions that might be blocked, so the helpdesk needs to be aware of the CSA troubleshooting escalation procedure that you have developed.

Operational Maintenance

Now that the agent deployment is complete, treat CSA like your other enterprise systems management applications. Because SQL Server is integral to the CSA MC, follow your organization's standards for database maintenance and backups. Create a backup schedule, maintenance windows, and update/upgrade procedures for your environment.

Database Maintenance

Most of the security administrators responsible for managing CSA do not have advanced database administrator (DBA) skills. Large CSA deployments that use a remote or dedicated SQL Server will likely take place at organizations large enough to have a database expert or database management team. For smaller scale deployments, this might not be an option. Regularly check the Status Summary screen for database maintenance alerts. Most of the maintenance that needs to be done on the CSA database is basic and most administrators should have no problem following the online SQL Server help to perform routine and requested maintenance.

System Backups

Because CSA is a network application like any other, you should be sure it is backed up regularly as part of your organization's normal backup rotation. Backing up a small deployment with the database and CSA MC on the same server is as simple as creating a backup schedule under the Maintenance menu and backing up the target directory. Large scale deployments with remote database servers are somewhat more complicated because the Backup option is not available on the Maintenance menu. Follow your normal database backup procedure, whether that is backing up the database live, making dumps, and so on, and make sure to back up the entire Program Files\cscopx\CSAMC45 directory and all subdirectories.

Test System Patches in Lab

Microsoft released a patch during the fourth quarter of 2005 that addressed certain vulnerabilities in Terminal Services. This patch also had some incompatibilities with CSA 4.5 that caused servers running Terminal Services to experience the Blue Screen of Death.

Test all patches in a lab with CSA and note the interaction of the patches with CSA. Research the vulnerabilities that the patch is supposed to address. If CSA already addresses those vulnerabilities (and it does in most cases), you have time to test the patches in a controlled lab setting without rushing the patches onto your systems.

Test Non-CSA Application Upgrades in Lab

Often during upgrades, applications are installed in new directories or have new executable names. This is likely to cause problems with your application classes and file set variables. Make sure that all application upgrades are tested with CSA, particularly applications that have had exception policies built or that have application specific policies.

Run Application Deployment Unprotected Hosts Report to Find Machines Without CSA

This report is useful and lets you know what hosts on your network are not registered with the CSA MC. You mainly look for machines that are in the deployment scope but have not registered with the CSA MC. It is also useful to be aware of communications to hosts outside of the scope and machines that cannot run CSA, such as AIX or HP-UX servers.

Run this report regularly to see new hosts added to the network that do not have CSA installed.

CSA Upgrades

Cisco releases updates and patches throughout the year, and it is a good idea to stay on the current release whenever you can. The first time you upgrade or update a CSA MC, upgrade a lab or test CSA MC, so that you know what will happen to the existing groups and policies and how they interact and coexist with the current version groups and policies. Test upgrading agents to the new version, so that you know what to expect in terms of network traffic and the amount of time an upgrade takes. You can also see the interaction between the new agent and policies and any applications that run on the tested host.

Upgrading MC

When the CSA MC is upgraded, any existing groups, policies, and other objects that differ from the new version are preserved. Objects that are the same in the new version and the existing installed version are updated with the new version number. Custom policies, groups, and objects are preserved without a version number. Carefully review the differences in the new version and old versions. In most cases, exception policies need to be applied to the new updated groups and the respective older groups.

Upgrading Agents

The act of upgrading the agents is simple, but like everything else with CSA, it requires diligent planning. The agent upgrade kits are transferred using the HTTP protocol so they can be cached at your remote WAN sites using a cache engine or cache services and WCCP on the remote WAN router. Again, roll the kits out according to a schedule and do it group-by-group.

APPENDIX **B**

Cisco Security Agent 5.0

Cisco Security Agent 5.0 is the latest revision of the product and it has a few new features that are worth mentioning. This appendix covers many of the new features and provides screen shots to help you better understand the latest features and functionality that have been added.

Operating System Support

The Cisco Security Agent continues to support the same operating systems as in earlier versions but has added a few more current versions to the tally. In version 5.0, the CSA product now also supports Solaris 9, Windows Tablet PC, and VMware. As the product continues to evolve, you can be sure that new operating systems and version support continue to emerge. It should be mentioned that at the time of writing this, the CSA MC still required Windows 2000 as the base operating system. This is due to the fact that the base installation required for the CSA MC is the CiscoWorks VMS suite, which runs on Windows 2000.

System Warnings

The CSA MC now has the capability to produce warnings as pop-up messages when you log in to the CSA MC interface. Figure B-1 allows you to see what a common pop-up message looks like to the administrator. You can directly link to the appropriate location in the CSA MC by clicking the URL embedded in the Warning message or you can close the warning by clicking the X in the upper-right corner of the dialog box.

Figure B-1 *Warning Dialog Boxes*

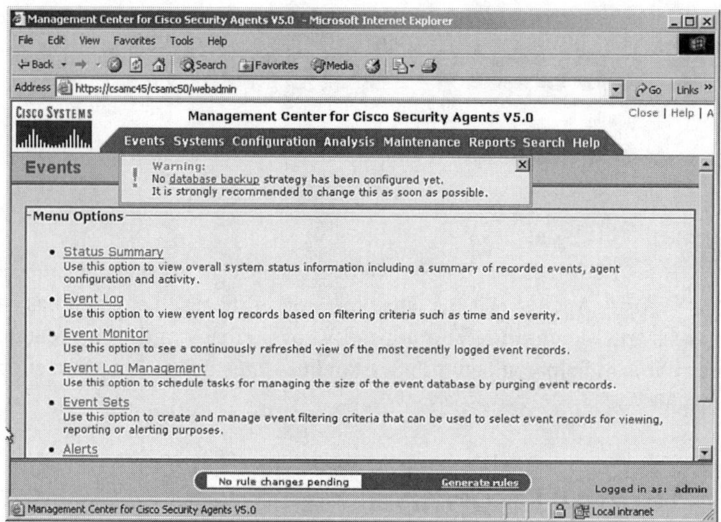

Status Summary Screen

The Status Summary screen has undergone a few changes that will make a CSA administrator's use of the product a bit more efficient. There are several new lines of data provided in the Network Status section and some apparent changes to the Most Active section of the screen.

Network Status

The Network Status section of the Summary page includes some new data and features. Following is a list of some changes and descriptions, as shown in Figure B-2:

- **Host History Collection Enabled**—You can now maintain Host history for two weeks. The information is viewable from **Systems>Hosts** and consists of the following:
  - Registration
  - Test Mode Setting Changes
  - Learn Mode Setting Changes
  - IP Address Changes
  - CTA Posture Changes
  - CSA Version Changes
  - Active and Inactive Changes

- **Active hosts with CSA Security Agent disabled**—Tracks hosts that are disabled on the endpoint.
- **Hosts running in learn mode**—Tracks hosts in Learn mode.
- **Hosts with BIOS supported boot detection**—Tracks hosts with BIOS boot detection.
- **Hosts in state *Insecure boot detected***—Can track hosts whose BIOS reported that it previously booted in a nonstandard fashion, such as from USB or CD.
- **Hosts in state condition *Untrusted rootkit detected***—Tracks systems in which a driver has attempted to dynamically load.
- **Query rules with saved answer in past 24 hours**—Tracks the number of rules to which users have responded and cached an answer.

Figure B-2 *Status Summary Changes*

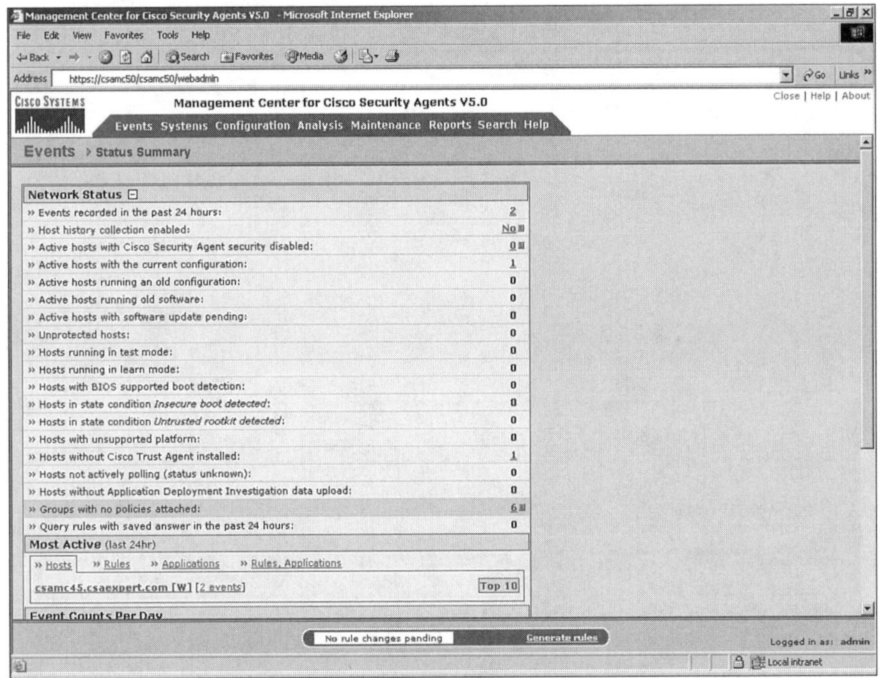

Most Active

The Most Active portion of the CSA MC Summary page has been a great addition since CSA 4.5 and has improved even more. In CSA 5.0, you now have easy access to the most active hosts, rules, applications, and rules/applications. Every CSA administrator is particularly interested in applications. You can now see which applications trigger the most events, regardless of which type of rule they trigger. This can be useful for locating a process that triggers many different rules, but rarely the same rule twice. Previously, the only option you had was to see what rules had been triggered most often, but there was never a way to correlate an application across multiple rules. Now you can see that information quite easily. An example of rules/applications is seen in Figure B-3 and the 10 most active applications view can be seen in Figure B-4.

Figure B-3 *Rules/Applications Most Active*

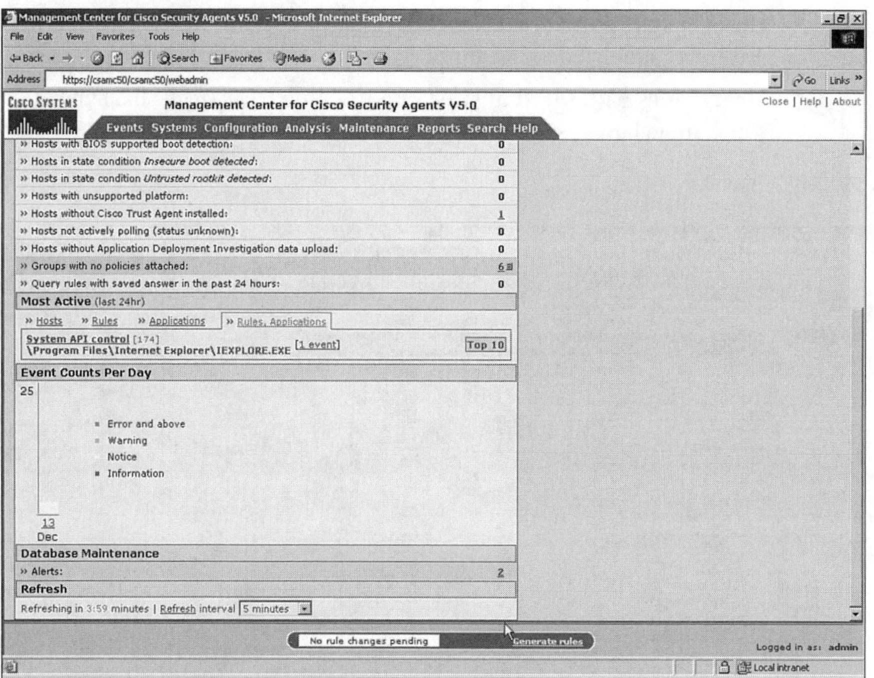

Figure B-4 *Top 10 Most Active Applications*

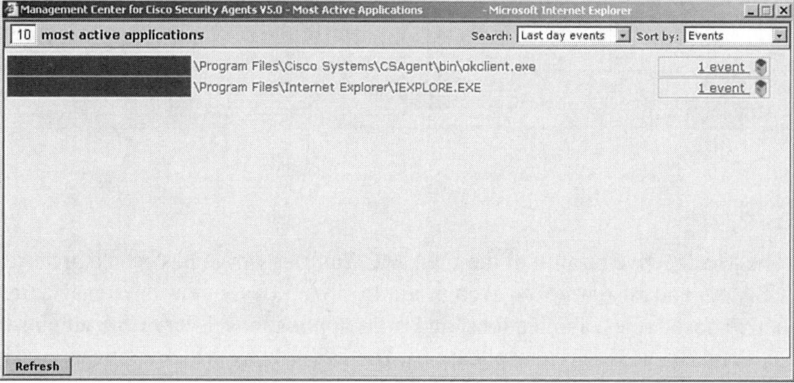

Event Log Changes

The event log has not changed much, other than a few options that are available when sorting the log. When using the Find Similar Events option to sort the log, as displayed in Figure B-5, you now have the ability to look for the same application. This is a valuable way to look for events that were triggered by the same suspect or troublesome application.

Figure B-5 *Find Similar Events with the Application Option*

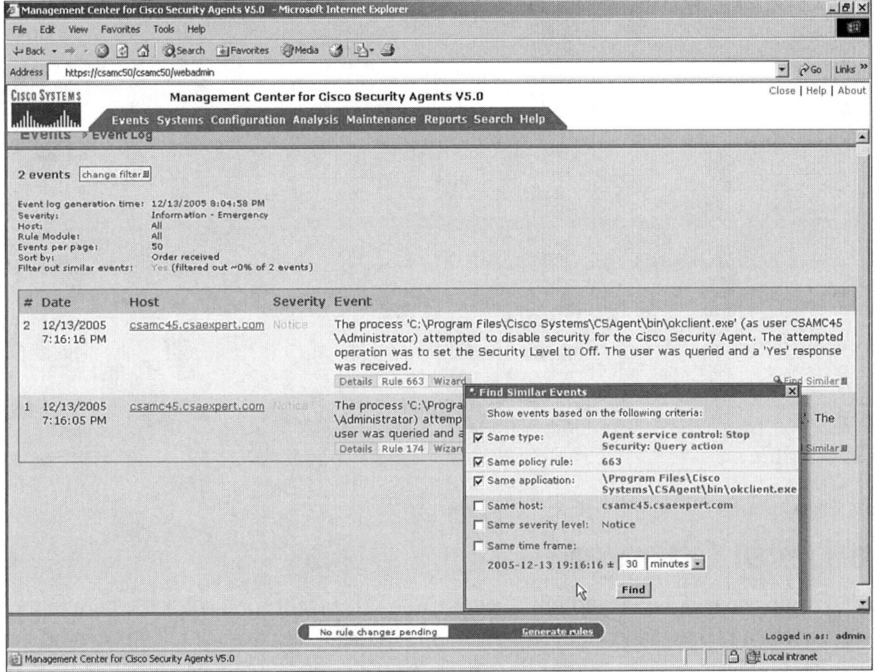

The Filter Events option of the event log also has a new option, as seen in Figure B-6. You now can sort the events by either order received or date. The events are placed in the database in the order they are received from the agents, which makes it easier to display if you view it the same way. If you wish to see the events in the order they happened, by date, the system needs to reorder them before displaying, which takes more time.

Figure B-6 *Filter Events Sorting*

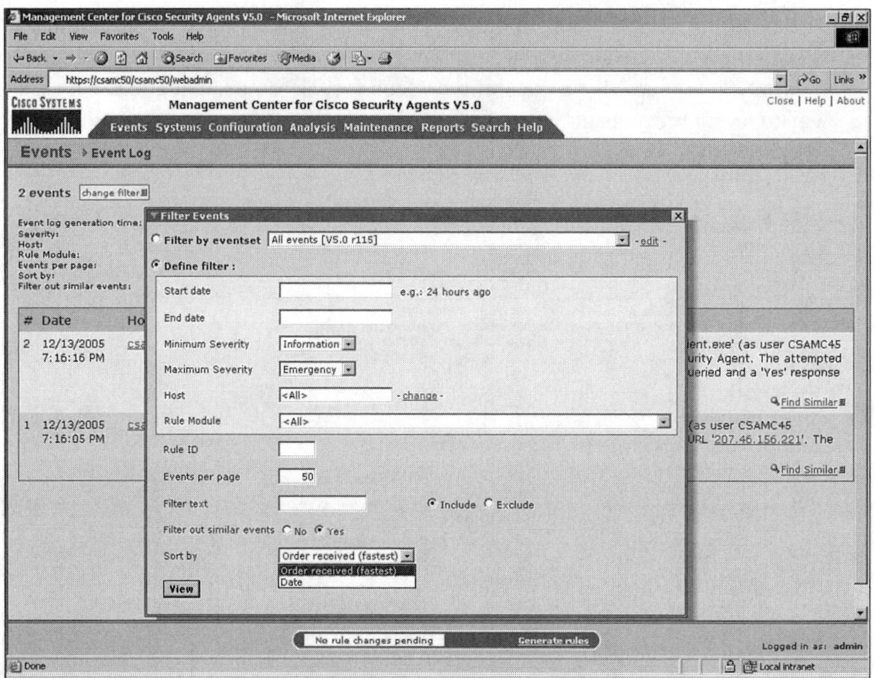

Group Level Changes

Groups have not changed much as of CSA 5.0, except for a subtle change in the overrides section and one in the view of the combined rules. The overrides have been broken into two categories, as seen in Figure B-7: Rule overrides and Log overrides. The Rule overrides area contains the Test mode and Learn mode options, and Log overrides contains Log deny actions, Verbose logging, and Filter user info from events. You can see that the new option here is Learning mode.

Figure B-7 *Overrides in CSA 5.0*

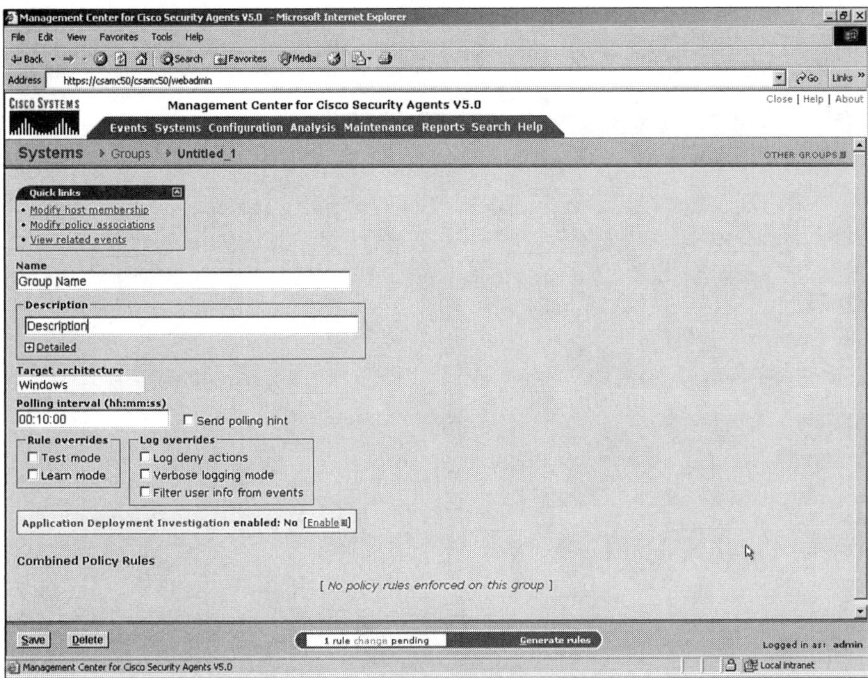

Learn mode is designed to limit the number of pop-up messages a new agent experiences after installation. During Learn mode, the agent automatically enters an allow response to queries without prompting the user if the query had an allow option. This will be cached until Learn mode is disabled and if the query had Allow as the default action, will remain as a permanently cached entry. This should lower the number of agent interactions after deployment and ease the user experience.

Hosts

Host configuration also is another feature that has not changed much during the migration to CSA 5.0. The biggest change is the Host Recycle Bin that was added as of this release. You can see the capability to move hosts to the Recycle Bin from multiple locations in Figures B-8 and B-9. In addition, there are a few simple changes, as shown in Figure B-9, that allow you to see state information from the Host screen.

Figure B-8 *Recycle Bin Option on Hosts Screen*

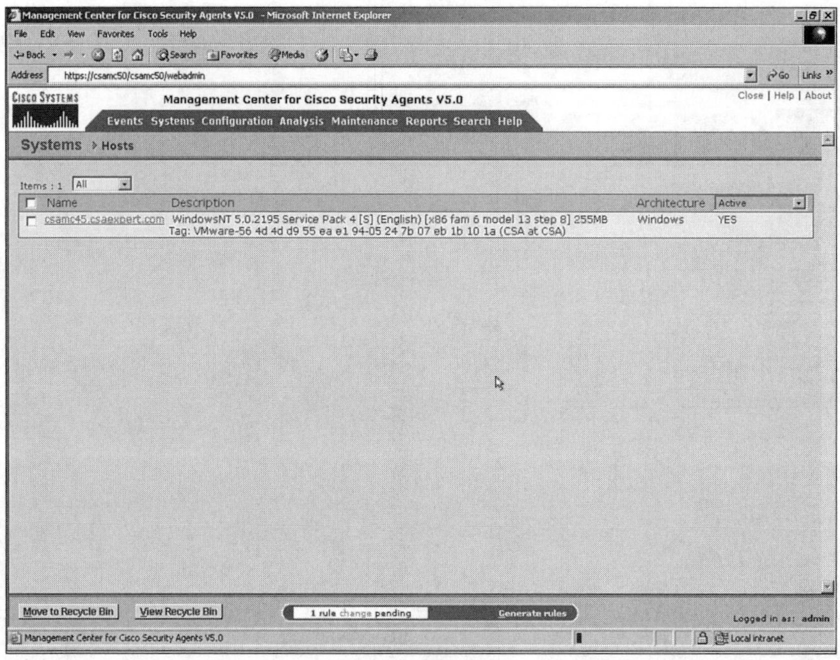

Figure B-9 *Recycle Bin Option and State Set Views*

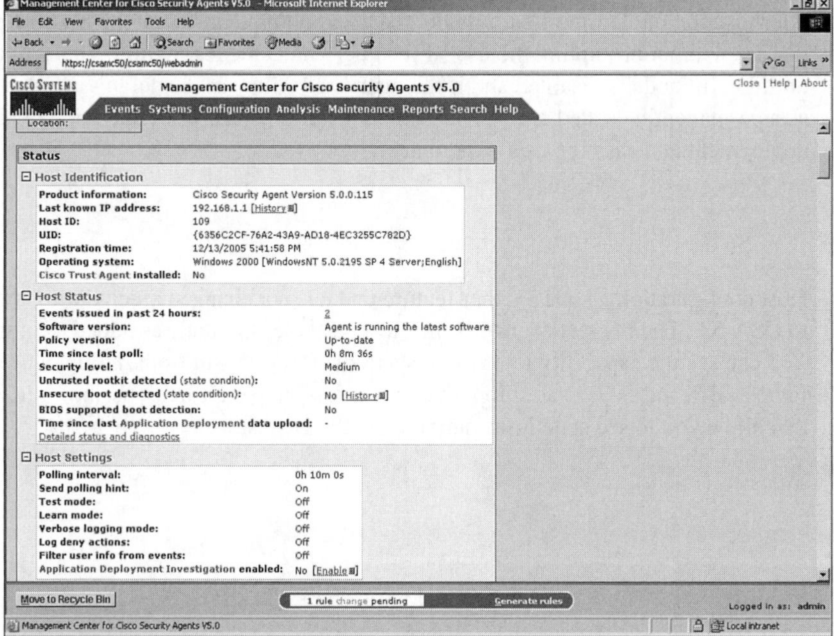

Recycle Bin

The Recycle Bin was added in version 5.0 to simplify the process of a host going dormant and coming back online without losing previous information. After 30 days, a host is removed from the visible CSA MC screens, but all information is still cached in the event that the system returns. The hosts will remain in the Recycle Bin for an additional 30 days, and then is purged from the system.

Host Management Tasks

Another addition that indirectly affects hosts is the configurable settings for new hosts tasks. You can now set up scheduled tasks to automatically perform the following:

- Add hosts from a group to another group after a set period of time
- Move hosts from a group to another group after a set period of time
- Remove hosts from a group after a period of time
- Regularly regenerate rules

This allows you to place a host in Test mode for a few days, and then automatically remove the host from that group and place it into another nontest mode group. The configuration screen for host management tasks is displayed in Figure B-10.

Figure B-10 *Host Management Task Configuration*

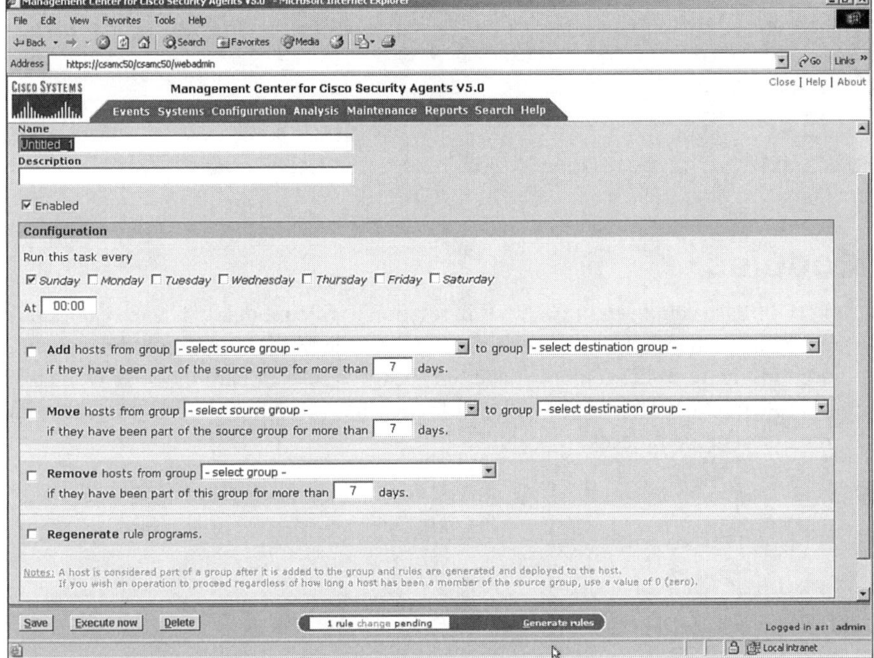

Combined Policy State Set Notation

A less visible but noteworthy additional feature is the graphical icon placed next to rules in the combined policy views to denote when a rule is a part of a state set and is not always applied as part of the currently enforced policy. You can see in Figure B-11 that there is an S icon next to each rule to which a set is applied.

Figure B-11 *State Set Notation in Combine Policy Views*

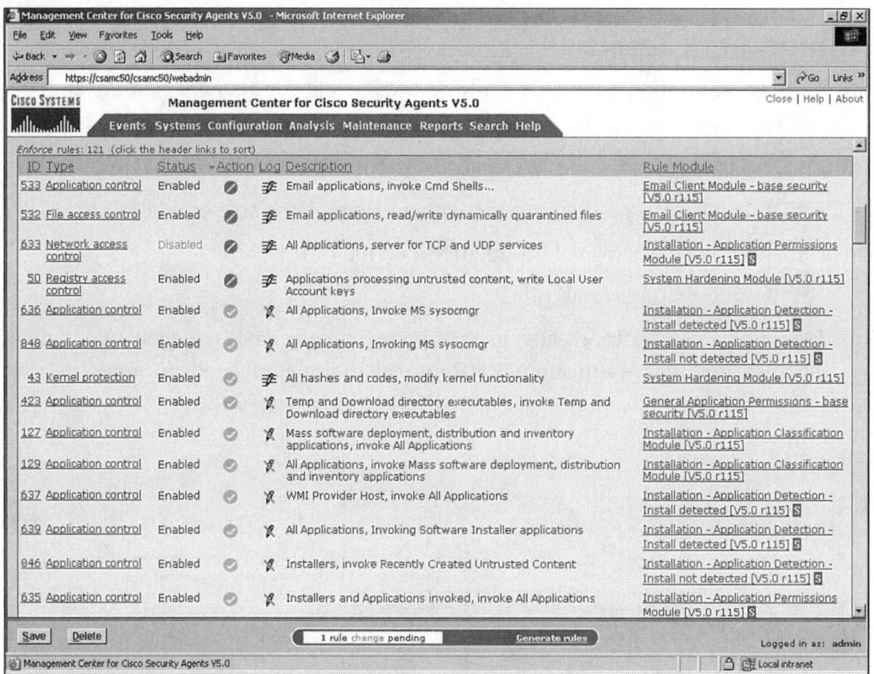

Rule Modules

Very little has changed in CSA 5.0 in relation to rule modules. The only noticeable change is visible in the Rule overrides section of the Rule Module configuration screen. As can be seen in Figure B-12, you now have the ability to select Learn mode as well as Test mode per rule module. This option at the Rule Module configuration level provides granularity to the Learn mode process.

Figure B-12 *Per Rule Module Learn Mode*

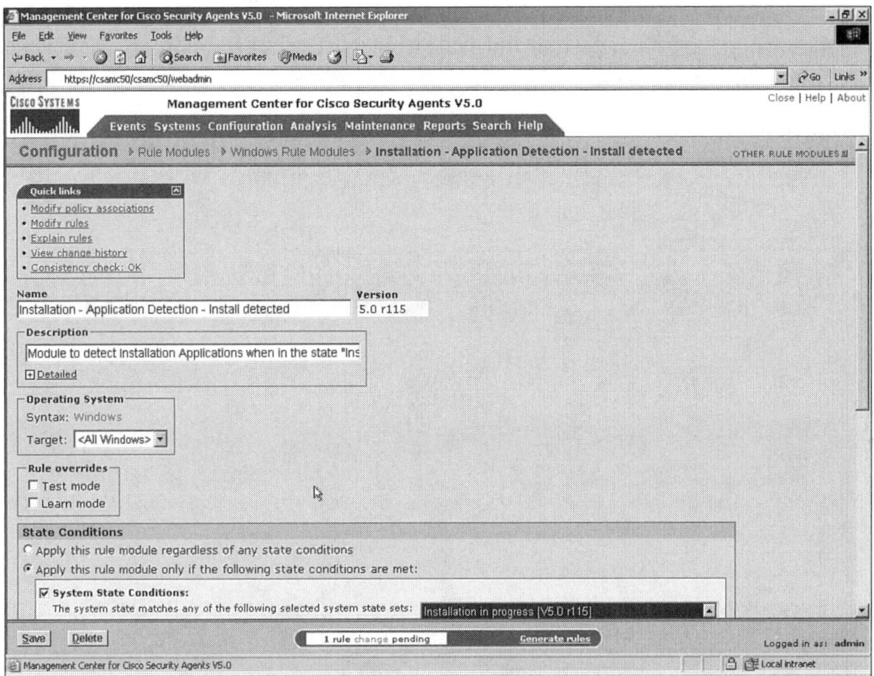

Rules

Some of the major changes made to the CSA 5.0 product are visible in Rule configuration screens. Most notably, there are some changes in the actions relating to the names of the actions and also to an additional action type.

Actions

A few of the actions have been renamed in the newest product revision. The higher precedence actions are now all Priority actions, such as Priority Allow and Priority Deny. There are no longer any High Priority rules. However, the order of precedence remains the same.

New Set Action

There is now a new rule action named Set. The Set action allows the administrator to set various options when the matching rule triggers. The Set action is available via the actions list on the various Rule configuration screens, as displayed in Figure B-13.

Figure B-13 *Set Action Option*

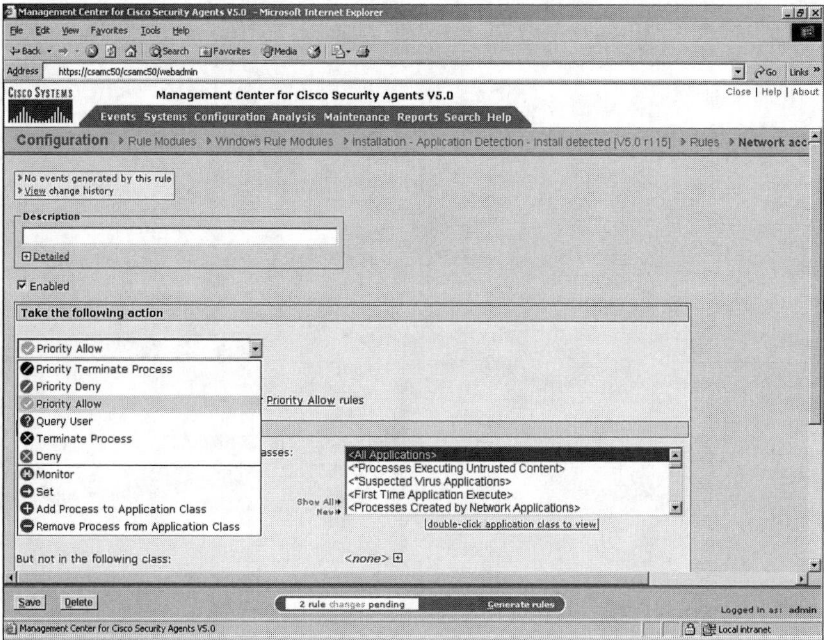

After you select **Set** as the action type, you are required to select the attribute you wish to set and then the associated attribute value. The attributes are listed in in the following and displayed in Figure B-14, and an example attribute value selection dropdown box is displayed in Figure B-15. The options are:

- **detected rootkit**—Can set the system state to rootkit detected if an Untrusted action is set by matching this rule. The options are:
  - **Trusted**—Set this matching module as a trusted rootkit.
  - **Untrusted**—Set this matching module as an untrusted rootkit.
- **detected boot**—This action can alert the administrator when the system's BIOS, if it supports this feature, reports a previous insecure boot has been detected. An example is booting from a CD or USB key. It can also be used along with state sets to change the system state. This rule can also detect a previous Safe mode boot. The options are:
  - **Secure**—Can alert or trigger when a secure boot is detected.
  - **Insecure**—Alerts as insecure if detected.

- **detected access**—Allows you to receive an event notification and/or change the system state when unprotected access occurs to a system without a corresponding protected rule.
  - **Protected**—Set the access that is protected on the system, possibly to a specific web server. Include this rule in the Web server policy.
  - **Unprotected**—Set all other web server access (as defined, TCP/80 access) to alert you to unprotected web servers when there is no protected access rule in the combined system policy. In most cases, the unprotected access rule should exist in the base policy, such as <All Windows>, to ensure the rule is applied to all systems.
- **Security level**—Use this setting to force a system to move into High, Medium, or Low system states. The system will then immediately begin to enforce rules that are tied to that particular state. The options are:
  - High
  - Medium
  - Low
- **File**—You can tag a file as Trusted or Untrusted and cause it to be displayed in the Untrusted Applications section of the Agent UI. In addition, this file—if marked untrusted—will be added to the dynamic application class <*Processes Executing Untrusted Content>. The options are:
  - Trusted
  - Untrusted
- **Host Address**—You can cause an IP Address to be marked as untrusted and quarantined either locally or locally and globally:
  - **Untrusted Host (Locally and Globally)**—Causes the IP Address to be added to the local @dynamic variable used in other policy rules. In addition, the IP address is sent via an event to the CSA MC, which could then become a globally quarantined IP address.
  - **Untrusted Host (Locally)**—Causes an IP address to be added locally to @dynamic, which can be used by other rules.
- **Differentiated Service**—You can now mark or remark IP packets with the Differentiated Services tags (QoS) with the CSA Agent. This allows you to provide your network trusted QoS, as the endpoint applications will not be able to override this setting. It is not unusual for applications to attempt to set these parameters to gain access to extra network bandwidth and priority. The parameters set by CSA are Differentiated Services Code Point (DSCP) and Per Hop Behavior (PHB), as indicated in the list that follows by (DSCP, PHB). The options are:
  - priority Best Effort (0,0)
  - priority Scavenger (8, CS1)

— application specified—Allows the application to define the settings as necessary.

— IP routing (48, CS6)

— Voice (46, EF)

— Interactive Video (34, AF41)

— Streaming Video (32, CS4)

— Mission Critical Data (26, AF31)

— Call Signaling (24, CS3)

— Transactional Data (18, AF21)

— Network Management (16, CS2)

— Bulk Data (10, AF11)

— Best Effort (0,0)

— Scavenger (8, CS1)

NOTE The CSA Agent continues to apply the QoS tags even when in Test mode.

Figure B-14 *Set Action Attributes*

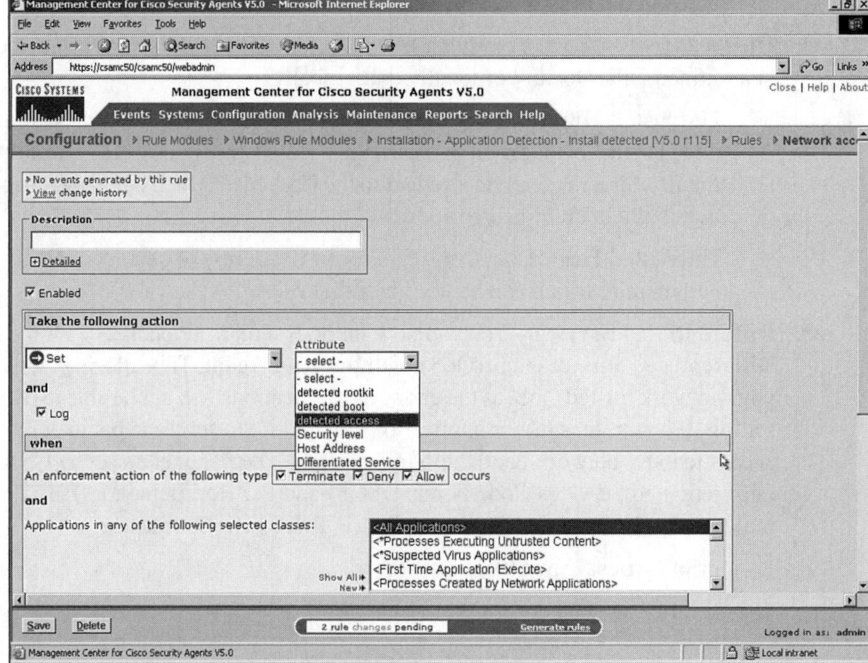

Figure B-15 *Set Action Sample Attribute Values for QoS*

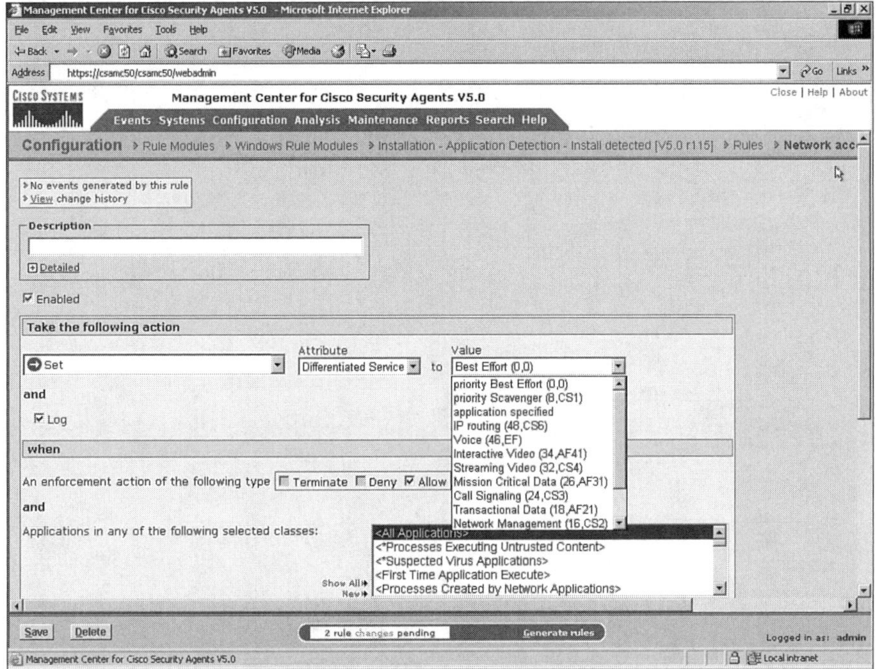

Searching

When attempting to locate objects within the database, the CSA Search functionality is a crucial component of the product. Searching has been enhanced to include a few new search parameters that ensure you can isolate particular objects.

Hosts Search

You can now more granularly search for hosts in the CSA MC database using several new options in the Hosts Search Criteria menu. The new options and original options are displayed in B-16. You can now search for:

- Hosts with a specific security level or disabled
- Hosts by OS platform
- Hosts using desktop or server licenses
- Hosts attached to a group for a specific timeframe
- Hosts having a certain state condition
- Hosts that support BIOS boot detection

Figure B-16 *CSA 5.0 Hosts Search Options*

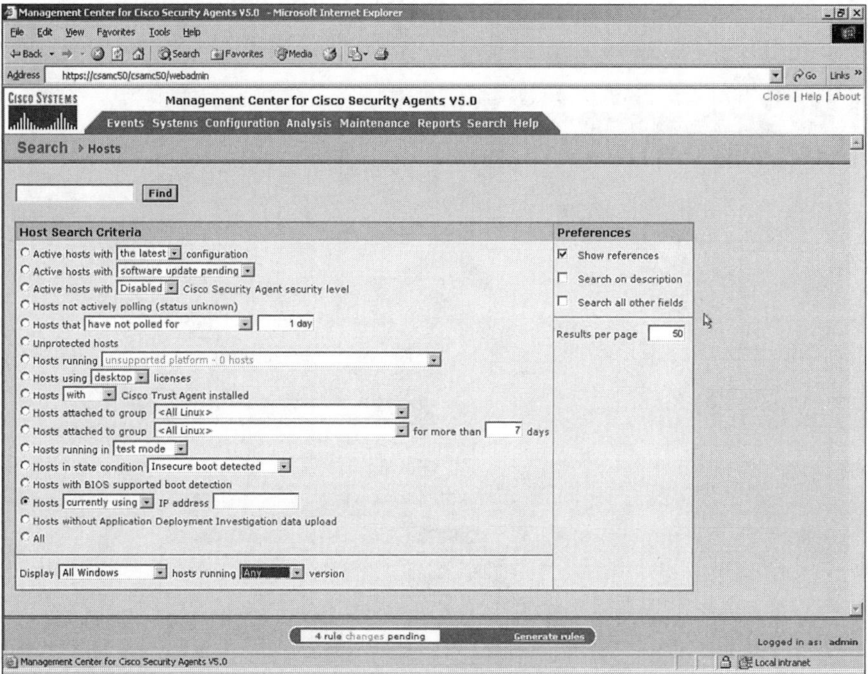

Rules Search

The Rules Search has been changed slightly to include some new features as well as an important search criterion. In addition to the previously available option, you can look for the following, as displayed in Figure B-17:

- Rules in Learn mode
- Query rules that have saved answers from a host within a certain timeframe

Figure B-17 *CSA 5.0 Rules Search Options*

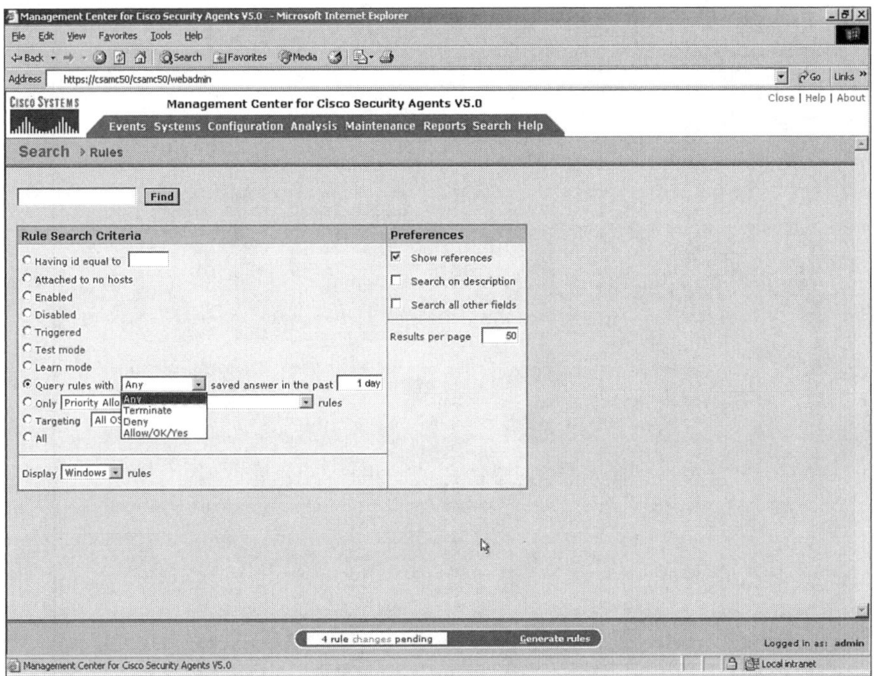

Agent Diagnostics

You now have more detailed host diagnostics in CSA 5.0, as shown in Figure B-18. This includes disk space available information for the system queried. You now have the capability to see the diagnostic history of a host if it is being collected in your CSA deployment. This includes diagnostic data collected previously, so you can compare it to the currently available diagnostic data.

Figure B-18 *Agent Diagnostics in CSA 5.0*

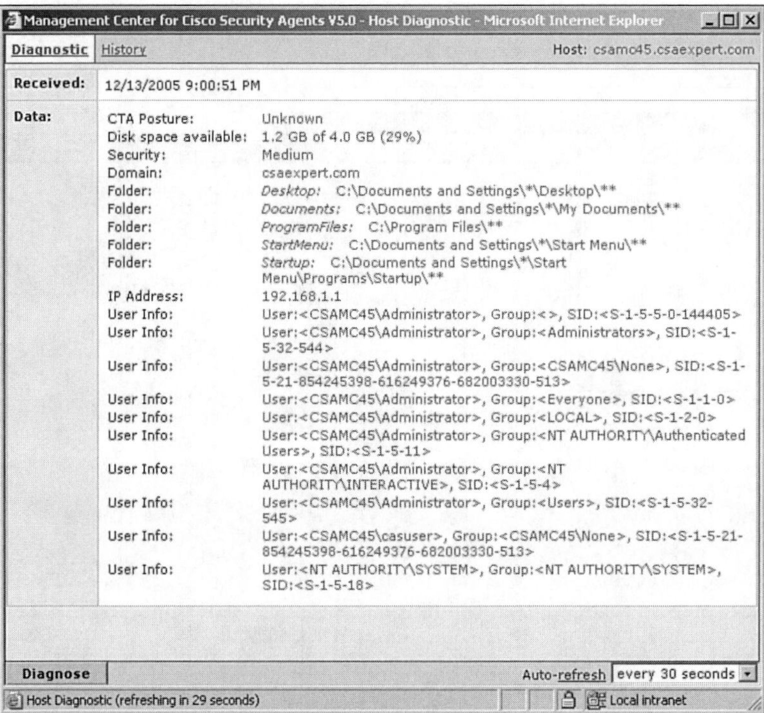

Database Maintenance Information

The connected CSA database information is available via the CSA MC GUI, as displayed in Figure B-19. You now have the ability to see the connection parameters, such as DB Server, DB Name, and Connection type.

Figure B-19 *Database Information*

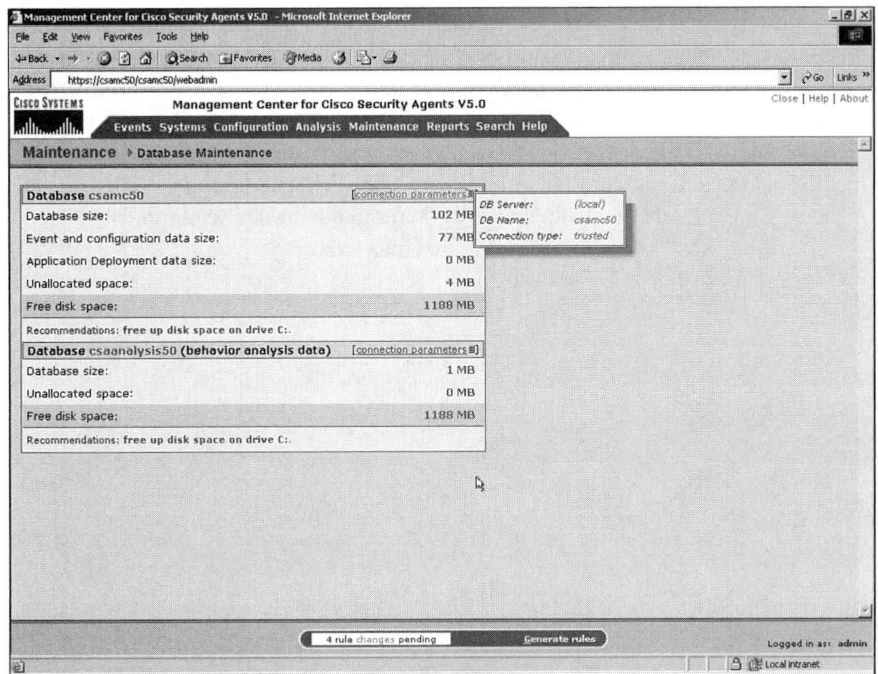

Resetting the Security Agent

Before the release of version 5.0, if you wished to reset certain agent functions or settings from the CSA MC, you had to reset the entire agent. In 5.0, you now have more granular reset options on a per agent basis. You can reset the following parameters:

- Cached Response and Logging
- Local Firewall Settings
- Learned Information
- System Security
- System State
- Untrusted Applications
- User Query Responses

Summary

You can see many exciting new features in the CSA 5.0 product that may warrant an upgrade to your existing CSA deployment. These features, such as Learn mode, can assist in the deployment of the product and also in the maintenance of the product. For example, you can use the new search parameters and agent reset options. One of the most exciting new features is the Set action that allows you to provide new security functionality, such as trusted QoS and insecure BIOS boot detection. For specific functionality included in the latest CSA 5.x release available to you, refer to the latest release notes.

INDEX

A

B

C

D

E

K-L

M

N

O

P

Q

R

S

T

U

V

W

Cisco Systems

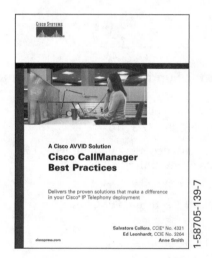

THIS BOOK IS SAFARI ENABLED

INCLUDES FREE 45-DAY ACCESS TO THE ONLINE EDITION

The Safari® Enabled icon on the cover of your favorite technology book means the book is available through Safari Bookshelf. When you buy this book, you get free access to the online edition for 45 days.

Safari Bookshelf is an electronic reference library that lets you easily search thousands of technical books, find code samples, download chapters, and access technical information whenever and wherever you need it.

TO GAIN 45-DAY SAFARI ENABLED ACCESS TO THIS BOOK:

- Go to **http://www.ciscopress.com/safarienabled**
- Complete the brief registration form
- Enter the coupon code found in the front of this book before the "Contents at a Glance" page

If you have difficulty registering on Safari Bookshelf or accessing the online edition, please e-mail customer-service@safaribooksonline.com.